AF477984

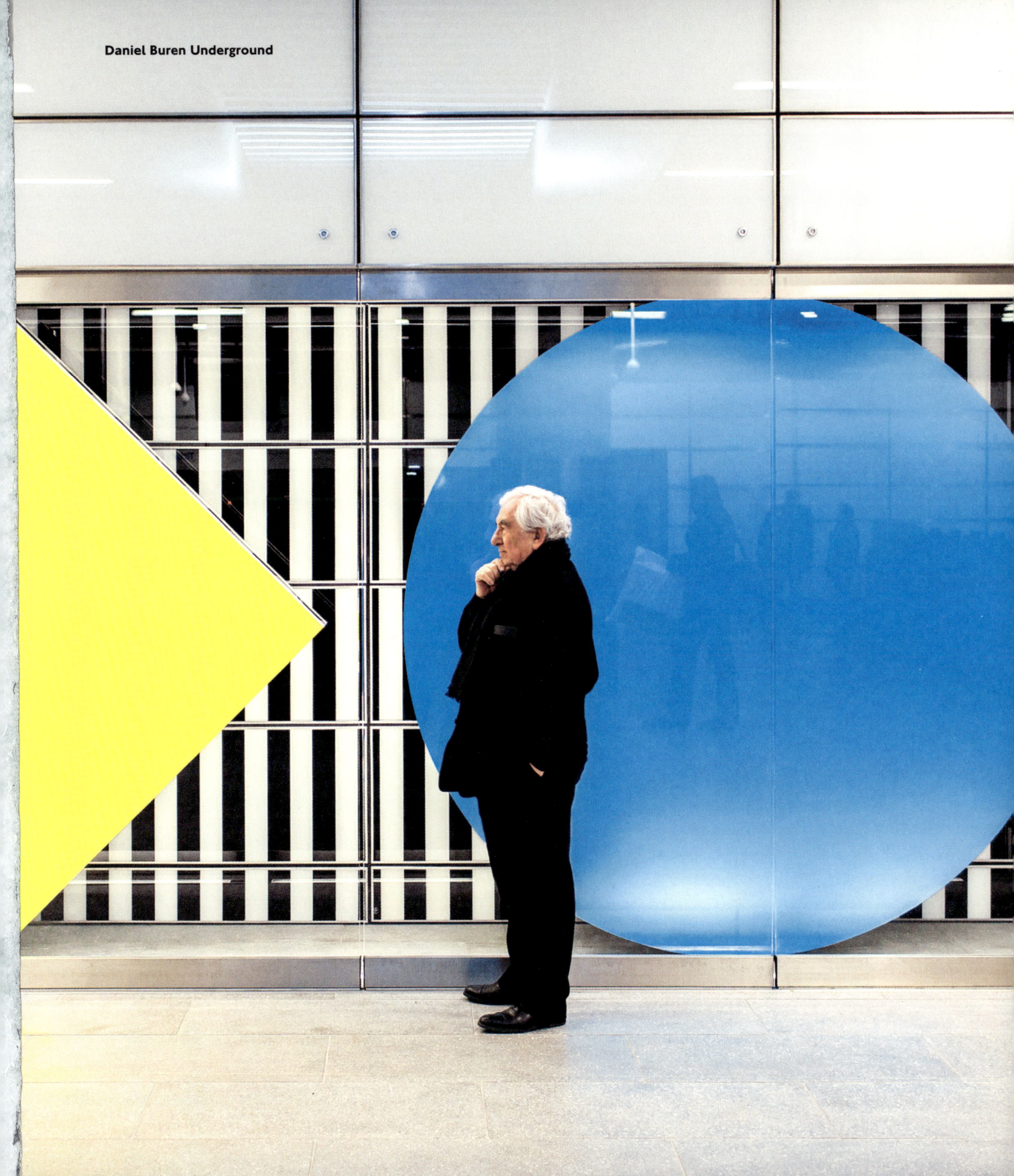
Daniel Buren Underground

Edited by Eleanor Pinfield
Texts by Tamsin Dillon, Hans Ulrich Obrist, Eleanor Pinfield and Mark Wild
Interview with Tim Marlow

Underground

Daniel Buren

ART/BOOKS

First published in the United Kingdom in 2017
by Art Books Publishing Ltd

Art Books Publishing Ltd
77 Oriel Road
London E9 5SG
Tel: +44 (0)20 8533 5835
info@artbookspublishing.co.uk
www.artbookspublishing.co.uk

British Library Cataloguing-in-Publication Data
A catalogue record for this book is available
from the British Library

ISBN 978-1-908970-29-9

Designed by The Studio of Williamson Curran
Repro by JK Morris Production AB, Värnamo
Printed and bound in Latvia by Livonia

Distributed outside North America by
Thames & Hudson
181a High Holborn
London WC1V 7QX
United Kingdom
Tel: +44 (0)20 7845 5000
Fax: +44 (0)20 7845 5055
sales@thameshudson.co.uk

Available in North America through
ARTBOOK | D.A.P.
155 Sixth Avenue, 2nd Floor,
New York, N.Y. 10013
www.artbook.com

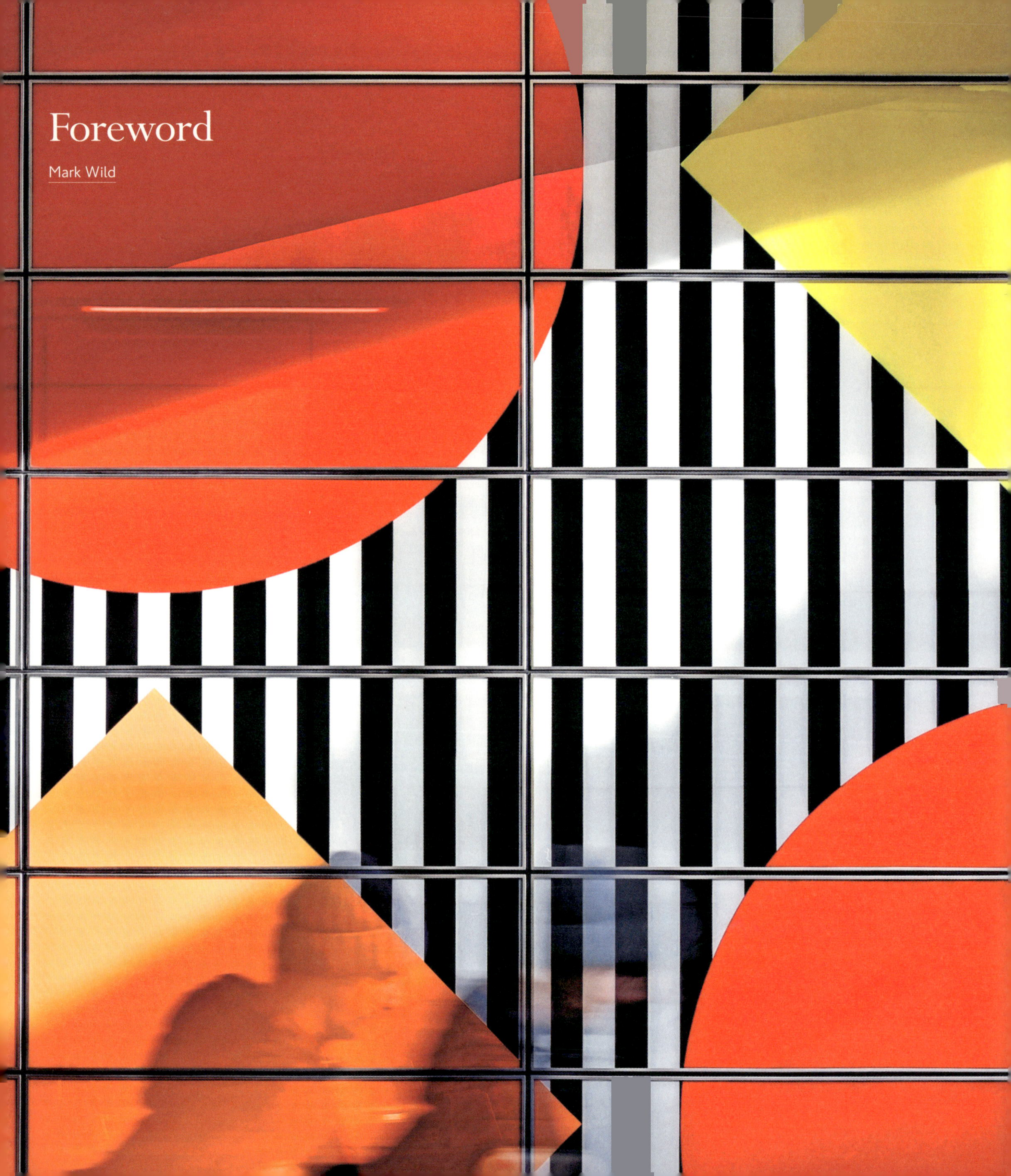

Foreword

Mark Wild

As we move about this busy city, bustling with tourists and commuters alike, why bother with art? What does it bring to a transport network striving to be the most efficient and advanced in the world? The answer is clearly demonstrated at Tottenham Court Road, a station long at the heart of London Underground's commitment to working with renowned artists. Art changes spaces; it changes our perceptions; it changes how we feel as we travel. Art does not just enliven and decorate stations, it leaves a trace. At Tottenham Court Road, it leaves a trace of our past, but also points to the future of our city.

The Underground has a rich history of collaborating with the leading artists of the day. Paul Nash, Man Ray, László Moholy-Nagy, Enid Marx, among many others, were all enticed by the opportunity to speak directly to the people of this great city. Involving artists in our major projects is a challenge, but one that we continue to embrace. Art on the Underground, Transport for London's contemporary art programme, commissions the most significant artists of the twenty-first century to create works of excitement and vision that none of us can anticipate.

Tottenham Court Road embodies the power of art in a public space. In the 1980s, Sir Eduardo Paolozzi was invited to imagine a work on a grand scale, resulting in his extensive mosaic designs. In 2007, as the station's modernization was being planned, Daniel Buren conceived of an expansive work, taking over the new space with a deceptively simple combination of stripes, colours and shapes.

I am immensely proud to celebrate the completion of his outstanding art work, *Diamonds and Circles*. Tottenham Court Road station has been a hub for more than a century and will soon welcome the new Elizabeth line in 2018, strengthening its privileged position as a pivot between east and west. As we look to this future, we do so with the sophisticated perspective of Buren's work. It seems right that his first permanent public commission in the United Kingdom sits here, in London, at the centre of the capital. It is world-class art for a world-class city.

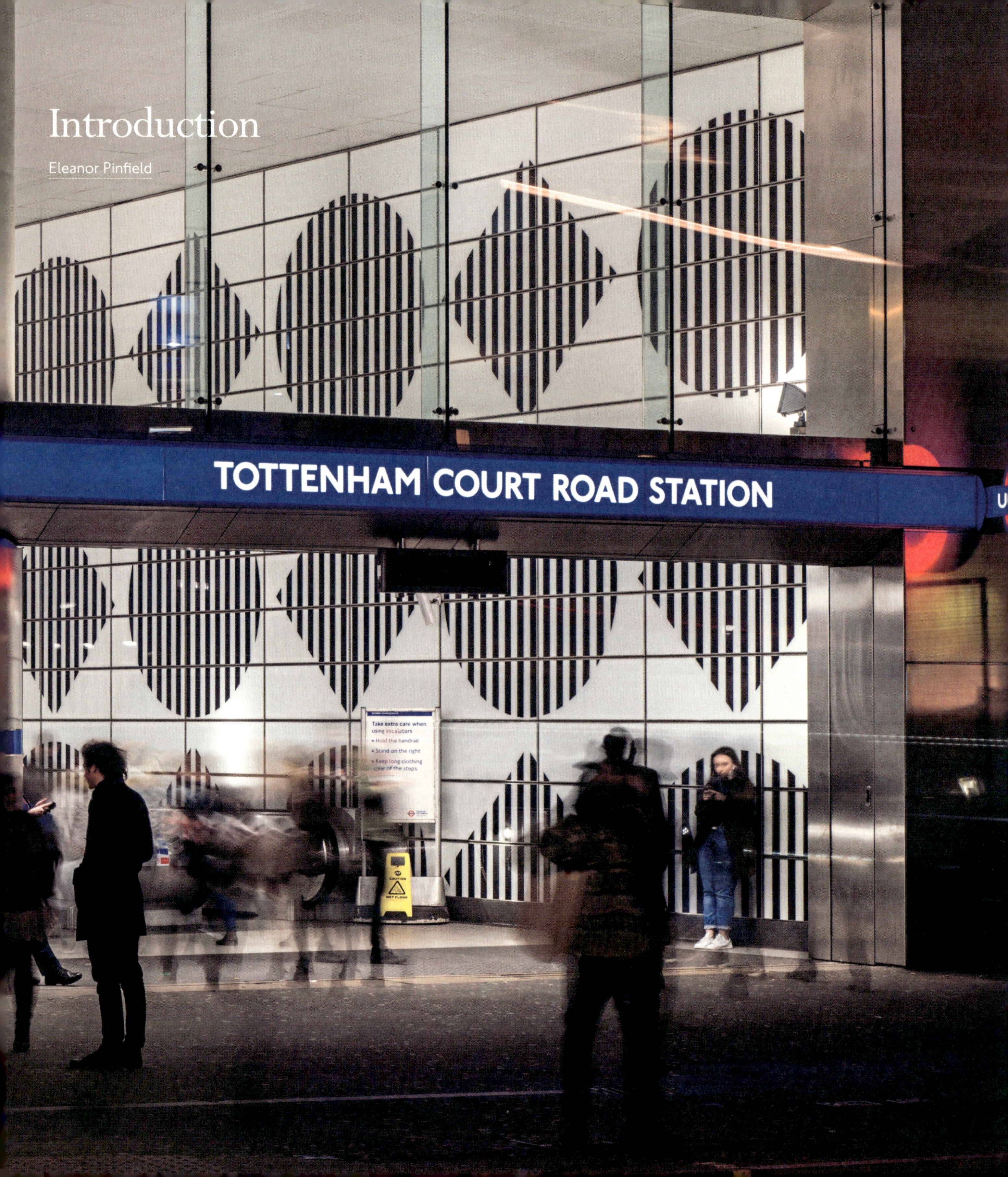

Introduction

Eleanor Pinfield

For more than a century, Tottenham Court Road station has been at the centre of London's transport network. Opening in 1900 on the Central London Railway, it forms part of the spine of the Underground that cuts through the city from east to west. And yet despite its central location, it has never asserted its place above ground. Today, the transformation is complete. Following a major redesign by architects Hawkins\Brown and Stanton Williams, it is boldly present for the first time. Towering glass porticos rise above Charing Cross Road, drawing light into the subterranean spaces; and on Oxford Street, the station has its own imposing glass box entrance, one of several new ways into the expanded ticket hall. It was as part of this reimagination of Tottenham Court Road's architecture that in 2007 Art on the Underground selected French artist Daniel Buren to develop a permanent work for the station. Now, in 2017, we can appreciate the commission in its entirety. As the modernization reaches completion, Buren's works *in situ*, entitled *Diamonds and Circles*, carry us from street to concourse. Our movement through space is at the heart of the artist's concept.

In his early career, Buren used striped fabric bought in the textile markets of Paris as a canvas on which to paint, an escape from the confines of traditional painting. The stripes varied slightly in size, averaging 8.7 centimetres in width. As he developed his practice in the late 1960s and 1970s, the 8.7-centimetre stripe – which he describes as a 'visual tool', as Hans Ulrich Obrist writes in these pages – became a fixed and constant feature, appearing in works ranging from interventions in city streets to installations in museums and galleries and public commissions. In 1970, for instance, in a work called *110 Stations du Métro Parisien*, he pasted white-and-blue-striped posters among film and theatre advertisements inside Paris Métro stations. He repeated this self-initiated intervention three years later with an orange-striped poster. He then collated photographs of each station in two volumes, presenting the sites in alphabetical order as a coded guide to an expansive work. This early project embodies a number of key concepts relevant to his long career: disruption of public space; simplicity in form; and the use of arbitrary systems of organization. A transport system translates a sprawling city into station, line and network, a concept that we use to 'read' the city. Akin to this, Buren's work organizes physical space with his concept – a stripe fixed in size, a tool to measure space. What is unique becomes part of a larger system. And yet, through this very process of systematization, our gaze is disrupted. This 'visual tool' causes us to look more closely at the environment around us and to see it afresh with new eyes.

The mark of the artist

A detail of *The Big Wall, Up and Down, Diamonds and Circles, Black and White*, the component of *Diamonds and Circles* at the Oxford Street entrance (opposite), shows Daniel Buren's signature motif, the 8.7-centimetre stripe, at actual size.

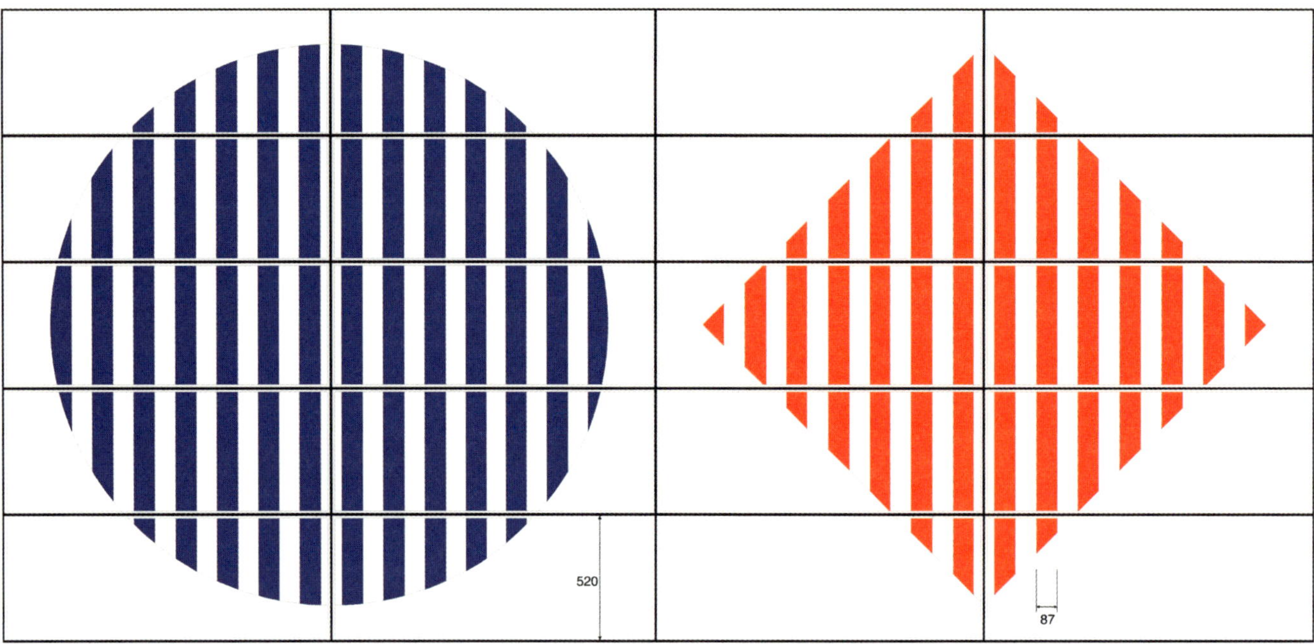

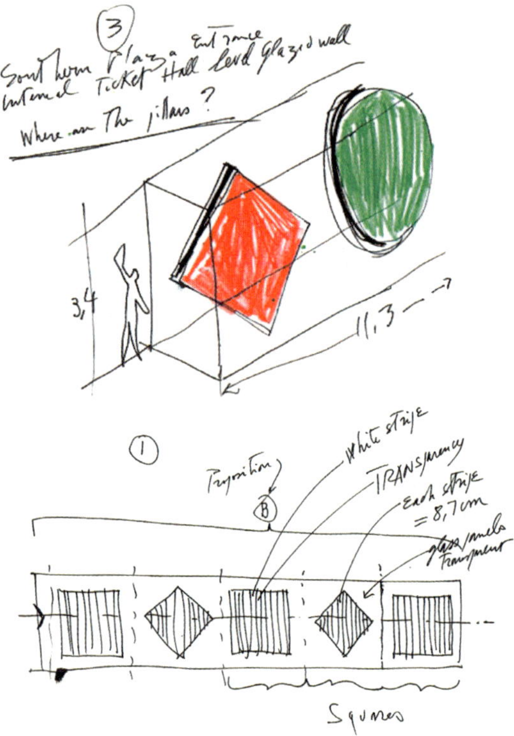

The concept takes shape

These initial ideas reveal that Buren considered applying his stripe to the diamonds and circles, before settling on solid forms for the coloured shapes.

Buren has often employed transport as a way to introduce movement into his work. In 1980, for example, at the Art Institute of Chicago, he pasted stripes onto the doors of trains running past the museum. A window overlooking the railway, normally kept hidden, was uncovered, and a timetable was provided so that visitors would know when the striped trains were passing. Entitled *Watch the Doors, Please!*, the work could be seen from the window and other points around the city. And in France, he has worked with the tram systems of Mulhouse and Tours. In the latter, he applied stripes to the trams' doors and platforms to create a perfect alignment when the vehicles come to a rest. The simplicity of the scheme makes the motion of the tram visible, even when it is not present, while having the practical benefit of letting passengers know where to stand for the next arrival. Through works such as these, the artist creates conditions to allow people to encounter art beyond the gallery wall, often accidentally or unknowingly. As he discusses with Tim Marlow for this book, what does it mean to meet a work in this way? Moreover, how can an artist contend with what he describes as the 'basic futility' of art in a metro?

At Tottenham Court Road, he provides an answer, for he has taken on a space where contemplation of art is not the primary or even the intended activity, and has done so with dramatic results. The main components of the work are the diamond and the circle, each 2.3 metres in height and diameter, which appear through the station. In certain locations, the shapes are solid; in others, they are made from the artist's trademark stripes. By using these repeating forms, the art 'walks' with you, marking time as you travel through the space. Starting its presence at street level against the noisy backdrop of Oxford Street, the black-striped diamonds and circles act as a beacon to the station entrance. The monochrome elements cut through the frenetic environment of the street, the stripes capturing rich reflections of passing buses, multitudes of people and surrounding architecture. From Charing Cross Road, a dramatic frieze of block colours draws you down the escalator and stairway: blue, green, orange, red and yellow diamonds and circles, applied over a striped background. The colours are alphabetically ordered, aesthetic decisions dictated by the choice of an arbitrary system. From the Dominion Theatre entrance, a glass partition bearing white-and-transparent-striped circles and

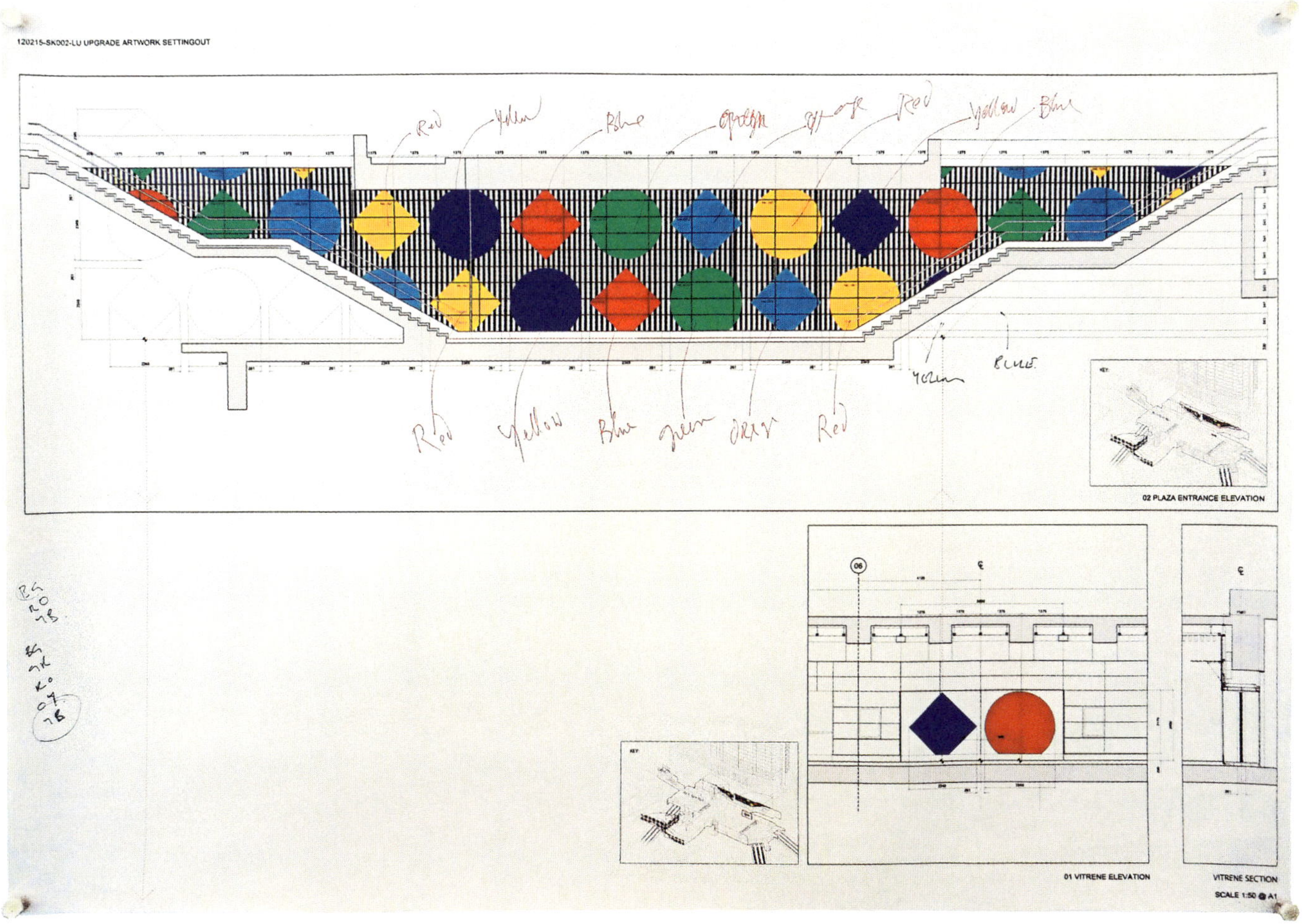

A wall of bold colour

A site drawing by the architects, Hawkins \ Brown, indicates the location of *The Big Wall, Up and Down, Diamonds and Circles, Blue, Green, Orange, Red, Yellow* at the entrance on Charing Cross Road.

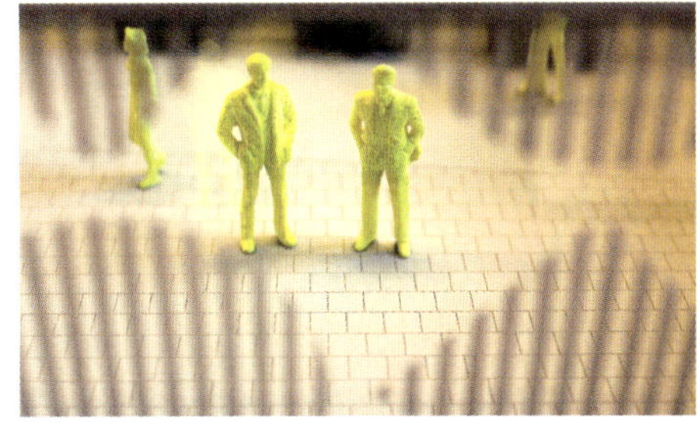

Light, glass and movement

A scale model shows *The Ticket Gate, Transparent Corridor, Diamonds and Circles, White Stripes* at the Dominion Theatre entrance to the station.

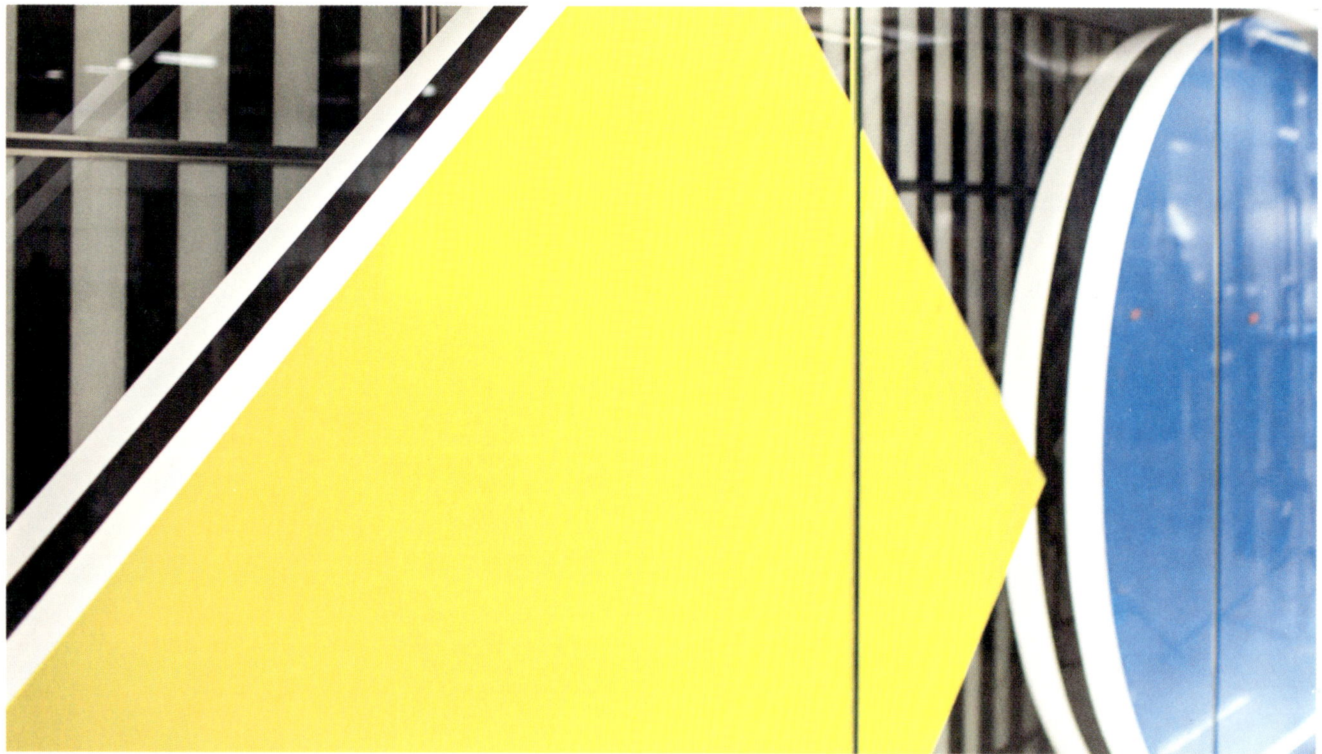

diamonds separates the access to the platforms from the ticket hall. The striped forms on the glass allow us to see both sides of the shape, while the 'colour' is provided by commuters as their busy forms rush past.

In the ticket hall, we find a peculiarity: a vitrine sitting alongside the ticket gates. Buren presents sculpture behind the glass: a yellow diamond and a blue circle, glossy, seductive, their depth marked with the ubiquitous black and white stripes. The sculptural forms contained within the box offer a new way of reading the two-dimensional shapes located throughout the upper levels of the station, for they seem to act almost as parents, the originators of the diamonds and circles applied to the walls. The glass box confounds expectation. Normally seen in a gallery or museum, the vitrine conventionally houses objects that are so delicate that they must be protected. Why have such a display cabinet in a ticket hall? What role does it perform?

It is a puzzle; here are the shapes that have followed you about the station, now in a privileged location behind glass. Are they the source or the conclusion of the work? To Buren, however, the most interesting question is will it make you stop and look? Will it divert your path?

Buren's scheme is a monumental addition to Sir Eduardo Paolozzi's celebrated mosaics deeper inside the station. Installed in the early 1980s, these works are among the most spectacular examples of public art of the late twentieth century, and evidence of London Underground's long-standing commitment to art. Descending from the new ticket hall, travellers are met in the lower passageways and platforms with bursts of movement from Paolozzi's complex urban industrial scenes. Stretching across all platforms, inhabiting interconnected tunnels and a unique rotunda space, the extent of Paolozzi's work is astounding. As part of the station's huge modernization, the mosaics

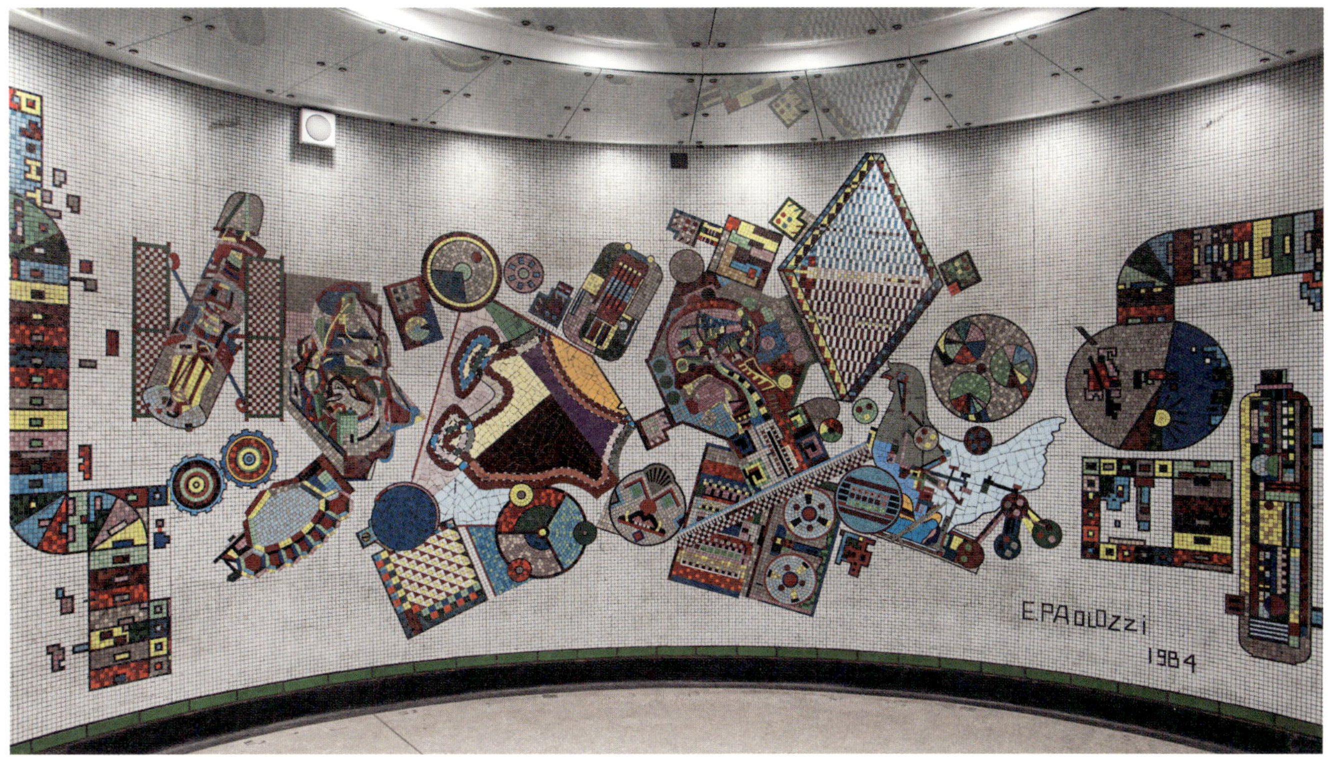

Masterpiece in mosaic

The unique rotunda space at the lower
level (the station's former lift shaft)
is home to one section of Sir Eduardo
Paolozzi's iconic mosiac scheme.

have undergone significant restoration and conservation work. The complexity of the task required a sophisticated approach to their repair. The majority of the mosaics have been left undisturbed, but in certain areas a more decisive response was required. With the raising of the ticket hall's ceiling, the 1980s escalator arches that descended from that space and featured Paolozzi's designs could not remain in place. These structures have been removed, but the legacy of the art work has been assured with this section of mosaic now forming part of the collection of Edinburgh College of Art, an institution renowned for its relationship with Paolozzi. Meanwhile, a major standalone mosaic element was preserved as the former Oxford Street entrance was taken out of use. With the support of preservation experts and specialists in the movement of art, this mosaic has been reinstated in the new tunnels at the lower levels of the station, ensuring that this intricate masterpiece remains on public view for decades to come.

As London changes and grows, so does our Underground system. With works by two of the finest artists of the past fifty years, Tottenham Court Road station is a testament to the power of art in public space. Now that his scheme is fully installed, we can celebrate the power of Daniel Buren's achievement as it measures out the redesigned station with stripe, with shape and with colour. Tottenham Court Road sits firmly within his illustrious practice, and yet presents something new. His work forces us to consider the pace and path we take as we pass through the station; it reminds us of the potential of artists' work to reimagine space; and it helps us to find beauty in the mundane and in the predictable: the transport hub, the throng of a shopping centre, the start, middle and end of numerous quotidian journeys. Buren has given us an extraordinary response to public space and the way we experience the city. It is an iconic work in an iconic location, a celebration of the extraordinary – and the everyday – in our daily lives.

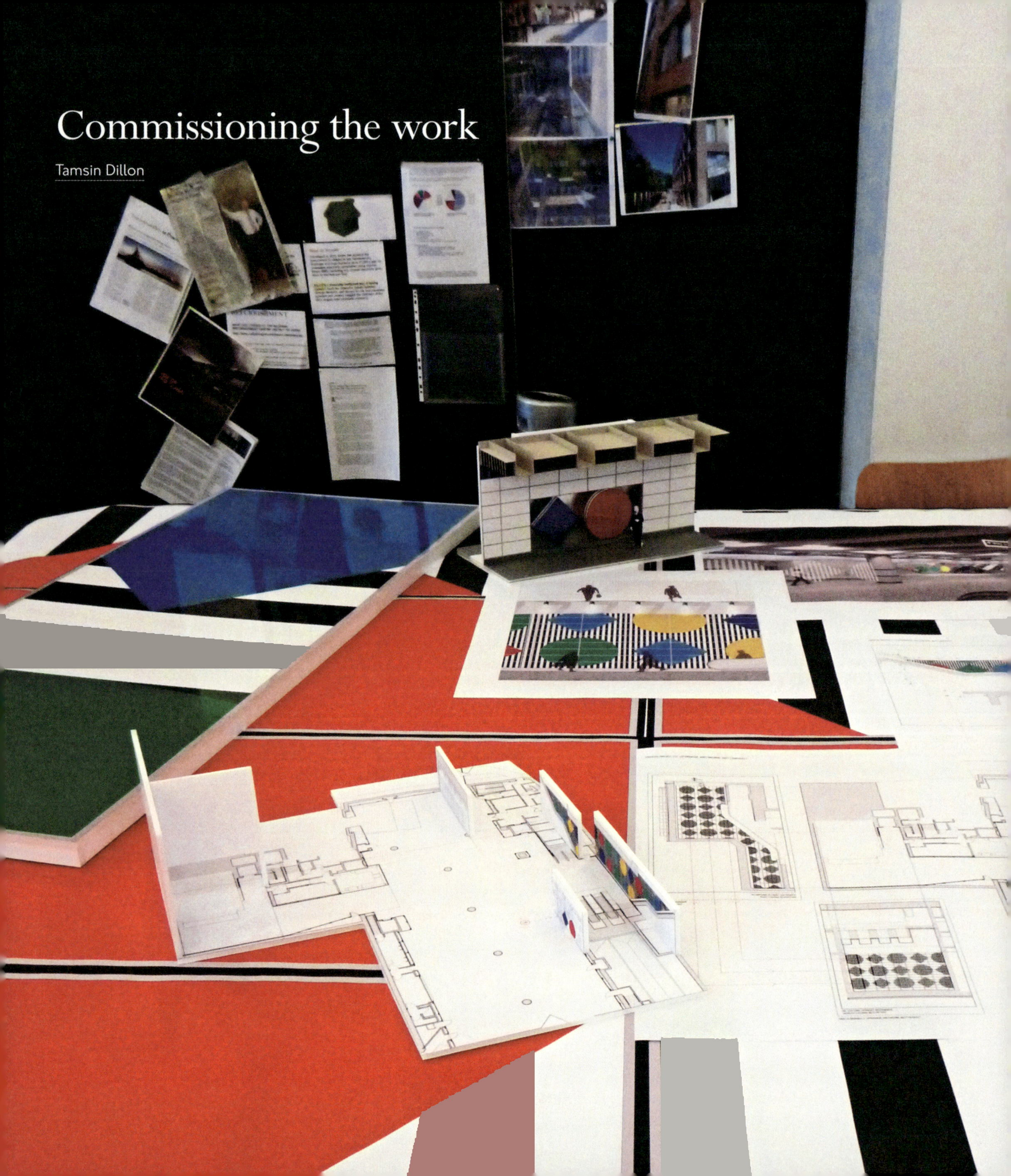

Commissioning the work
Tamsin Dillon

As an artist who has made many large-scale works in the public realm, including several as part of major building projects, Daniel Buren is accustomed to the length of time it can take to realize a commission. Even with that experience, however, the installation at Tottenham Court Road station has required an impressive level of commitment on his part, being almost a decade in the making. What is more, he is perhaps the only person who has seen the evolution of the work from start to finish.

The process began back in 2007 when I, as the then head of Art on the Underground, brought together a range of stakeholders to form a selection panel for the commission. In its first meeting, the group approved a brief and a longlist of candidates who might be considered. The brief outlined the challenge and opportunity for the artist: to create a permanent work for Tottenham Court Road that had a clear presence and impact on its architecture; to produce an installation that allowed the London Underground brand to remain prominent within the overall design, and would not detract from the signage guiding passengers around the station; and to develop a proposal that complemented the mosaics by Eduardo Paolozzi that were already in place. There were additional constraints, too, such as the use of only certain permissible materials, and the requirement to ensure a minimal level of maintenance. Such challenging conditions, typical of the complex nature of many public sites, would make the commission a demanding but stimulating experience for the selected artist. It was crucial that we arrived at a shortlist of individuals who could create world-class art under such constricted circumstances.

With all of this in mind, I invited Daniel to make a proposal. Because of his track record, approach and range of work since the 1960s, we were confident that he would produce a vision that was unique and striking. The sketches outlining his initial ideas confirmed that belief, and the panel received them enthusiastically. Our decision to award him the commission noted that his proposal would be bold and assertive, yet subtle; that it would work well as part of the architecture, yet would be unmissable and memorable.

From the beginning, the process was complicated, with many people at Transport for London and beyond necessarily involved in approving and moving forward the commission. Our selection of Daniel was the start of years of meetings, site visits, sample viewings and constant liaison between the artist, architects and contractors that has continued until this day. I and my team followed the upgrade works closely,

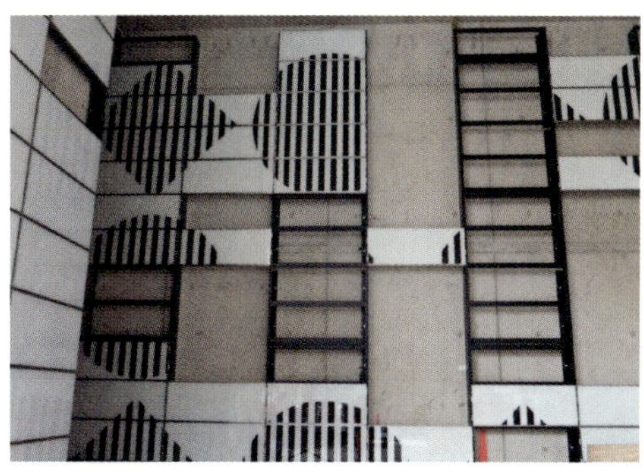

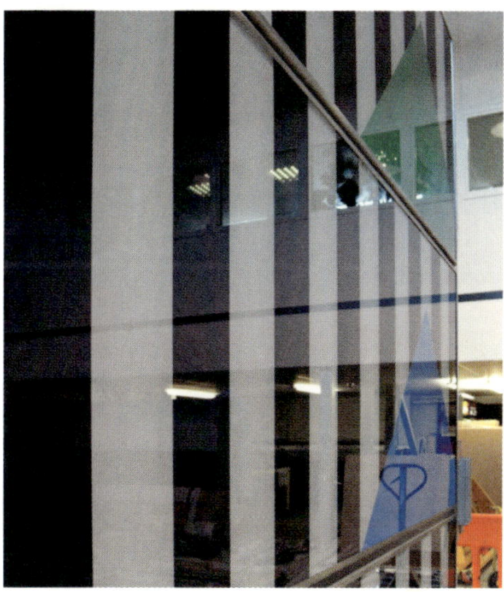

The scheme at the Oxford Street entrance begins to be installed in November 2013 (top), while test panels for the frieze at the Charing Cross Road are reviewed on site (bottom).

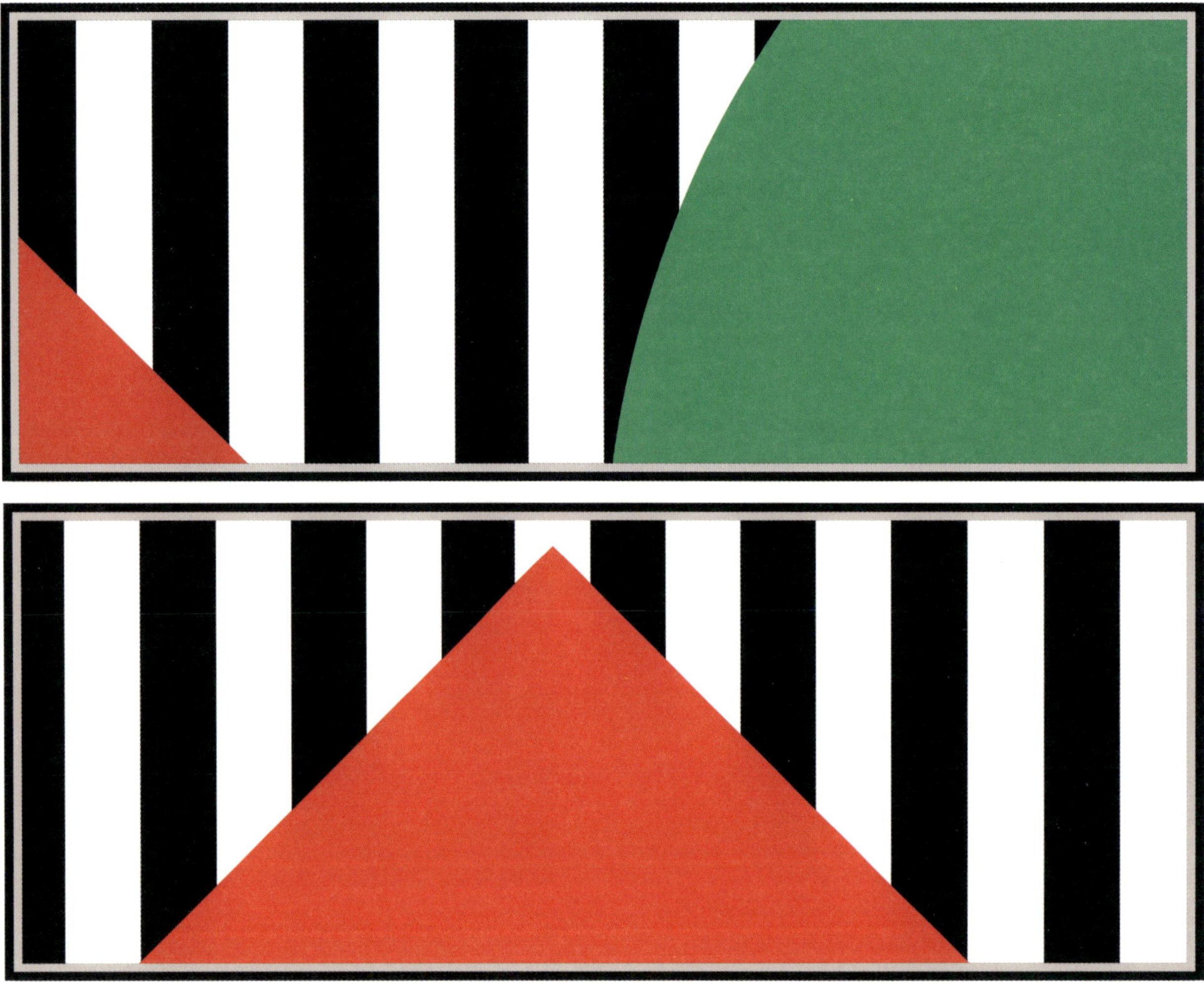

ensuring that his concept remained a central element of the plans, from the models and drawings through to the redeveloped station. It was important that everyone could envisage the proposed multifaceted installation, especially as we knew that it would take so long to come to fruition.

Having established the partnerships for the commission, and having put all the necessary elements in place to ensure the success of this ambitious project, I found myself handing over the baton to Eleanor Pinfield, my successor as head of Art on the Underground, just as the first part of the work, the black-and-white striped shapes at the Oxford Street entrance, was being completed and installed in 2014.

Since then, I have remained closely in touch with the process, keeping up to date with each of the latest developments, issues and changes, but above all anticipating the moment when this important permanent public art work could finally be unveiled in its entirety.

To view art works *in situ* years after they were conceived may be a frequent experience for Buren, but there is undoubtedly something uncanny about it. The architects' two-dimensional, computer-generated renderings of the station and the works within it were so accurate that encountering them physically in reality is a strange experience. There is an odd sense of familiarity that is not

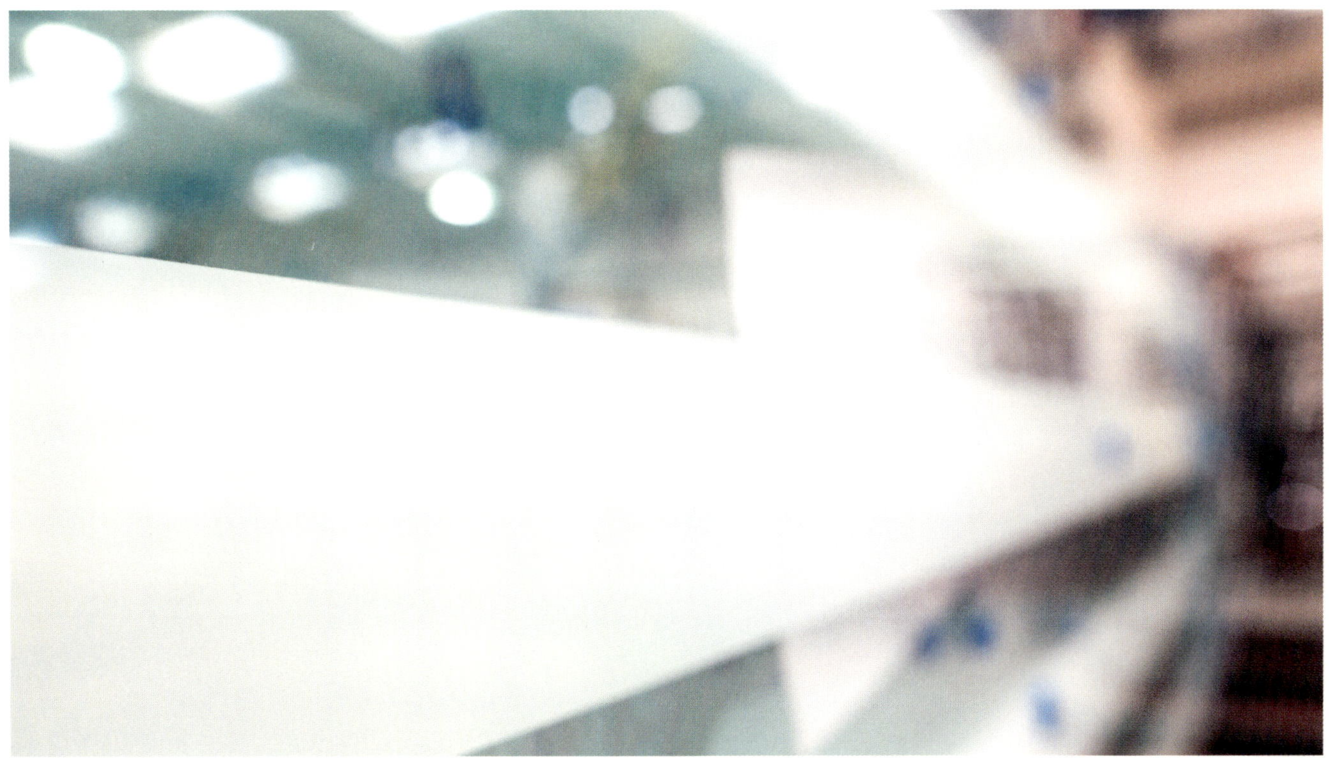

Glass panels for the Dominion Theatre
entrance partition, the last part of the
work to be installed in early 2017, await
delivery from the factory to the site.

in keeping with visiting a space for the first time — one that, until only recently, did not even exist.

Now that we can see the work installed as planned, we can reflect on the commission itself. It is possible to understand and admire Buren's ability to visualize the impact he would have on the architecture and to comprehend why his apparently simple proposition was chosen. The process has also unfolded in parallel with significant changes within Art on the Underground, in some way charting the growth and development of the programme over those years. The completion of this project represents a significant milestone in the history and trajectory of London Underground and its art programme, which, by building on the unique heritage of art and design on the Tube, has secured a clear and necessary niche within it. The realization of Buren's commission signifies a kind of coming of age for the programme, a maturing as it grows towards its firmly grounded future.

With the artist's vision now fully realized, it can at last enter the public realm and discourse: to be looked at and engaged with. This book is part of that process. Millions of people will pass through the station over the coming years, and they will encounter Buren's wonderfully simple but effective intervention as they do so. They will engage with it, or perhaps they will not; but if the art works resonate with the public as others before them have done, they will generate debate — certainly, Paolozzi's mosaics have been polarizing opinion since they were created. Personally, I hope that each time that people use Tottenham Court Road, they will take something from the work, even if it is simply to think a little differently about the space because of the intervention that Buren has made. I hope also that I will be just one among many, many people who will want to congratulate and thank Daniel Buren for taking so much time to bring us this wonderful permanent new work as part of the growing legacy and collection of art across London Underground.

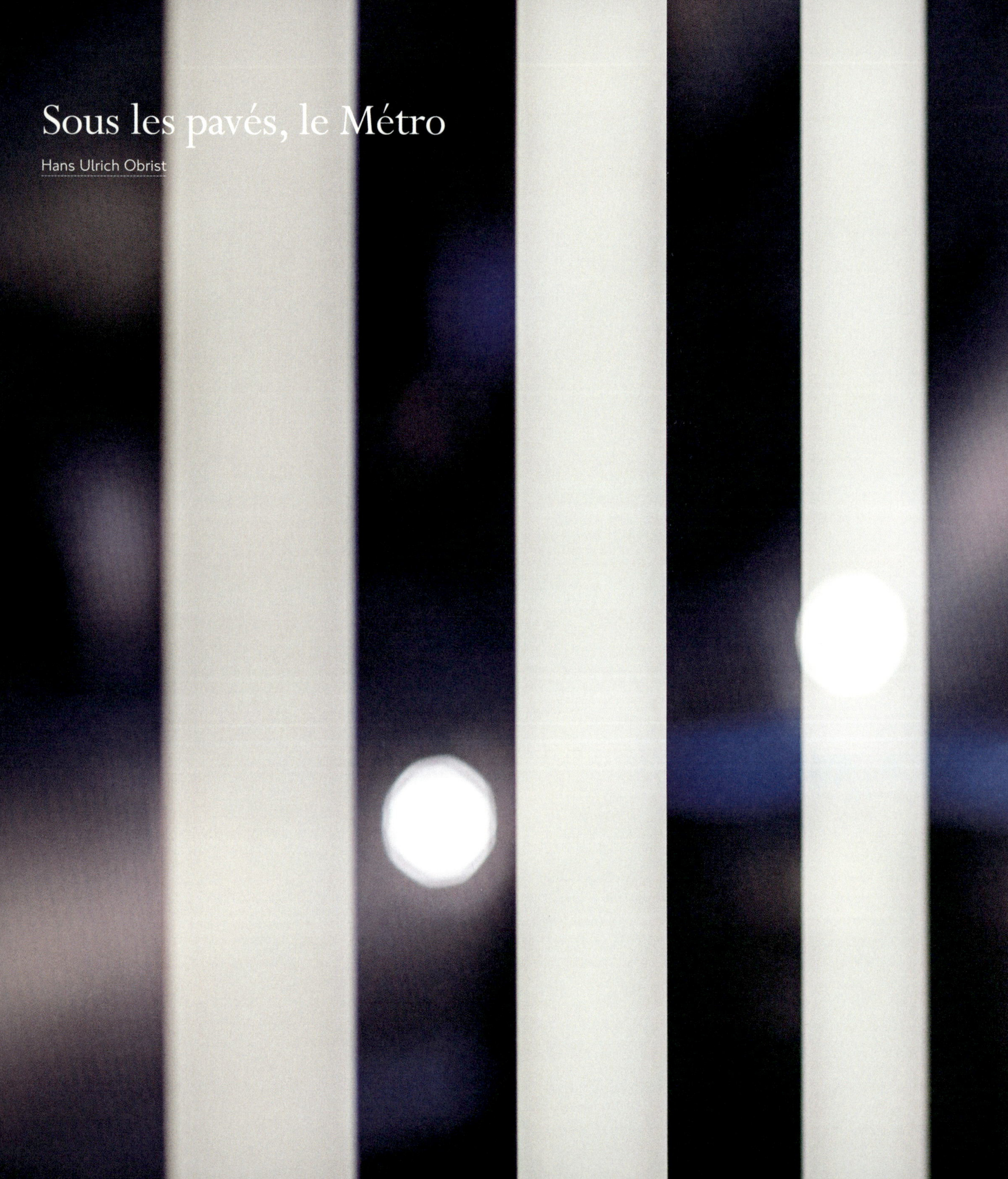
Sous les pavés, le Métro
Hans Ulrich Obrist

The poet, artist, designer and architect Vito Acconci once told me that a public space is not made public per se simply by virtue of being accessible to passers-by. A town square is designed as a place for congregation, for encounters, for experiences; a city-centre car park, on the other hand, while it might have comparable dimensions and be used by a similar number of people, is not (or not normally). It is the responsibility of those who create the space to imbue it with the special awareness and opportunity that is characteristic of a communal place. To make space public is an act.

Daniel Buren has long been a pioneer of public art. Since he began as a painter in the early 1960s, this prolific and innovative artist has accomplished many *in situ* interventions in the public realm, in cities and gardens, as well as in galleries and museums, always in response to the surrounding environment. He is best known for using regularly striped patterns to integrate visual surface and architectural schemes, notably on historical landmarks, as with the 1985–6 work *Les Deux Plateaux*, his celebrated sculptural contribution to the inner courtyard of the Palais-Royal in Paris. He developed his trademark stripes – always vertical, always the same breadth, always separated by the same intervals, and always painted in white and one other colour – shortly before he formed an association with Olivier Mosset, Michel Parmentier and Niele Toroni, which lasted from December 1966 to September 1967. The stripes invite us to consider the architecture (as found) of which they are a part as much as the image they present. Buren describes them as a 'visual tool' that is 'no longer a work to be seen, to be looked at, but the element that allows something else to be seen'. Thus he advances his aim of engaging the viewer with the architectural and symbolic elements of the space in which they find themselves.

Buren has used these trademark stripes consistently throughout the intervening half century to explore the alliance between painting and architecture. For his 1968 exhibition at the Galleria Apollinaire in Milan, he glued green-and-white-striped material to the exterior door. The piece obstructed the entrance to the gallery, drawing attention to the ways painting can function in and with the space in which it is presented. It forced viewers to look at the door, something that they might not otherwise have noticed. The effect was to remind them that their engagement with a work of art can never entirely be disentangled from its architectural context. This desire to investigate the relationship between art and architecture was apparent when the Art Institute of Chicago invited Buren

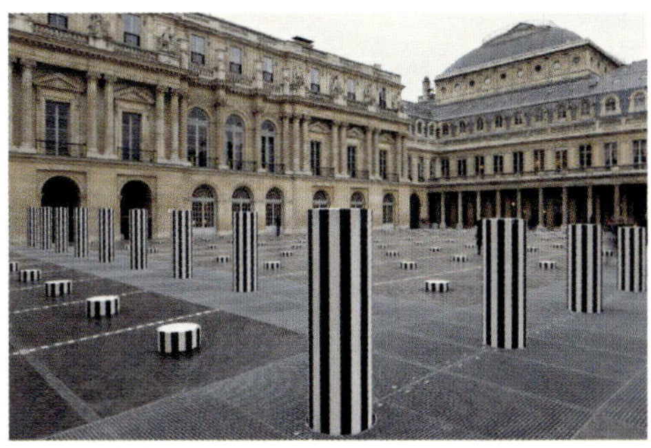

Photo-souvenir: Les Deux Plateaux

Permanent sculpture *in situ*,
Cour d'Honneur, Palais-Royal, Paris,
1985–6 (detail)

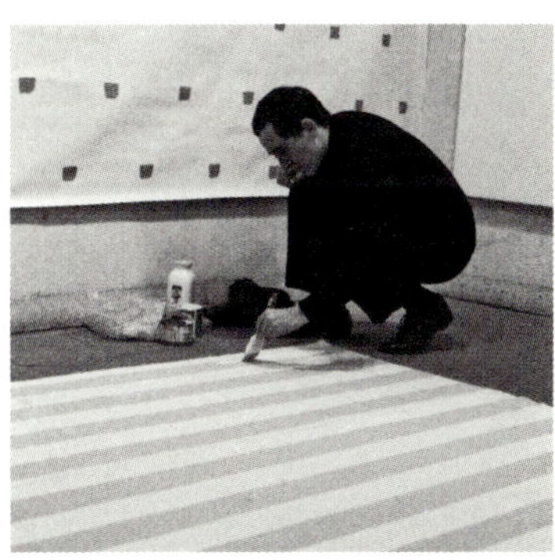

Photo-souvenir: Manifestation 1
Buren, Mosset, Parmentier, Toroni

18th Salon de la Jeune Peinture,
Musée d'Art Moderne de la Ville
de Paris, 3 January 1967 (detail)

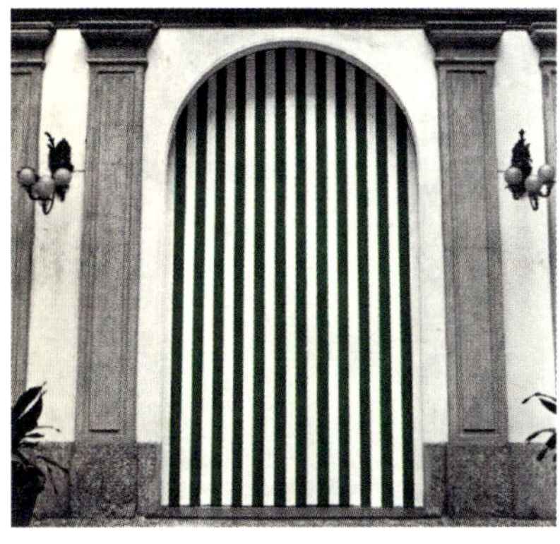

Photo-souvenir:
Papiers collés blanc et vert

Work *in situ*, Galleria Apollinaire, Milan,
October 1968 (detail)

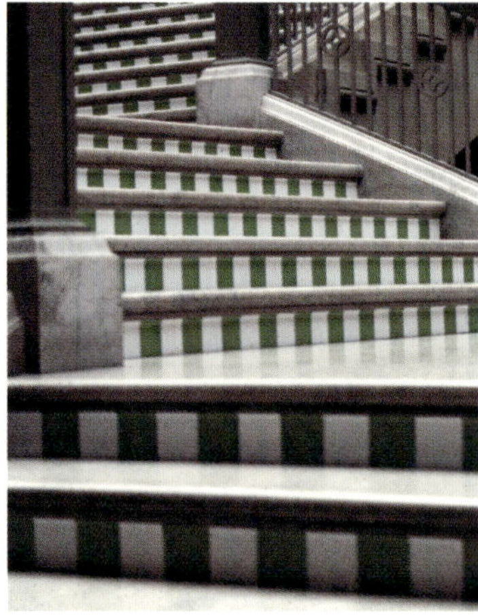

Work *in situ*, for the group show
'Europe in the Seventies: Aspects of
Recent Art', Art Institute of Chicago,
October 1977 (detail)

to take part in the exhibition 'Europe in the Seventies: Aspects of Recent Art' in 1977. Rather than present his work in the traditional exhibition spaces, he decided to make use of an architectural feature – the museum's grand staircase – that is typically treated as a purely functional part of the building, a means of getting from one place to another. By adding stripes to the risers of the steps, he transformed the staircase into a work of art in itself, to be treated and understood as such, rather than as a break or interval between the experience of art. The work is an example of how Buren changes the way we think of the spaces we inhabit, and is characteristic of his practice of working with unregarded or ignored elements: staircases, lobbies, exterior walls. More recently, he has reimagined Frank Gehry's radical building for the Fondation Louis Vuitton in Paris by transforming its billowing sails into a colourful stained-glass patchwork. By drawing attention to the shading and mirroring effects of the building's outer carapace, the intervention allows visitors to better understand and appreciate the feat of architecture. When we were speaking about his work with gardens in 2000, Buren told me that:

'I'm not someone who works in "untamed" nature, but only in landscapes transformed by man. For me there is not much difference in spirit between the rural landscape in which I work and the architecture or urban space in which things happen…. I don't think I would be interested in making a work in the desert, as many artists did in the 1960s. I wouldn't go. This is not an aesthetic point of view. I could go for a walk, but not to work. For those are places in which a human being is only a visitor and no longer a social being. It is a place without human encounters and without human history.'

Nancy Spero's 2001 mosaics of theatre-, dance- and orchestra-related subjects appear throughout the 66th Street-Lincoln Center subway station.

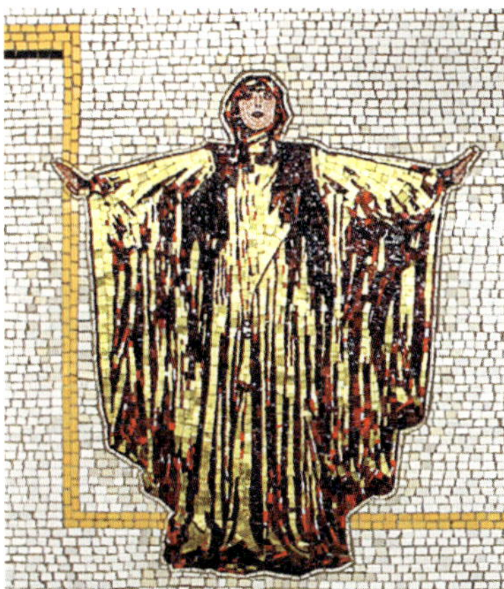
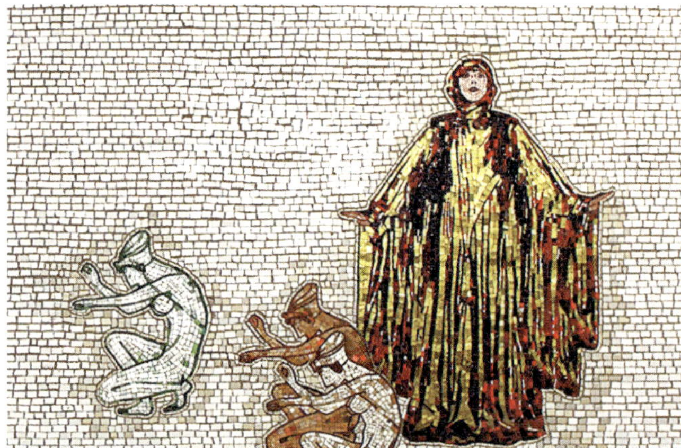
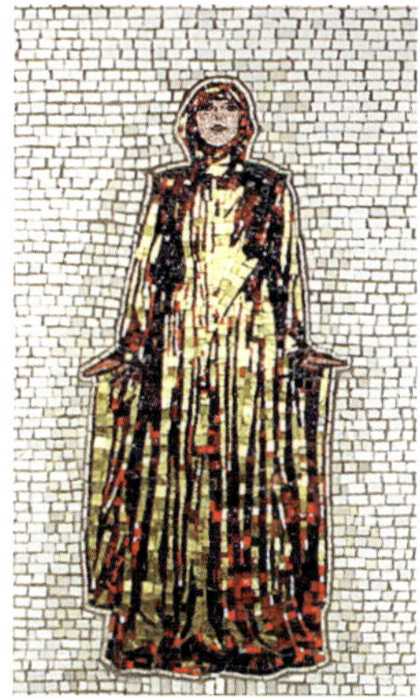

There are many artists who work *on* space, but Buren works *with* space, which makes him the perfect candidate for this commission at Tottenham Court Road. He adds something new to a long and distinguished history of artists working with underground stations, one of the most important chapters of which was written by Eduardo Paolozzi at this very location. Another great example of this strand of contemporary art is Nancy Spero's glass mosaic murals at 66th Street-Lincoln Center subway station in New York. These figurative works represent creativity: an opera star in a golden gown is depicted in several poses, now raising her arms, now singing. As the train goes by, the singer is animated so that her arms seem move to the side, and

Photo-souvenir:
L'Observatoire de la lumière

Work *in situ*, Fondation Louis Vuitton,
Paris, May 2016 (detail)

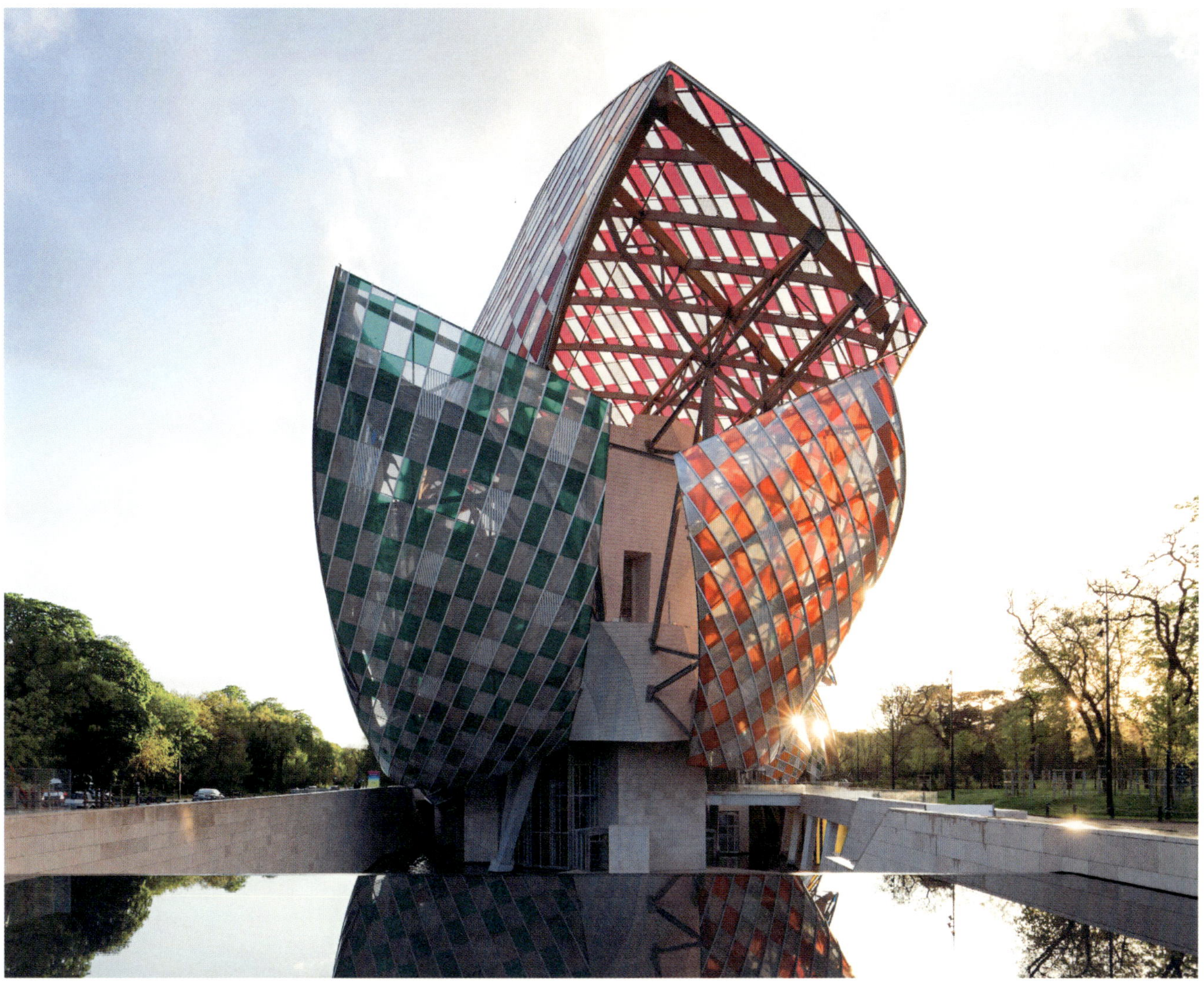

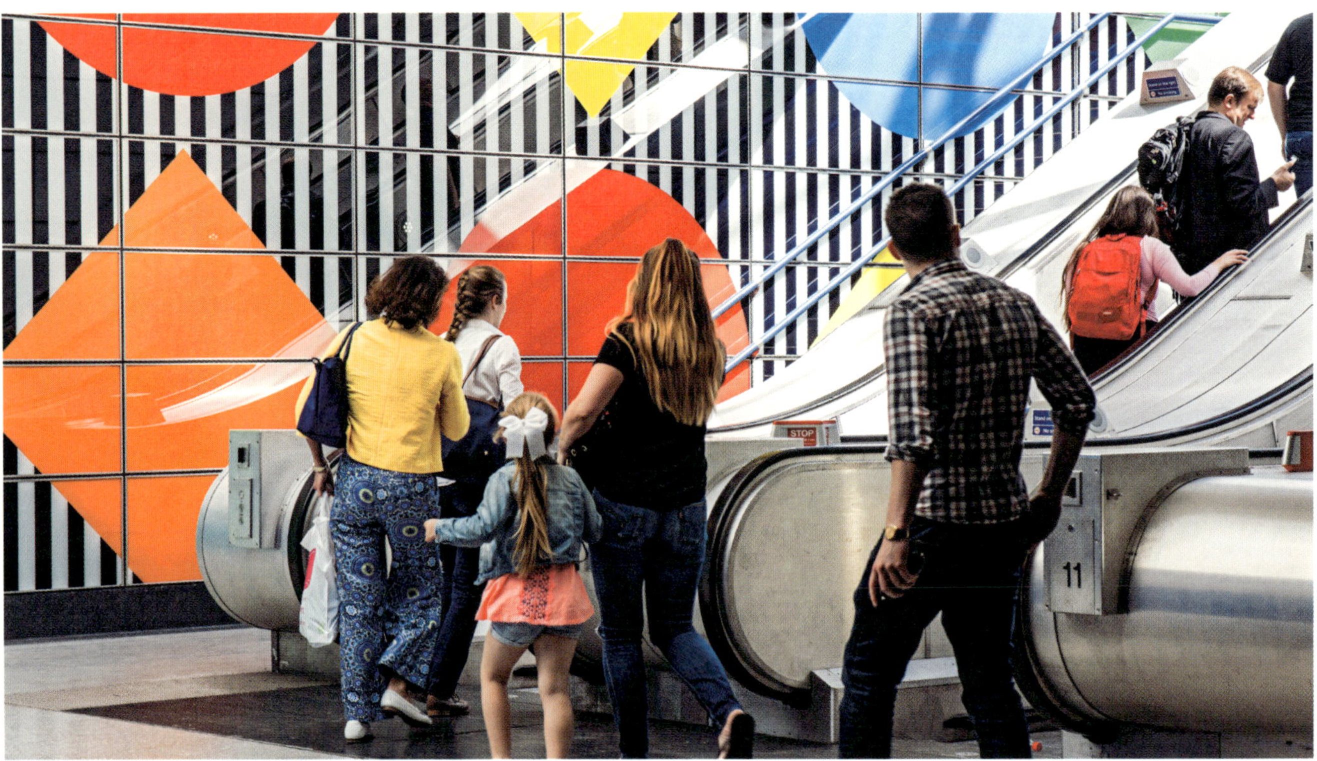

Moving through the space

Commuters make their way up the escalator onto Charing Cross Road past *The Big Wall, Up and Down, Diamonds and Circles, Blue, Green, Orange, Red, Yellow*.

then up and down. Spero incorporates the speed of the train into her work, using the passenger's experience to her own advantage, making the journey part of the work. Buren, too, uses the movement of the body through space as a central component of this intervention, not least on the escalators.

This is the essence of public art — to engage the visitor with the space — and while Spero and Buren might seem like very different artists in terms of their aesthetics or preoccupations, they both address this central purpose. Buren's scheme at Tottenham Court Road is to implement simple geometric shapes that issue from a number of stripes or colour blocks. These shapes pop up on different walls around the ticket hall and the entrances to the station. The idea came from working closely with the architects from the early stages of the project to understand how the spaces of the station would work, with its various interlocking floors, escalators, plazas and platforms. The artist describes it as a 'maze', a puzzle to be worked out in terms of how different spaces are interdependent, and how that concept could be used to enhance or draw out those spatial relationships.

As with the majority of Buren's interventions, this work was designed for and is only applicable to this particular situation. He has said that his art 'is never autonomous' because it relies on being seen in the space for which it was intended. The scheme at Tottenham Court Road is developed in response to, and is dependent upon, the architecture and the journey of the commuter through the station. It cannot be separated from those basic considerations. Thus we must think about the work not as something to be understood independently from every other aspect of the building, but as an integral part of our experience of it. The artist's practice is not only about working with the architecture, however; it is also about working with the people who create the space and those who move through it. This particular work is about the history of this part of central London, this vital hub on the transport network of one of the world's global cities, through which 230,000 people pass each day. The complexity of the space – the amount of different ways that someone can navigate it – means that each visitor enjoys a different journey through these repeating diamond and circle shapes, the original forms of which are realized in three dimensions in a vitrine in the ticket hall. The order in which the work of art is experienced, how you move around it, is decided by the specifics of your own journey – what platform you need to find, whether you need to top up your Oyster card. This openness to multiple movements through the space, which makes it possible for the viewer to pick their own way through and encounter the work from a variety of perspectives, reminds me of a discussion in which Hubert Damisch told me that in the experience of art there should be no predefined path, meaning that the visitor could enjoy a different experience each time, because new connections would present themselves. Buren's determination not to tell the viewer what path to take strikes me as a typically intelligent response to the specific situation – of commuting, travel, change – in which this work is installed.

In a conversation published in 2006, Buren told me that he admired the way the Mexican architect Luis Barragán – whose work he characterized as 'architecture at the limit of sculpture' – employed what he called 'offset entrances' [*entrées déportées*]:

> 'These entrances give the impression that the spaces are larger than they in fact are. They are placed in respect to the other features so that, when one goes through them, the apparent space is increased and tricks one's perception of the real space. There are also these games in the entrances, with colours reflected in bodies of static water which act as mirrors. And what is also very beautiful are these interior courtyards under the roofs, these patios … into which one emerges at the top of the house, and which give the impression of infinity.'

That notion of real and imagined space, circulation and the infinite – of moving around rather than following a single line – sheds light on Buren's intervention at Tottenham Court Road. From the start, he wanted to connect the ideas behind the work to the way that travellers move through the space: how they pass from under- to overground, or from one platform to another, through the series of tunnels, escalators, passageways and open spaces. This theme also links to the station's function in London's transport system, carrying citizens around the city. A static presentation would not work, because people are constantly moving through the station, so the artist has elected against having a single point at which the viewer should stand and admire the work in favour of an installation that you walk through and with. He creates a choreography of connections between the constituent parts by playing with colour and form through repetition and difference. Although there is little obvious visual action, the change in patterning creates the experience of a continuous, joined-up work. Using ordinary forms, Buren creates something extraordinary. Simple geometric forms coalesce into a frieze, which accompanies the flâneur on the journey from outside to inside, and vice versa.

Buren's work draws attention to the ways our daily lives interact with built environments and circulatory systems. This piece of public art encourages us to be curious about the world around us even when we are engaged in the most mundane of acts – commuting – and to consider our place within these architectures and the broader operations of the capital. There is at the heart of the work a desire to transform our everyday experience of the city, to remind us that the inquisitive mind and eye can find surprises around every corner.

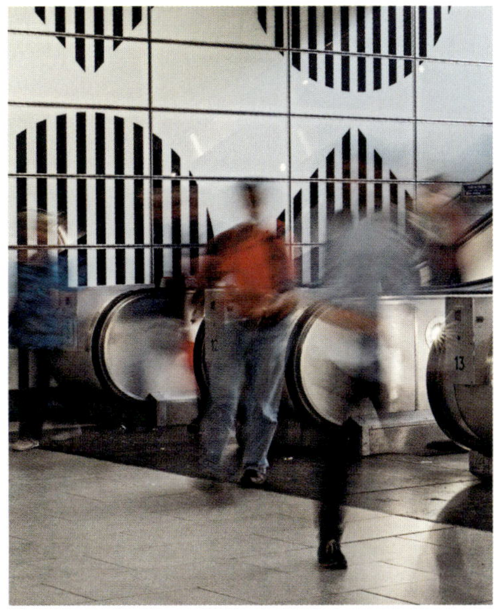

From outside to in

The regular and repeating pattern of geometric shapes and 8.7-centimetre stripes creates a continuous and rhythmic passage from street to concourse.

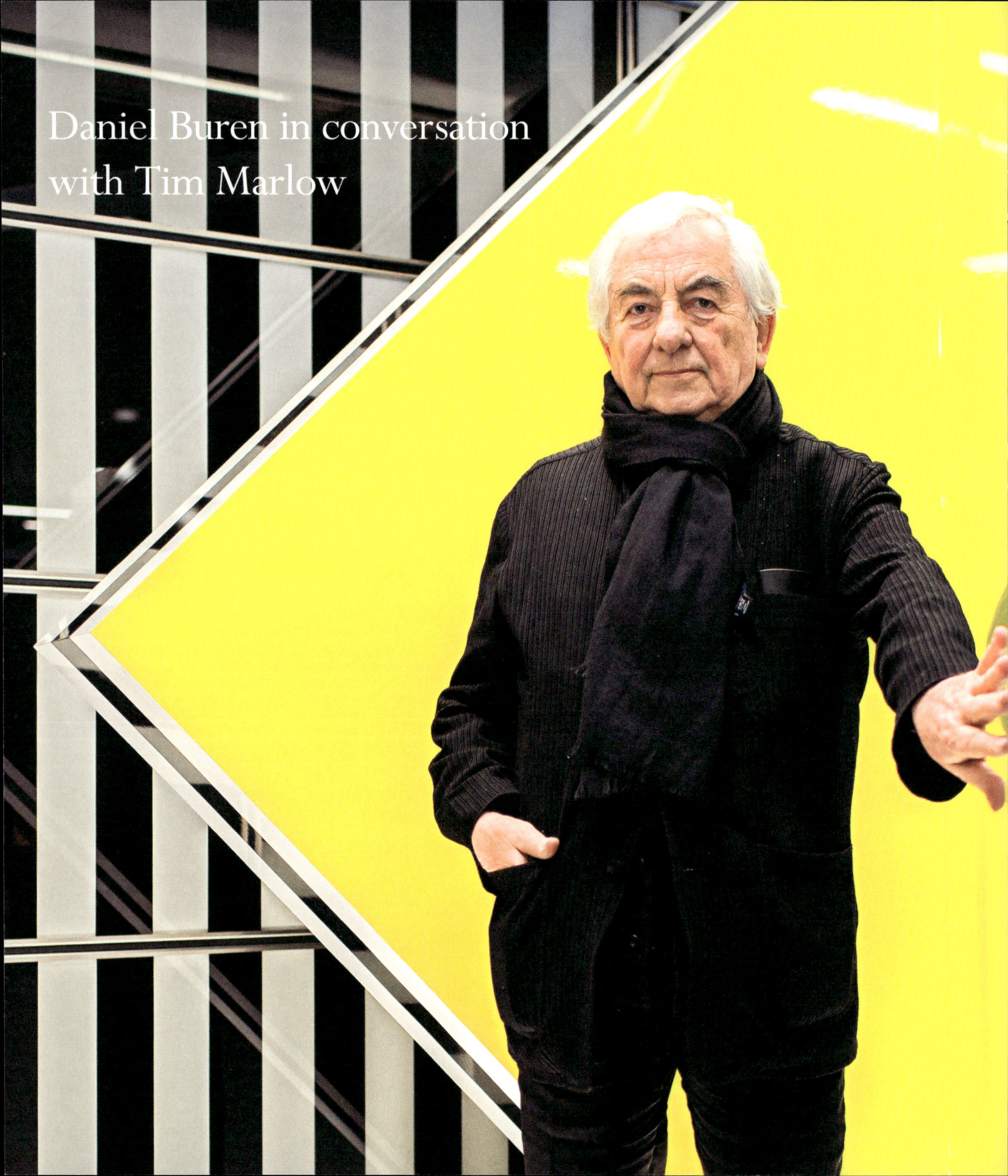
Daniel Buren in conversation
with Tim Marlow

TM: You seem to have developed a long and deep affinity with transport networks and metro stations in your work. It reads like a journey, from the *affichages sauvages* in the Paris Métro in the early 1970s via the Chicago train system in the early 1980s to the tram project in Tours in 2009.

DB: I have worked quite extensively, and one work leads to another. But I have never really paid much attention to the fact that I have worked so often with transportation. Most of my projects, especially the public art works, are the result of an invitation to participate in a competition of some kind. I have no idea if the people who invite me to take part have understood better than myself that I have a special 'talent' to deal with such topics or if it is just a series of coincidences.

It is true, though, that I have been involved with circulation, transport, signalization for a very long time. Some of my earliest attempts, from the end of 1967 up to the early 1970s, were my first striped posters, which I glued onto the sides of trucks when they were in parking lots or waiting on red lines. And in March 1970 I did a work in all 110 stations of the Paris Métro. For one week, I placed a blue-and-white-striped poster in the top right-hand corner of those large rectangular panels where they put adverts for the coming fortnight of shows and films. Three years later, I repeated the exercise but with a different colour stripe, this time orange. I then made two books of photographs of the pasted-up pieces of striped paper *in situ* in each station, which I presented by station name in alphabetical order. One volume was called *Legend I* and the other was *Legend II*. I wrote a text that was printed on the covers in six different languages: English, French, German, Italian, Japanese and Spanish. The books were published inside a simple box through Warehouse Publications in London, thanks to the generosity of Peter Townsend, then the editor of *Studio International*.

All of these works were done because of my own interest. I had no authorization, no request from anyone. I was lucky during this period – from 1965 to 1983 – to have supporters who helped me with invitations to exhibit or to publish books and texts in the United States, Canada, Japan and all over East and West Europe – everywhere except in France, where resistance against my work was extreme and sometimes violent, to say the least!

Later on, I continued to work with many different means of public transportations. For example, I did a large cycle of work with all the buses in Reims over more than one month, which changed from week to week. And in 1980, I did an

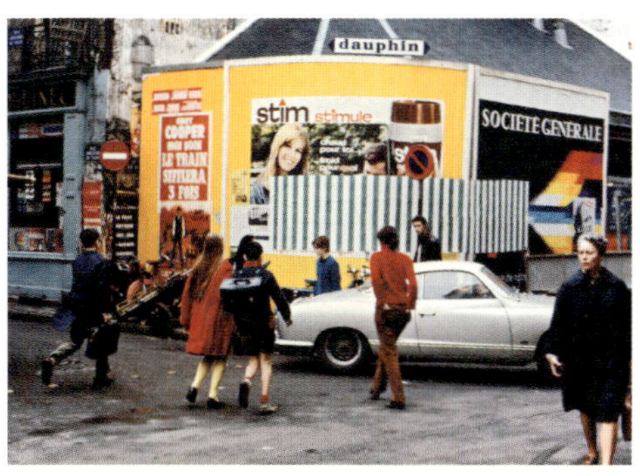

Photo-souvenir:
Affichage sauvage

Work *in situ*, Paris,
April 1968 (detail)

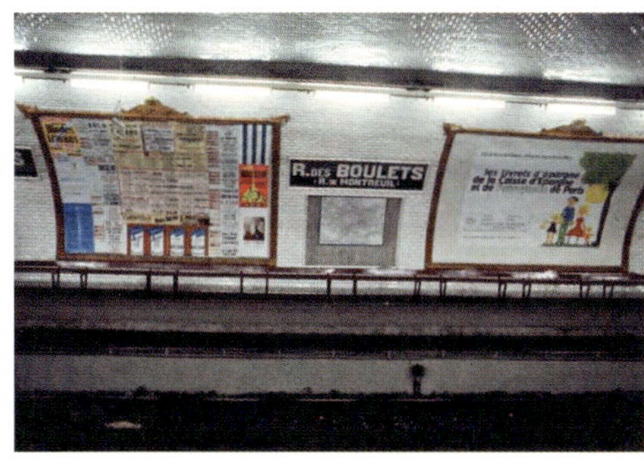

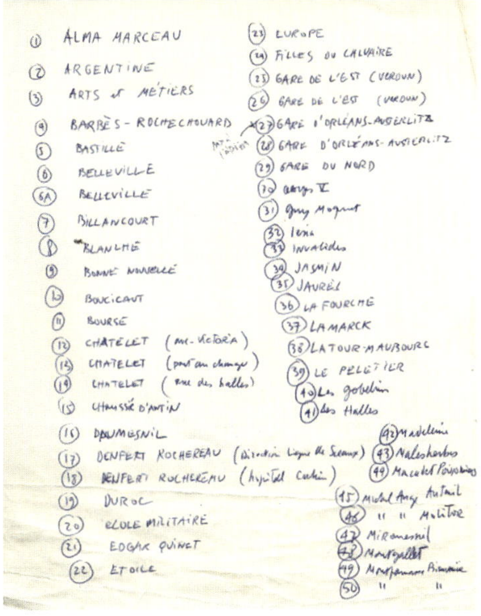

Photo-souvenir:
110 Stations du Métro Parisien

Work *in situ*, Paris,
April 1968 (details)

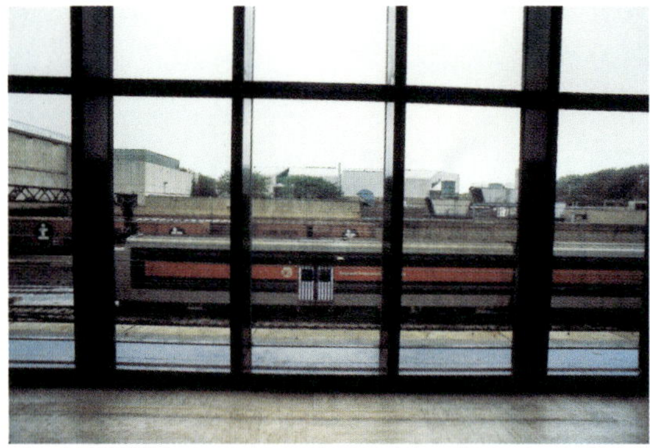

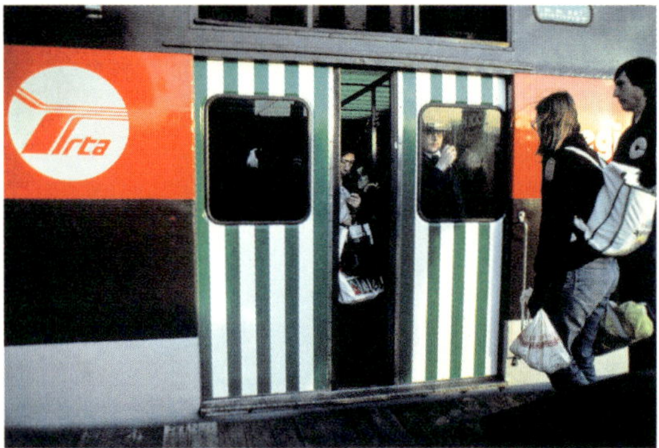

Photos-souvenirs:
Watch the Doors, Please!

Work *in situ*,
Art Institute of Chicago,
October 1980 (details)

important intervention on the doors of trains in Chicago. While preparing my project for the group show 'Europe in the Seventies' at the Art Institute of Chicago, I realized that this major museum was overlooking a railroad and that its biggest gallery was in fact a bridge passing right over the top of the tracks. And when looking at the exterior of the building, I realized also that it was a totally enclosed box of grey stone with the exception of a huge window facing onto this railway. I immediately got the idea of doing something to connect the trains and the museum through this enormous window. But try as hard as I might, I couldn't find it from inside the museum. It was invisible! I asked the staff where it was and they told me that years earlier it had been blocked up by a large internal wall, which was used sometimes to hang paintings. I asked if it would be possible to pull down the wall and thus open up the view of the tracks, the bridge, and beyond the railroad to the art school just behind. Of course, it was impossible to manage that for the group show, so I ended up doing something else. But the curator organizing the exhibition, Anne Rorimer, liked my train idea and continued to work hard to realize it. Finally, after three years, she succeeded and we were able to go ahead. We glued striped vinyl in five different colours onto all the doors of the trains that would pass by the museum. Inside the building, we removed the wall and made the surround of the window look exactly like the back of a canvas on stretchers, and just in front of the window we placed two small pillars just over a metre high, joined together by a red cord like those you see in front of important paintings. Then on the two adjacent walls there were written panels opposite each other: one gave the title of the piece, *Watch the Doors, Please!*, and the other had the complete timetable, giving the exact times the trains would pass in front of the window. Each passage lasted only ten or twelve seconds, after which the train was completely out of sight. The project remained on show for almost two years.

This long description highlights one important aspect of my approach. The project is so specific to that place that it could not work anywhere else. The work is not about just any train doors anywhere in the world, but only this unique occasion of the criss-crossing existence of two specific entities that are completely foreign to each other: a train system and one of the largest art institutions in the United States. And yet the paradox is that this specific dialogue leads us to ask questions about art in general. How much time do we need to see a painting? What are the meanings of frames in museum? Is a museum a place for information, observation, instruction or contemplation? What kind of dialogue happens between the reality of art and the reality of daily existence? Are the doors

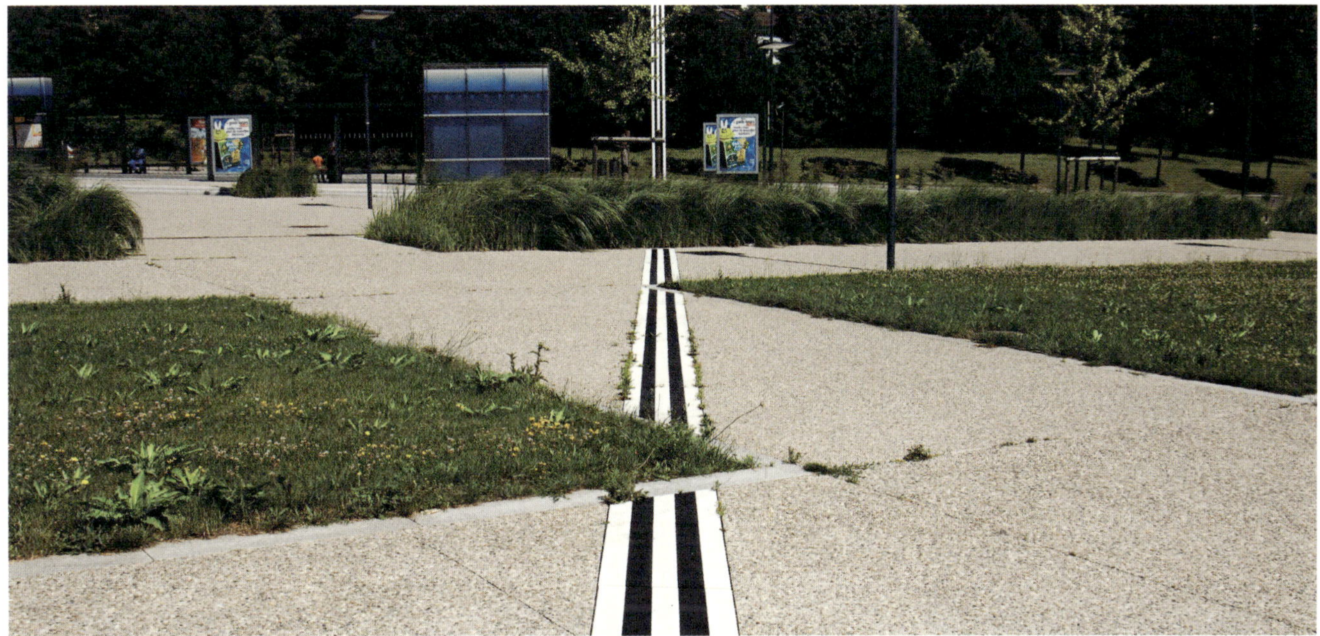

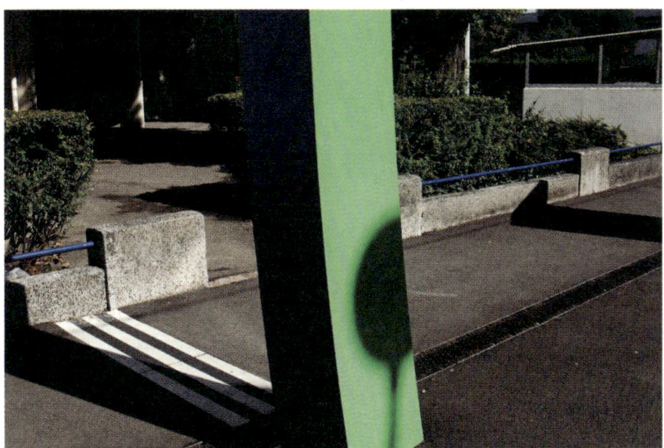

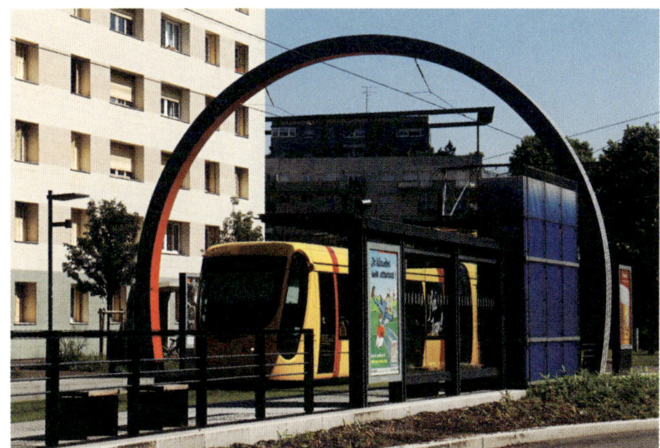

Photos-souvenirs: Tram / Trame

Permanent works *in situ* in two and
three dimensions, realized for
Tram / Train, Mulhouse, 2006 (details)

an art piece only when they pass in front of the museum window but just pure decoration when the train is in a station or out in the suburbs? And so on.

Over time, I have won some big commissions, like the one that involved working with all the tram stations in Mulhouse, France. More recently, with a large team of architects, designers, landscape architects, geographers and engineers, we created the entire tramway in the city of Tours, also in France, from the stations, to the trams themselves, as well as five places along the route. To mention just one detail, the cars are completely covered with a reflecting material that reflects the city, the street, the people, the river … only the doors are marked with black and white stripes. These stripes not only mark the rhythm of the moving vehicle, but also, when the full tram arrives, they connect with the black and

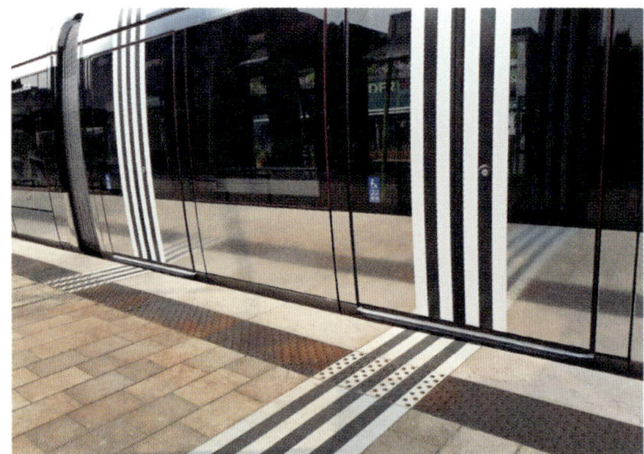

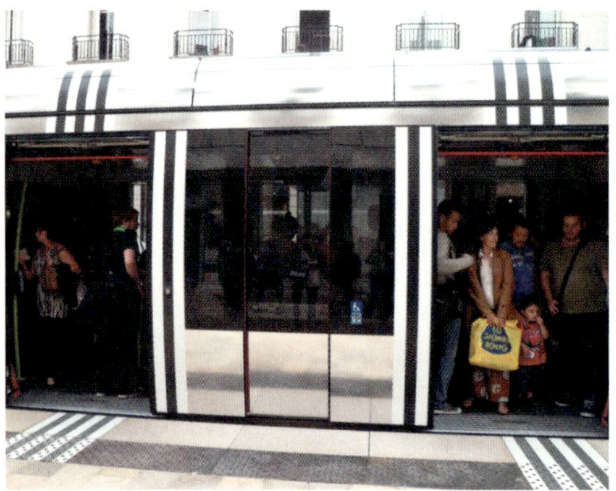

Permanent work *in situ* and mobile,
realized for the metropolitan tram
system of Tours et Joué-lès-Tours,
2013 (details)

white stripes in stone and marble on the floor of the station. The visual result is multiple: people can see exactly where the car will stop and can wait at the correct position, but also, when this moving object stops inside the station and the connection of the doors and floor is made, it seems to be fixed there for ever.

So, when you look back, it's true that I have been particularly interested with the idea of transportation in general and everything around it: movement, signalization, articulation between stations and trains or buses or boats.... But if you understand that each of my works is made in response to a

specific context, it discounts the caricature of my practice that you sometimes hear: 'Buren is just gluing stripes anywhere – in buses, trains, boats, trucks, stairs, walls, balloons, chairs, pavements, vitrines, skylights, etc.' Of course, after fifty years, someone might summarize my work in that way, but the reality is very different.

TM: How consciously did you work with this history when you began to think about Tottenham Court Road station?

DB: Tottenham Court Road has more to do with the circulation of people and what they can see when they move in a place like a station. When you realize how everyone walks, and more often runs, inside a subway, either to enter or to go out, you know that most people will have only a very short time or even interest to look at what you have made. If you accept such a situation, and if you know well that nobody in such a place is there to look at an art piece, you start to understand the challenge. So I tried to adapt my way of thinking for such a special configuration and activity. Millions of people moving all the time in front or against colours and forms with no intention to contemplate them at all! That was the challenge.

TM: People move at very different speeds in a subway station and, as you intimate, they will experience your work in a variety of fleeting ways. The escalator is particularly interesting in this regard – some people race down it and others stand (on the right, a London tradition). The work is therefore passive or active, fluid or static.

DB: Escalators are an interesting tool because they are maybe the only situation, after being inside a carriage travelling to the next station, where people are immobile and moving at once. That said, the movement of the escalator is not too fast and everyone is free to look at what is on the walls from very close up. I like this situation in the midst of the turmoil. A smooth, regular speed of ascending or descending in the middle of an otherwise frenetic and zigzagging activity. I agree totally with what you said about the different registers of the work. If someone paid attention to the elements presented at different levels, perhaps from a distance or extremely close by, they could realize the various stages from active to passive, from fluid to static.

TM: The site was not built when you began to develop the project in 2007. How does the physical, visceral experience of what you have created compare with your initial drawings and plans?

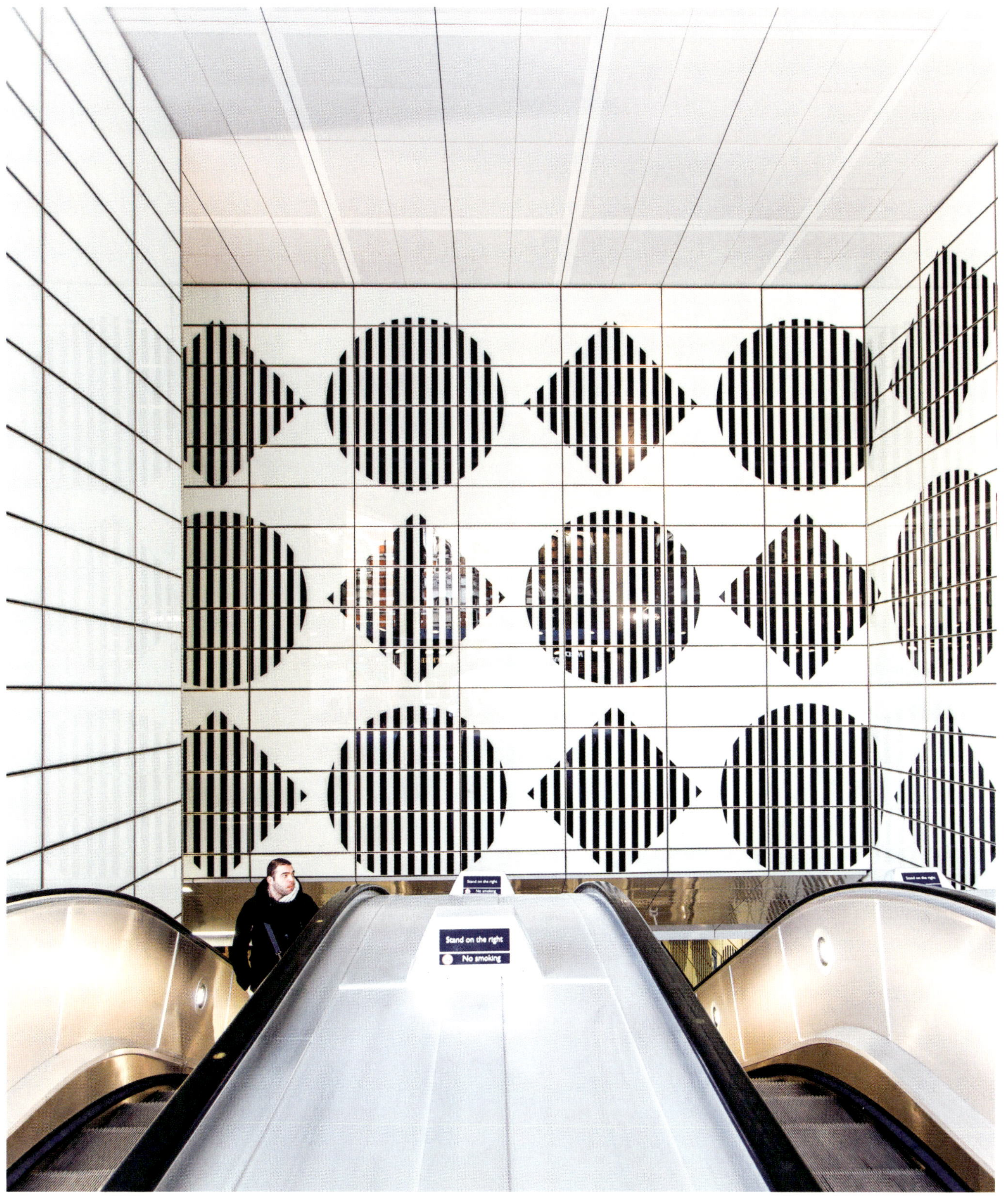

Stand on the right
No smoking
Stand on the right
No smoking

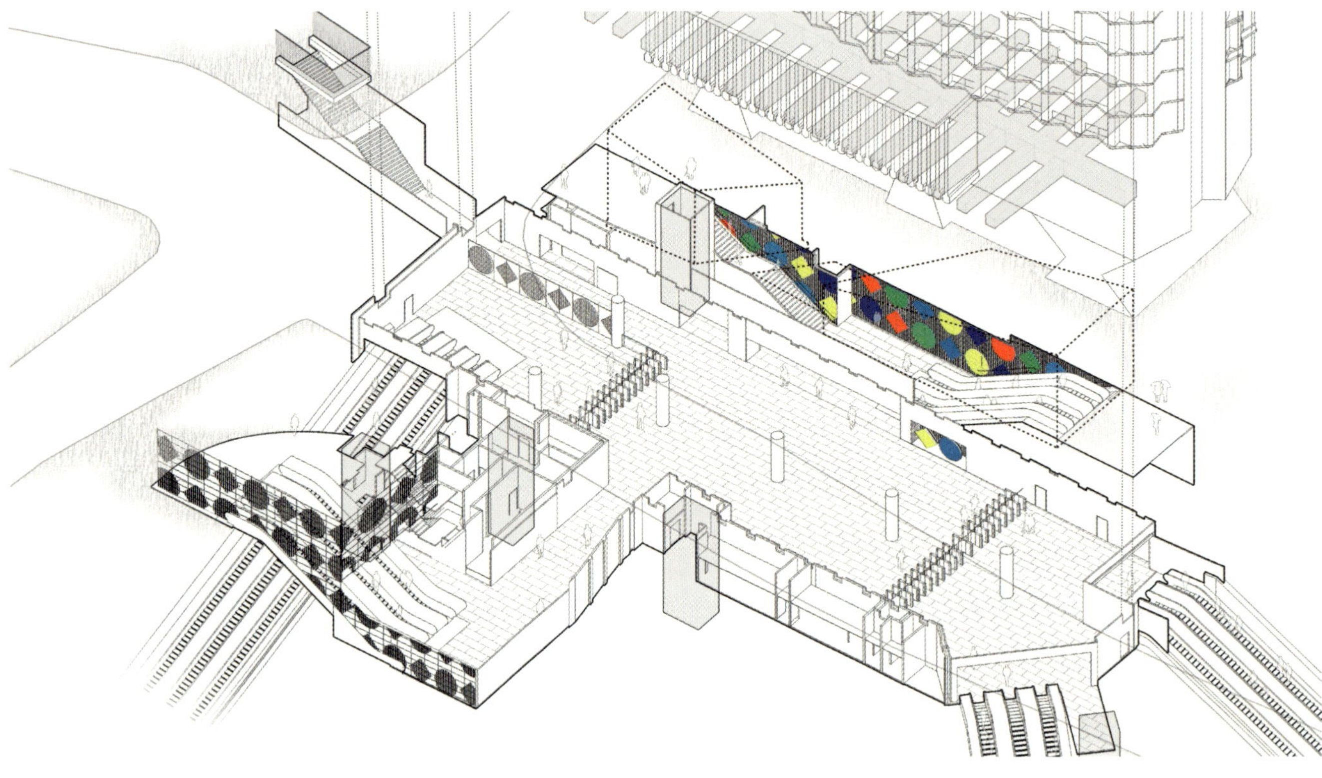

An expansive art work

*An axonometric projection shows
the four elements of Diamonds and Circles
as they spread through the redesigned
station's architecture.*

DB: I must say that in such a project, the most difficult thing is to imagine what the physical situation will be. The plans are extremely complex at the first glance, and it took some time for me to understand how the full operation of the station was going to work. On which floor were we compared with the platforms, for example? I was helped, I must admit, by the fantastic team of young architects working on the development, who reduced the difficulties and helped me, step by step, to build the project. To understand how this particular Underground station will function is one thing, but it was also important to comprehend how subways in general operate. What are they? Why do people use them? Why, even, should we add a work of art in the middle of these necessities remained a basic question for me, wherever and however the subway is constructed or restructured, before I could even think of what form it might take. That was my main concern, and knowing the basic futility of visual art in

such a context continued to guide my thinking throughout the entire project. How does one make something to be visible to millions of people who are certainly not walking, running, climbing and descending in order to appreciate or criticize works of art?

TM: How much does rethinking the notion of landmarks and monuments interest you, in this project and more generally?

DB: As much as the physical, mental, political, historical, social context of a place is important in framing what you can do anywhere, the work produced can in turn transform that place. Both influence each other in a constant backward-and-forward motion. In this respect, the notion of landmark is really interesting. You can work inside a situation that is already a landmark in its own right (the courtyard of the Palais-Royal in Paris comes to mind here) or you can create

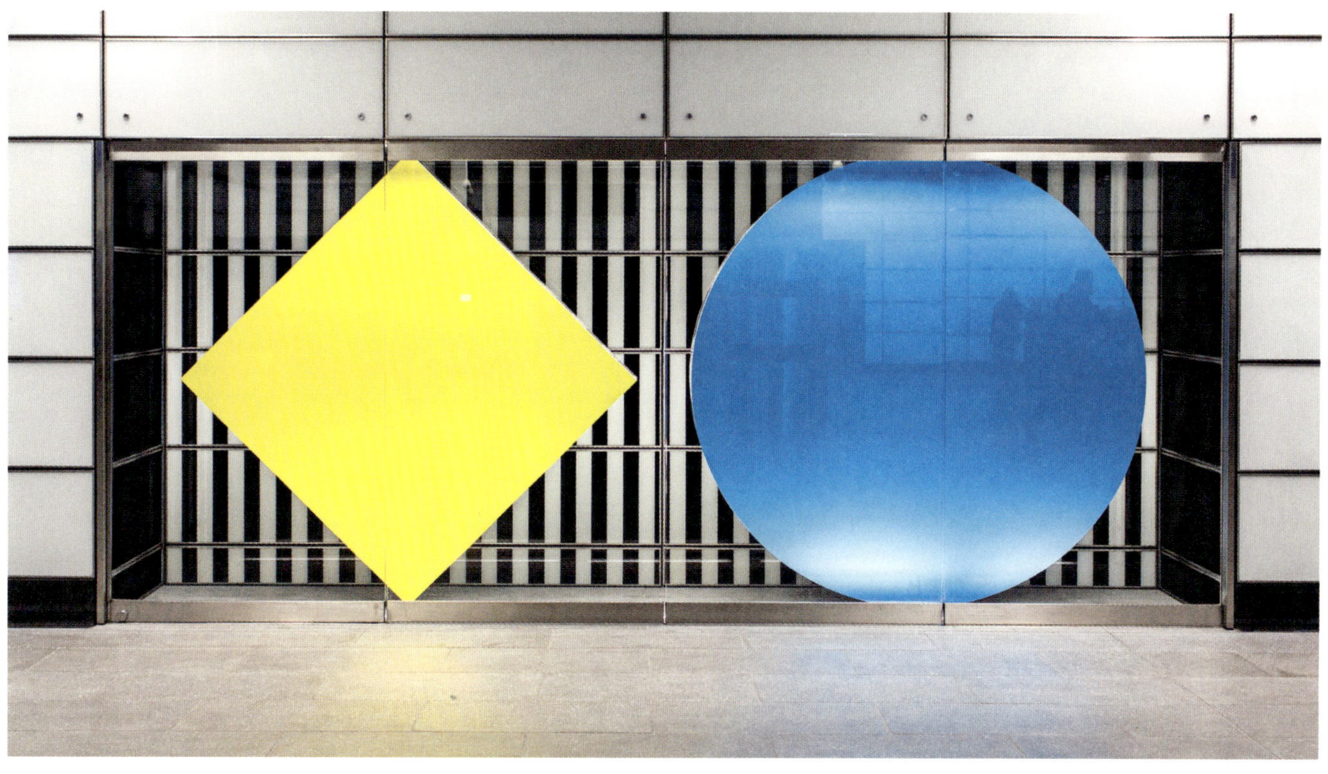

a work in a less well-defined location that becomes the landmark itself of the place. The work I made in Nantes in 2007, *Les Anneaux*, is an example of the latter.

TM: You have rarely, if ever, used vitrines in any of your gallery exhibitions and yet you have installed one in the new ticket hall at Tottenham Court Road. Is this a playful subversion of the idea of the museum to some extent?

DB: I have used the vitrine two or three times before, but in a very specific manner and also because of the context of the specific space. For example, I did a series of them in 1987 at the Musée des Arts Décoratifs in Paris, where the use of vitrines is rather extensive. Instead of containing objects to look at, they were covered with vertical-striped paper glued directly inside the glass. It was certainly another way to see something 'inside'! At Tottenham Court Road, my idea was to bring into the Tube a vitrine where we can see in three dimensions the two basic elements of the scheme — the simple geometric shapes — equal in size to the ones shown in two dimensions on the walls, as if the latter were escaping from their original forms. I can add that all the work in the station is playing in one way or another with glass and with the idea of protective vitrines. Everything is under glass. So the actual vitrine accentuates this general aspect of the work developed all over the station. Kept in a state as pristine as if they were in a museum, these works under glass mirror certain aspects of spectatorship inside museums; and if such a thing can be said, they are like that because I believe that the Underground deserves the same type of attention as any institutional place devoted to visual art.

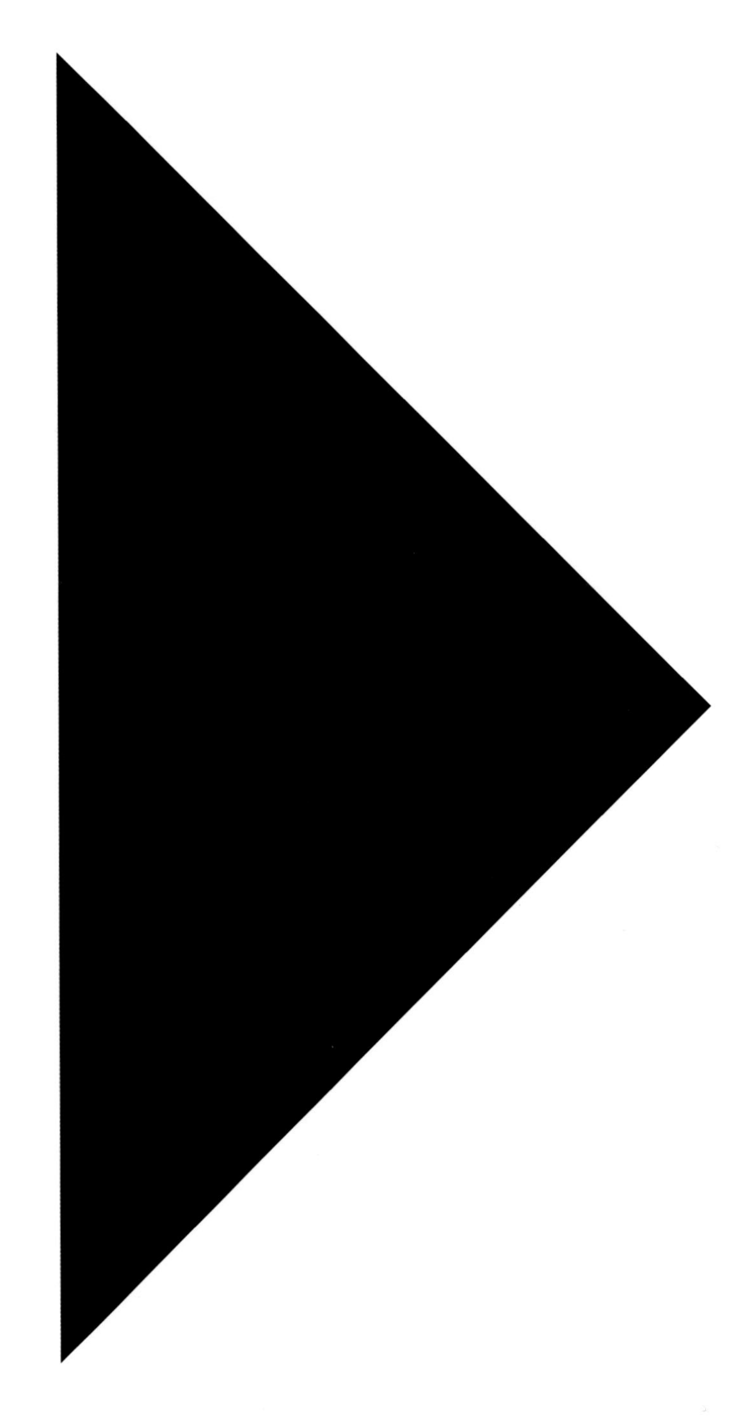

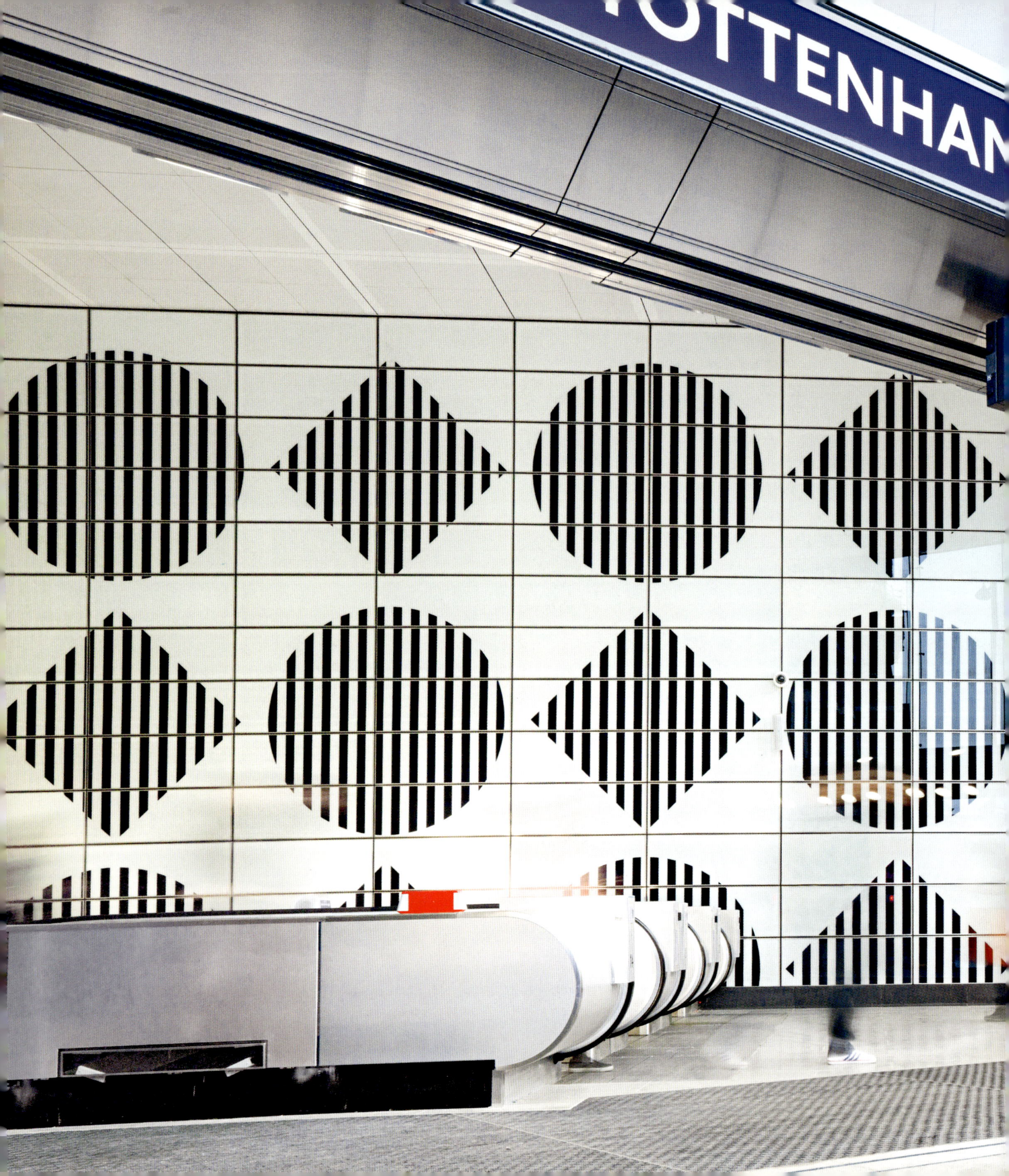
OTTENHAM

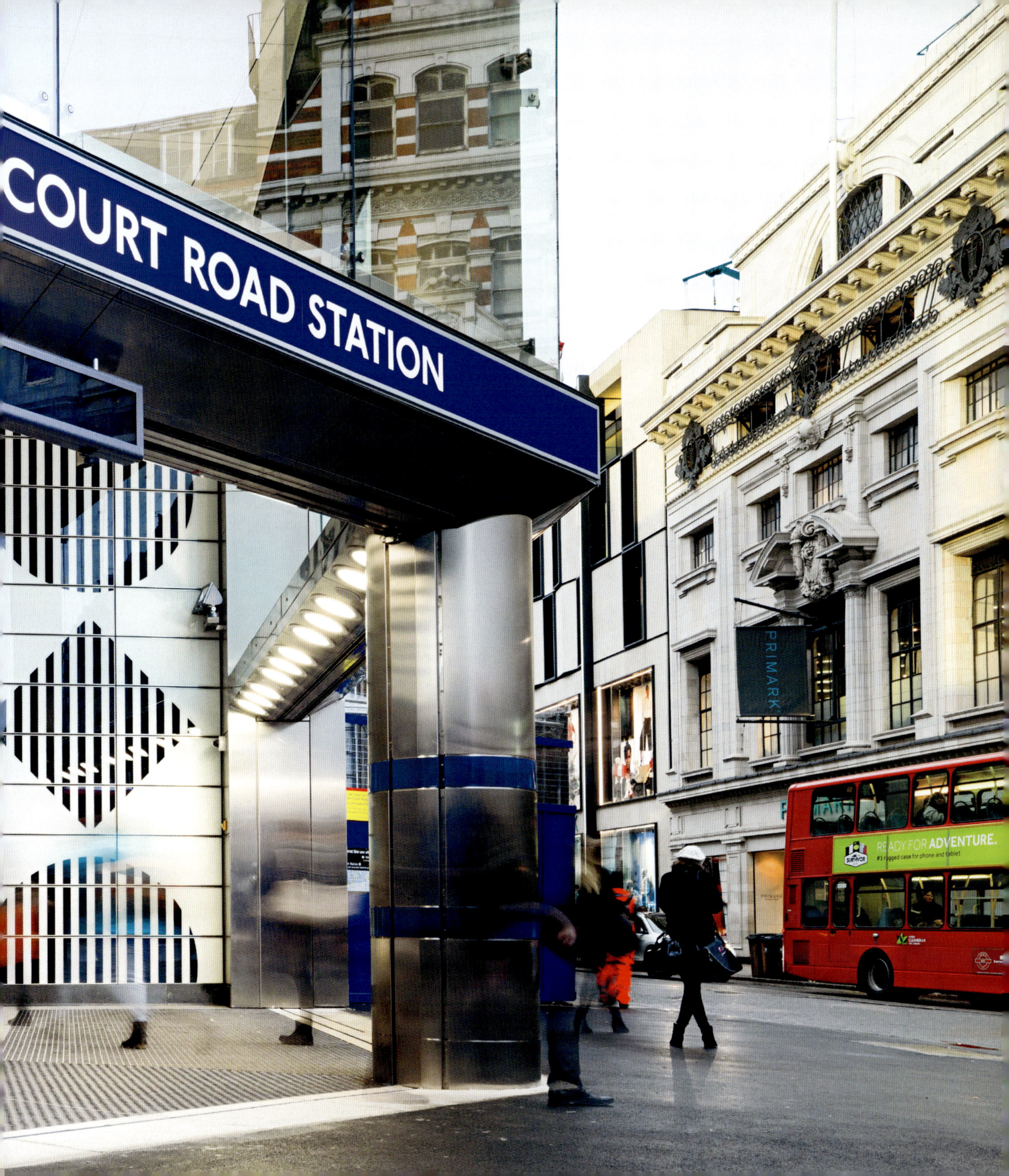
COURT ROAD STATION
PRIMARK
READY FOR ADVENTURE.
#1 rugged case for phone and tablet
SURVIVOR

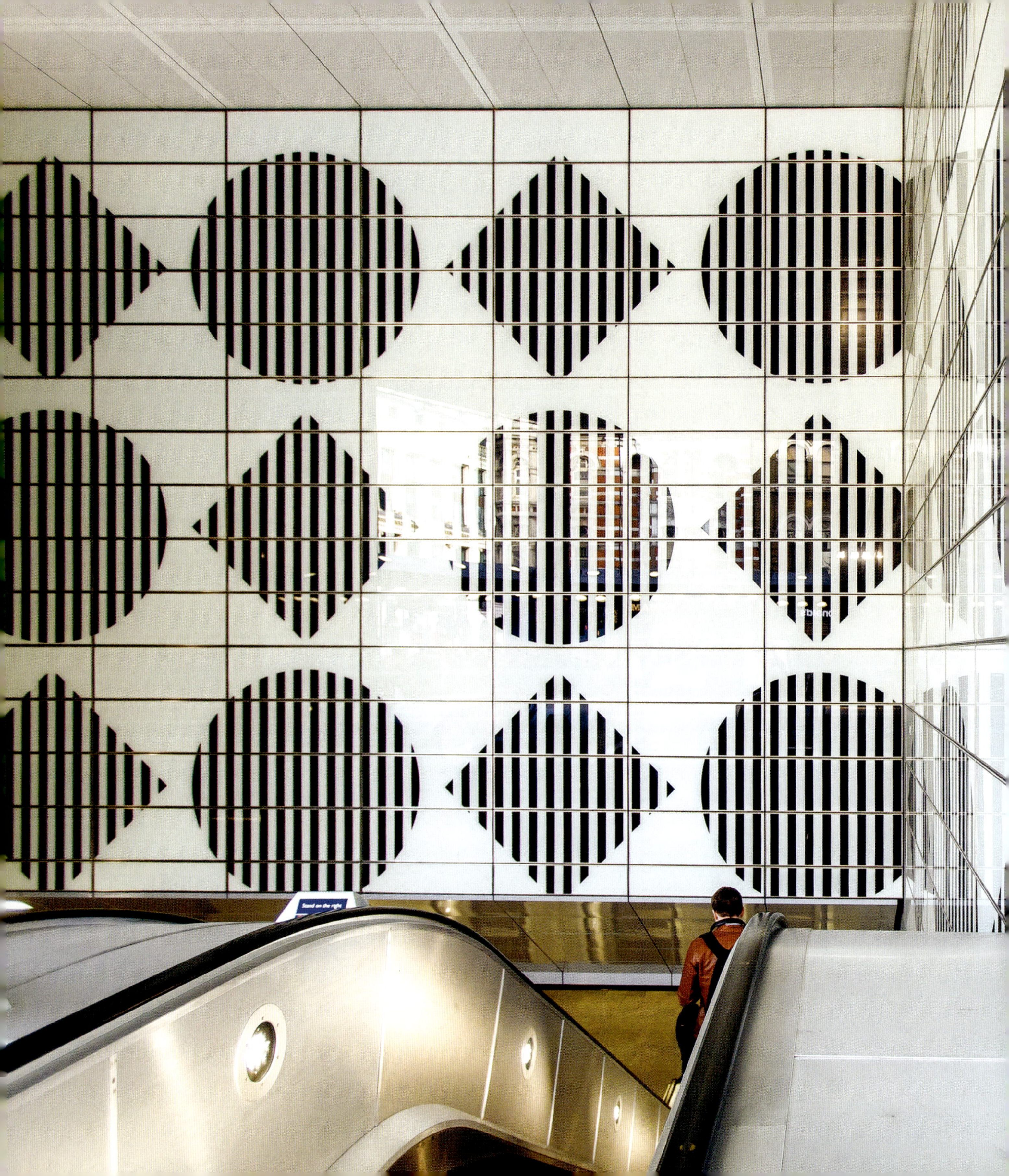

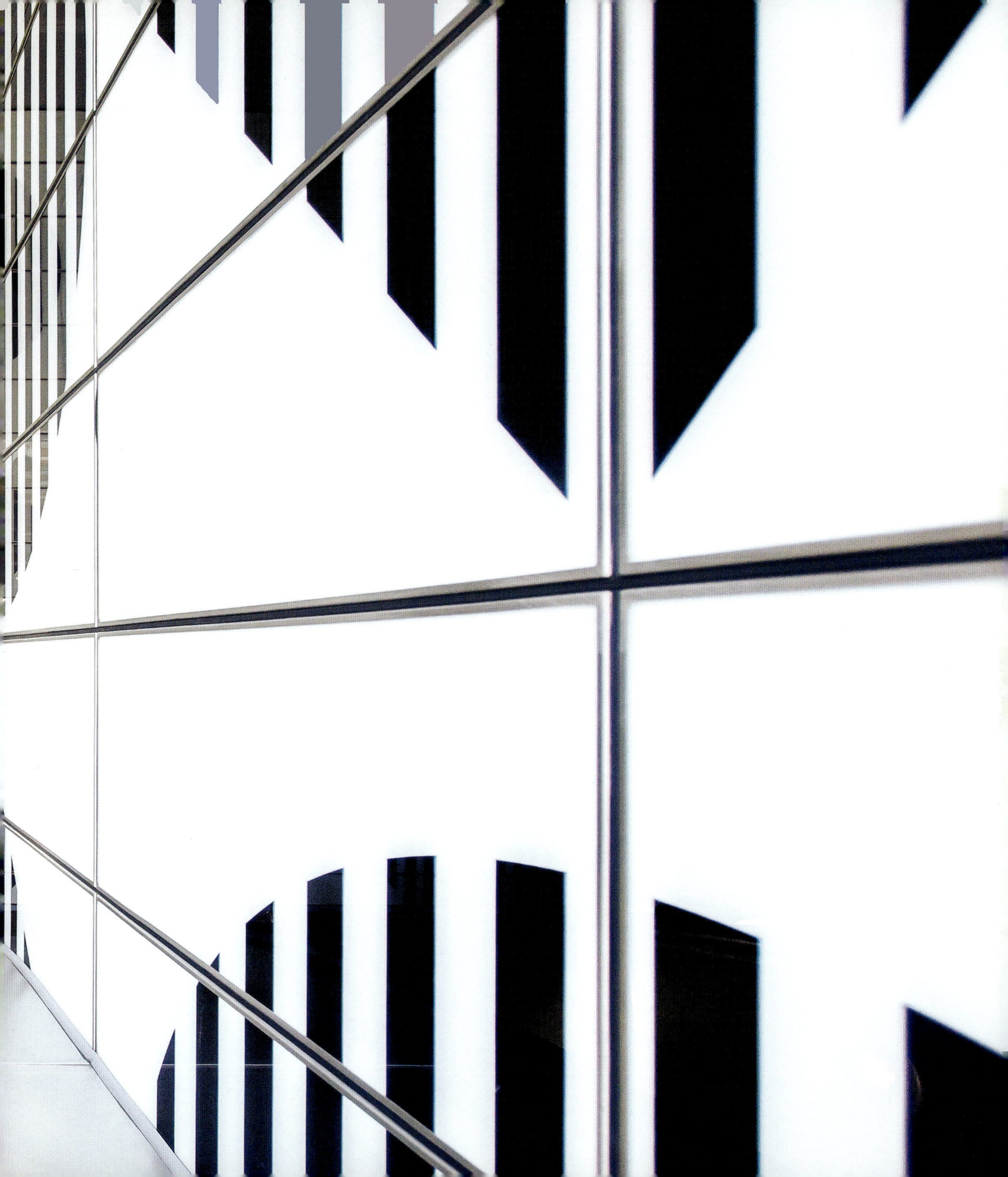

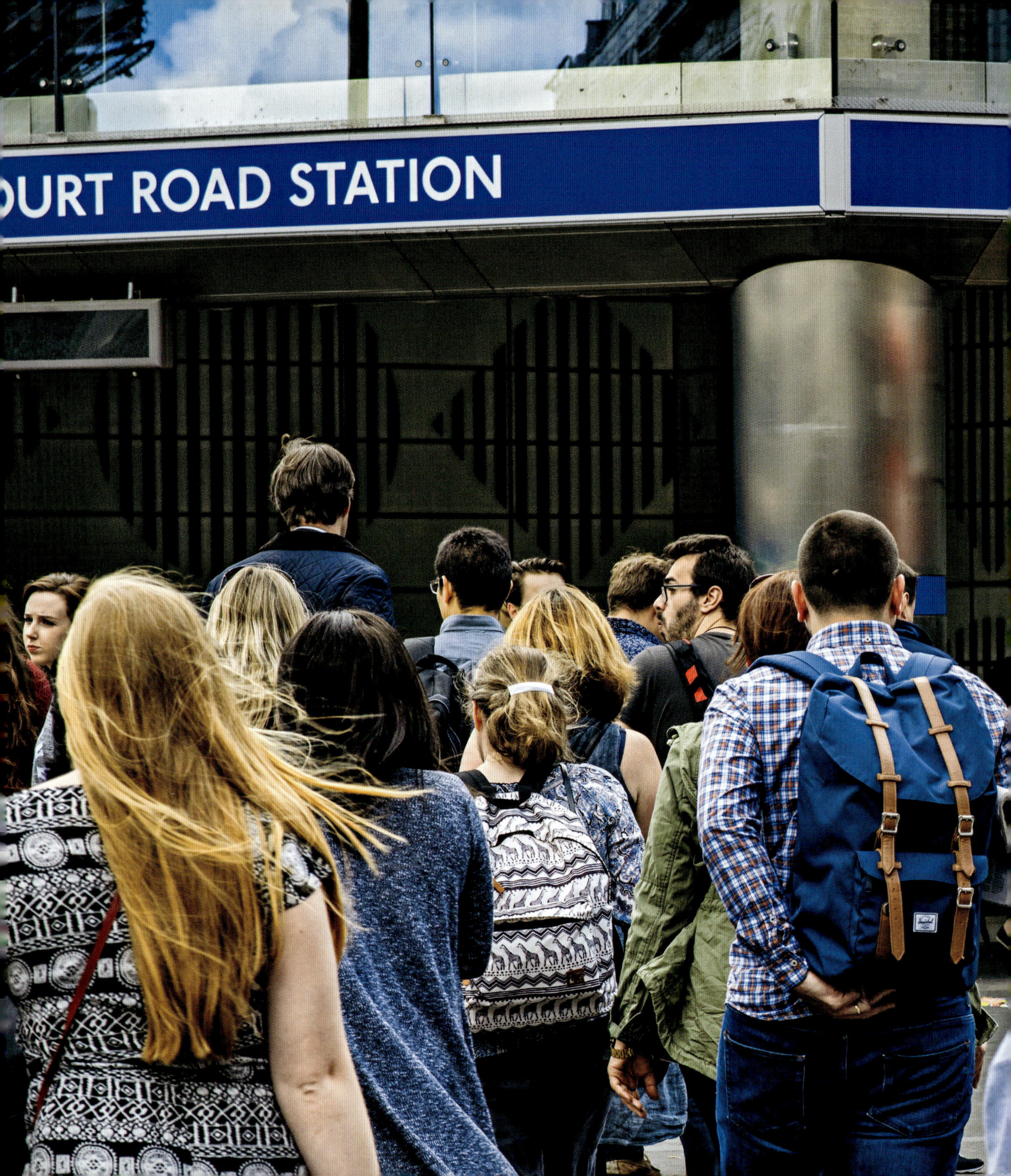

OURT ROAD STATION

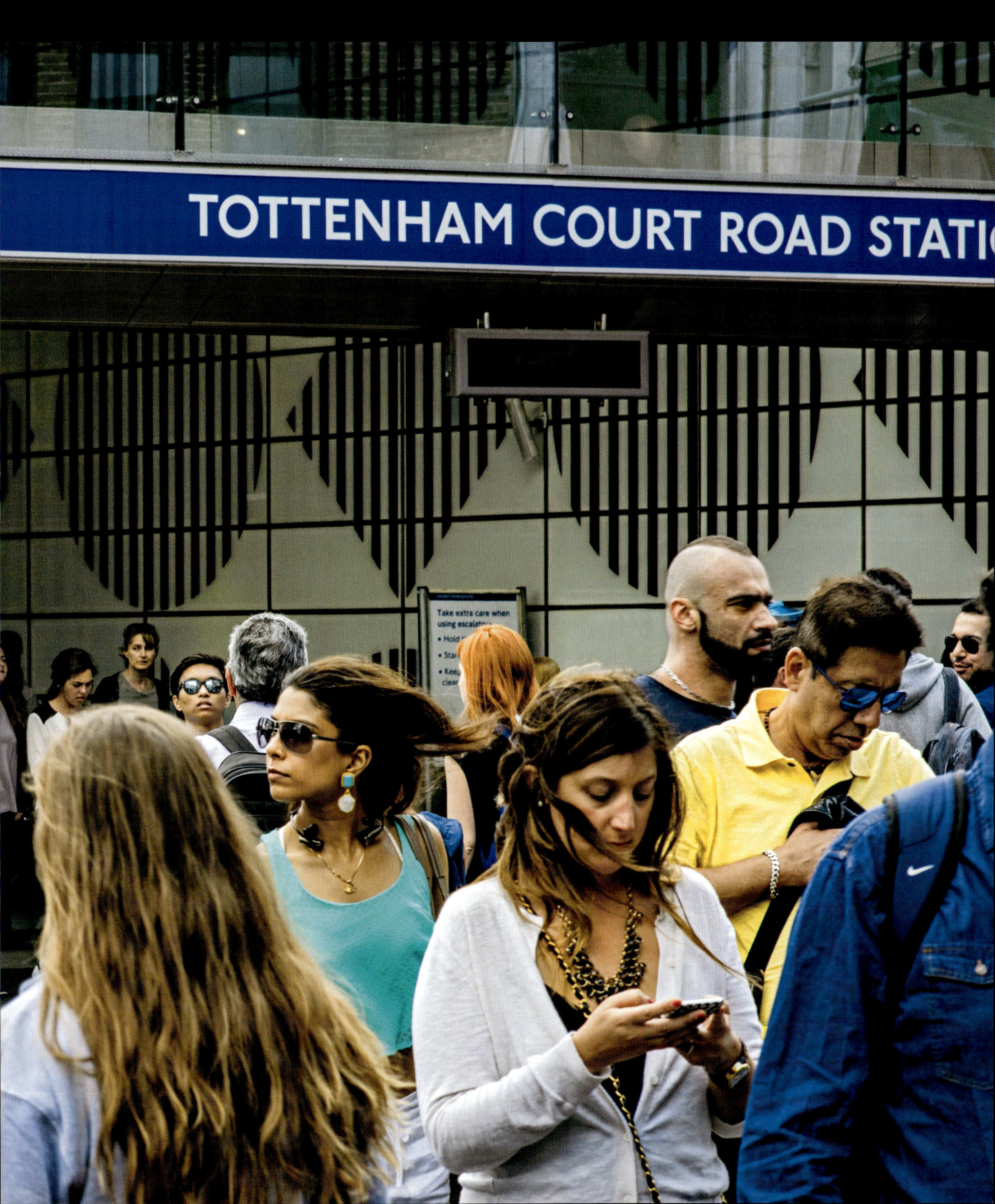
TOTTENHAM COURT ROAD STATION
Take extra care when
using escalators

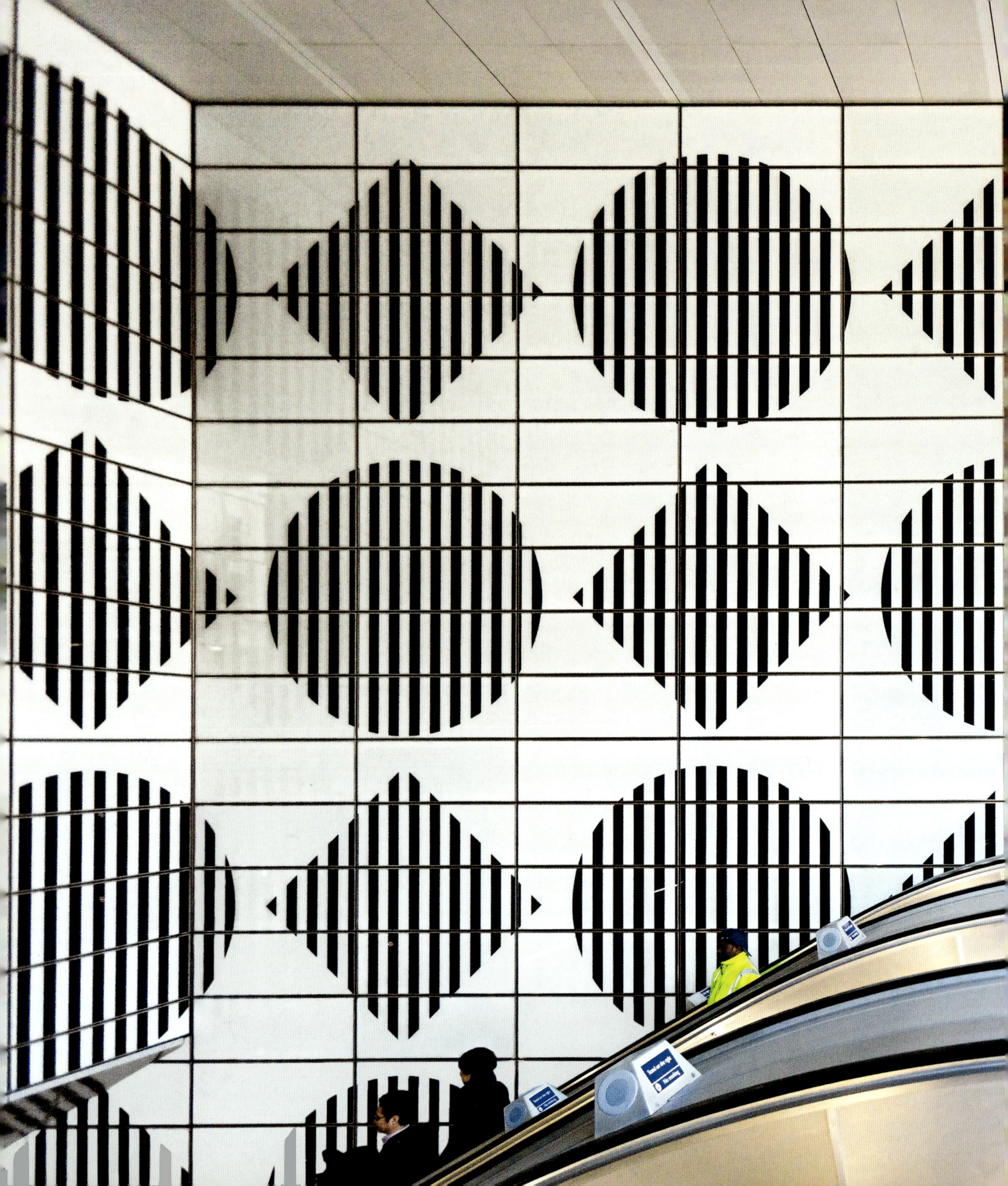

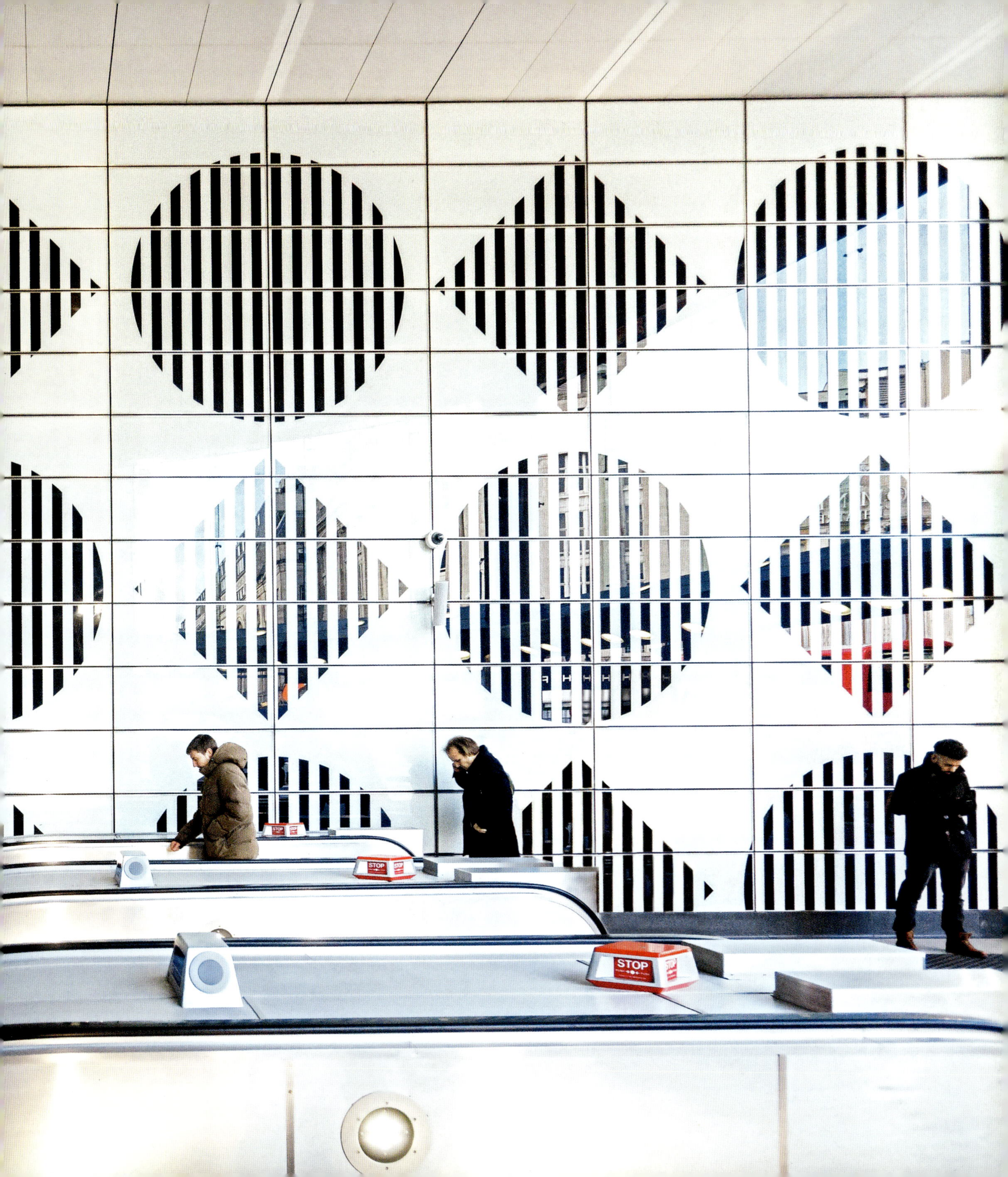

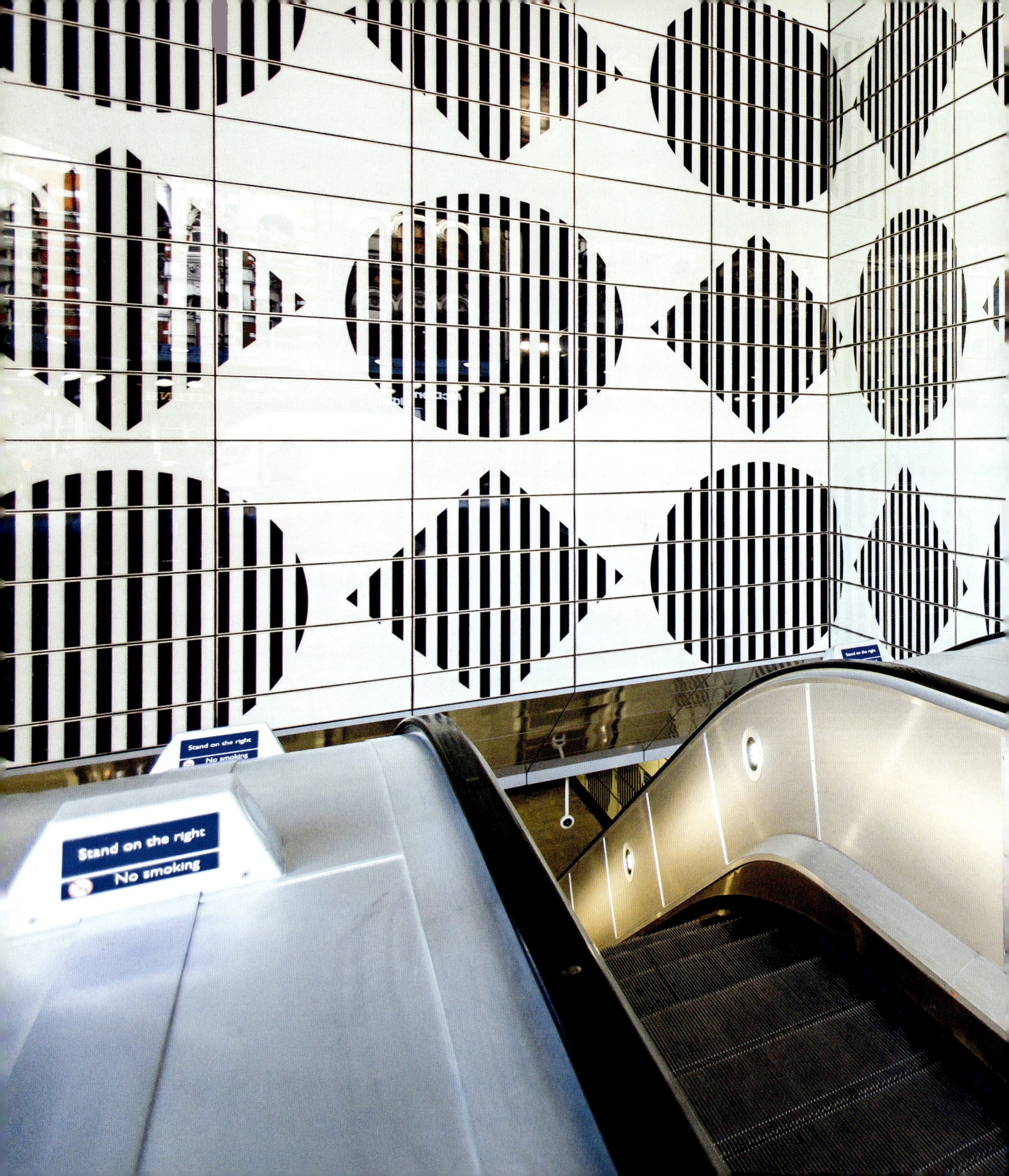
Stand on the right
No smoking
Stand on the right
No smoking

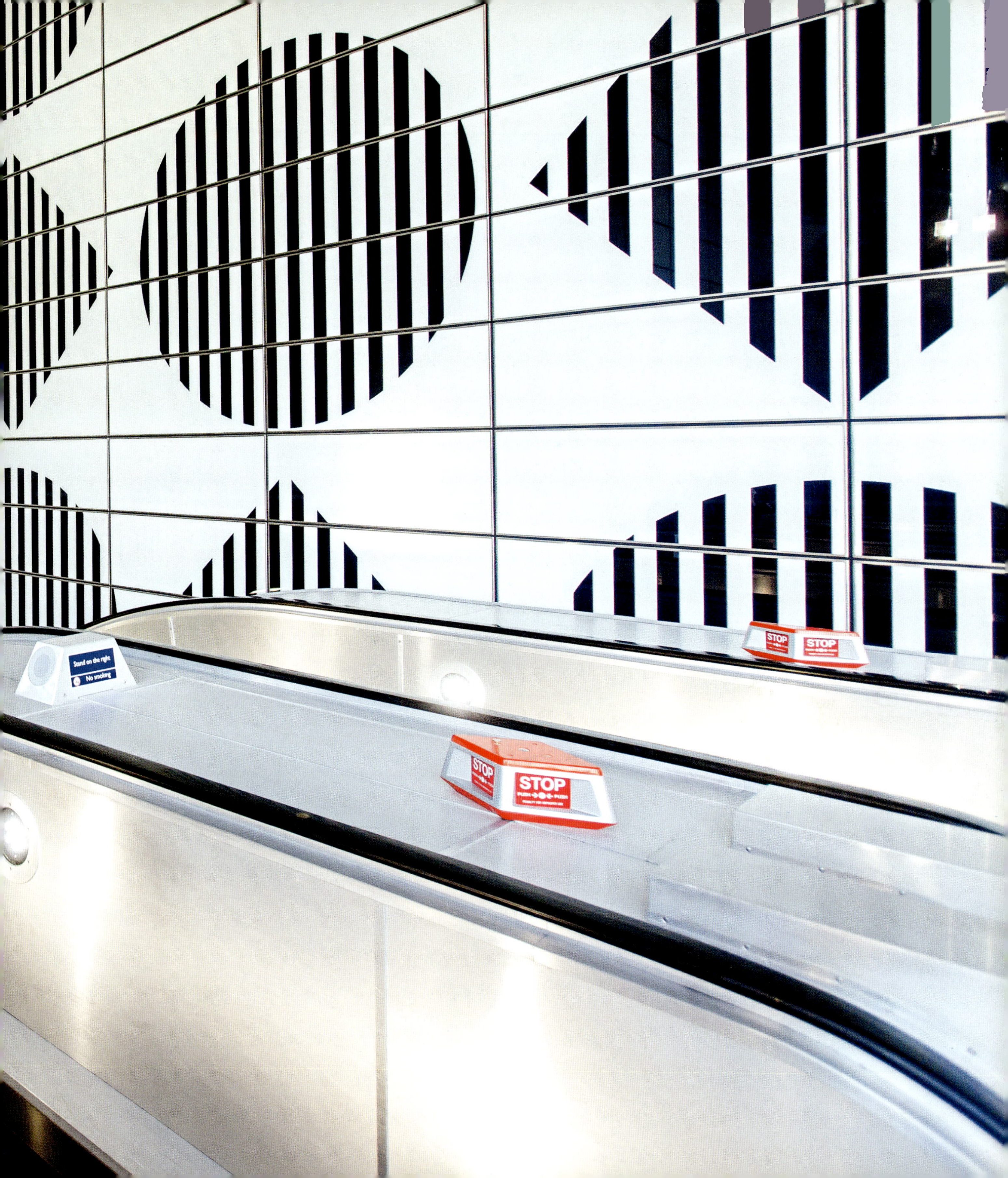

Stand on the right
No smoking
STOP
STOP
STOP

I play with very simple forms that repeat themselves and change through the use of colour or not and by the presence of the stripes, which are sometimes the form and sometimes the background. And I tried to work with the configuration of the subway, from the street level to the deepest part of the station. I knew that some of the works would be next to the escalators so that by definition you would have movement. The person is both static and moving, so it's a kind of difference. When you walk, everything has movement. When you are on the escalator, the body is static.

Daniel Buren

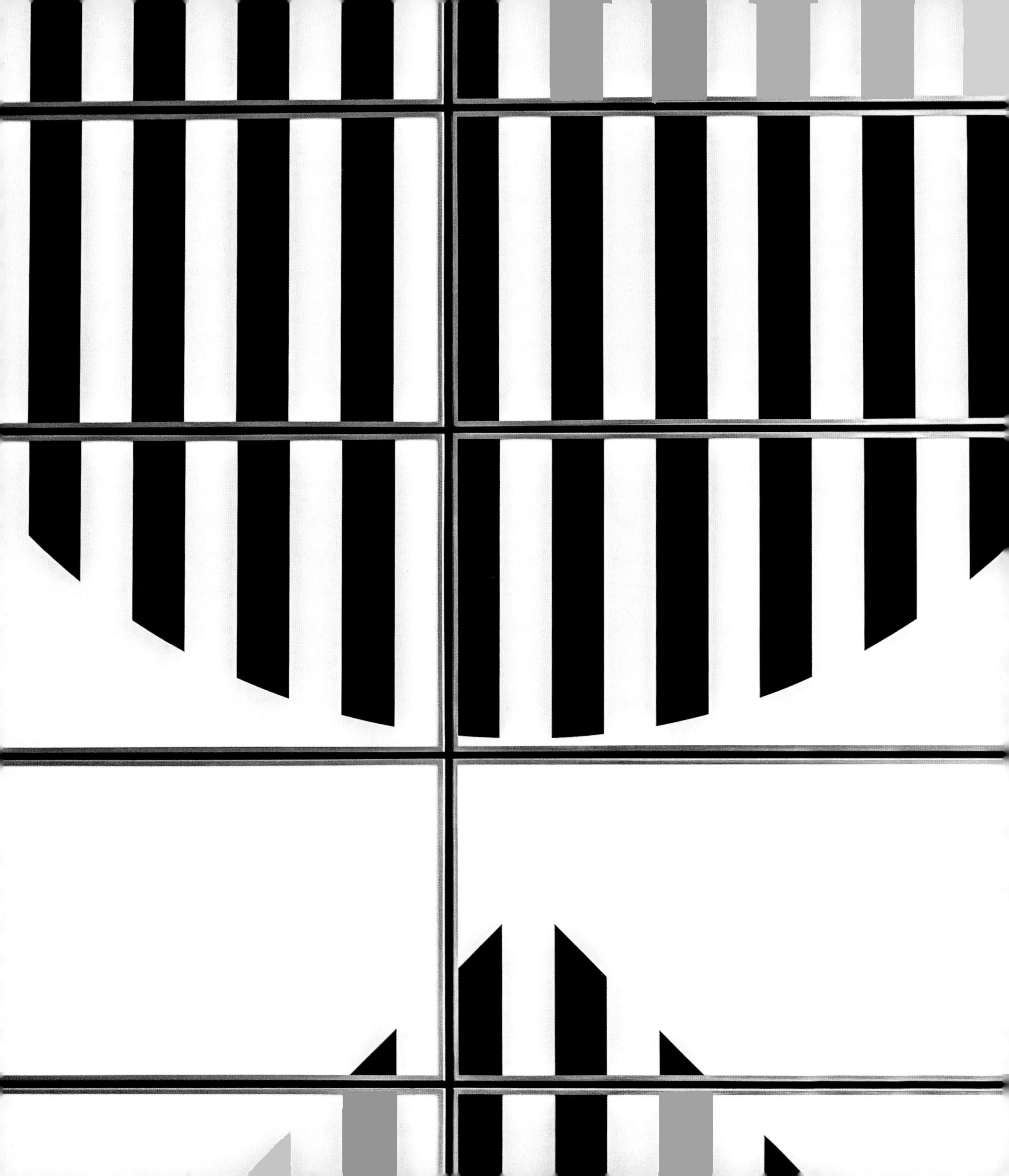

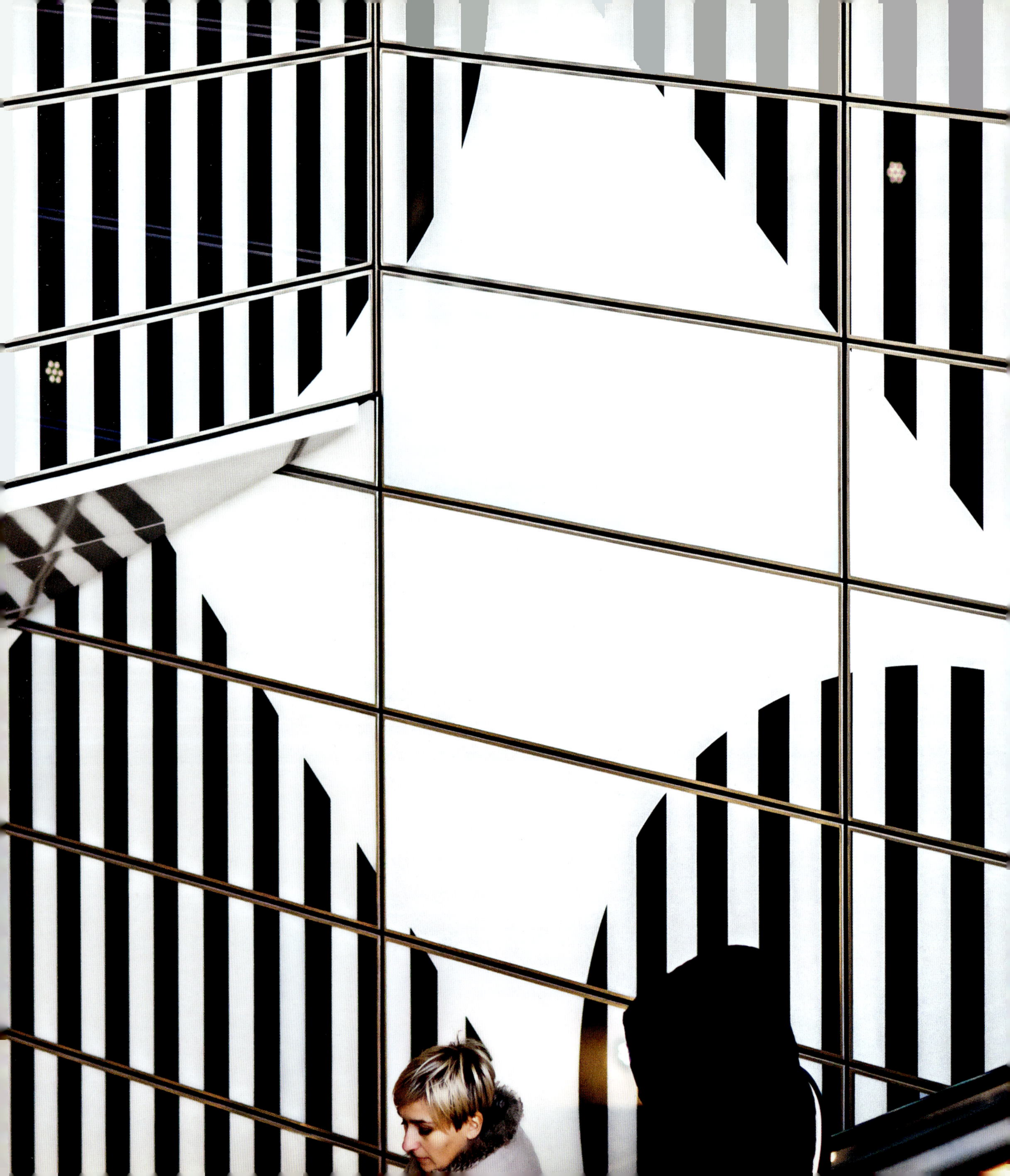

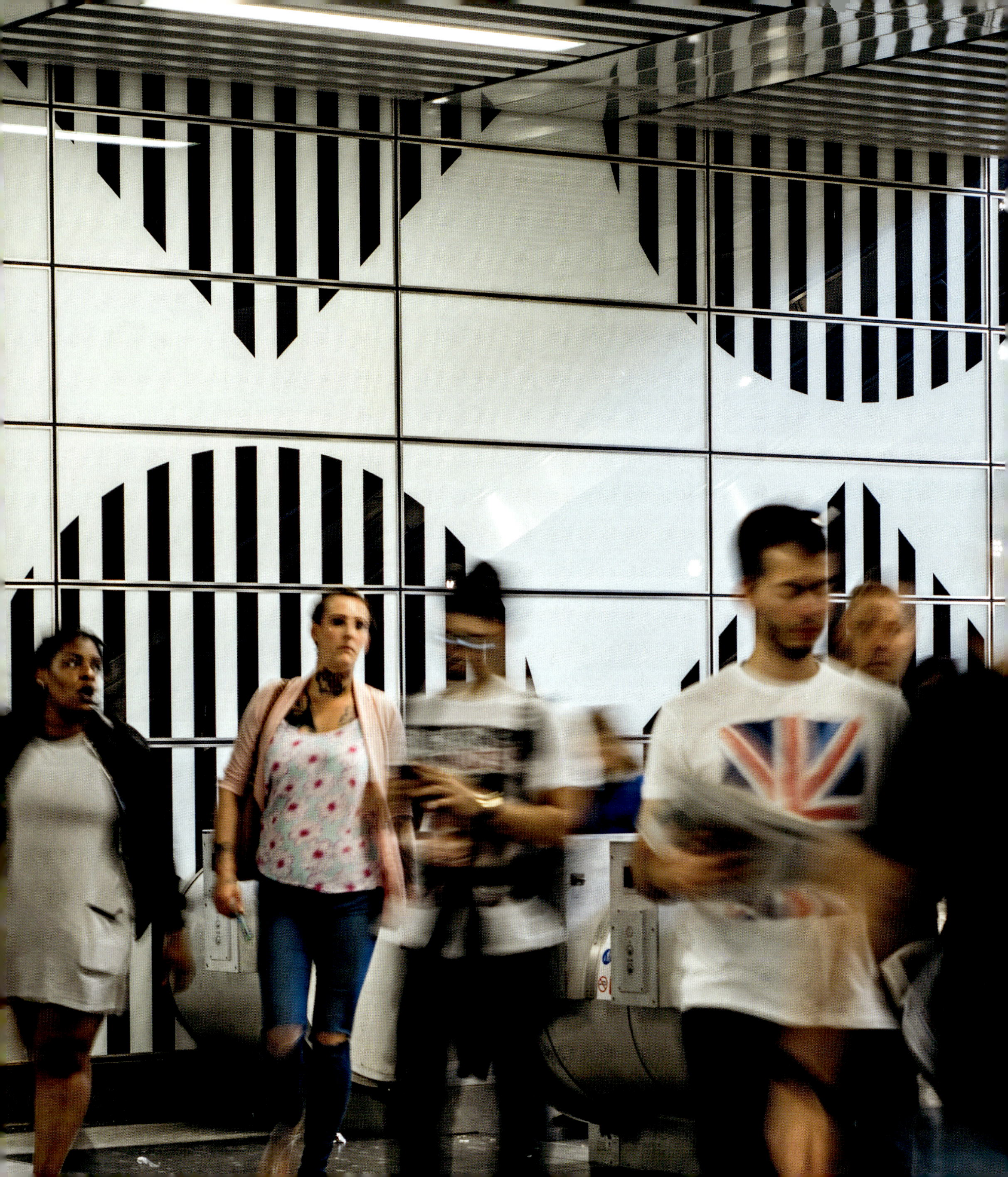

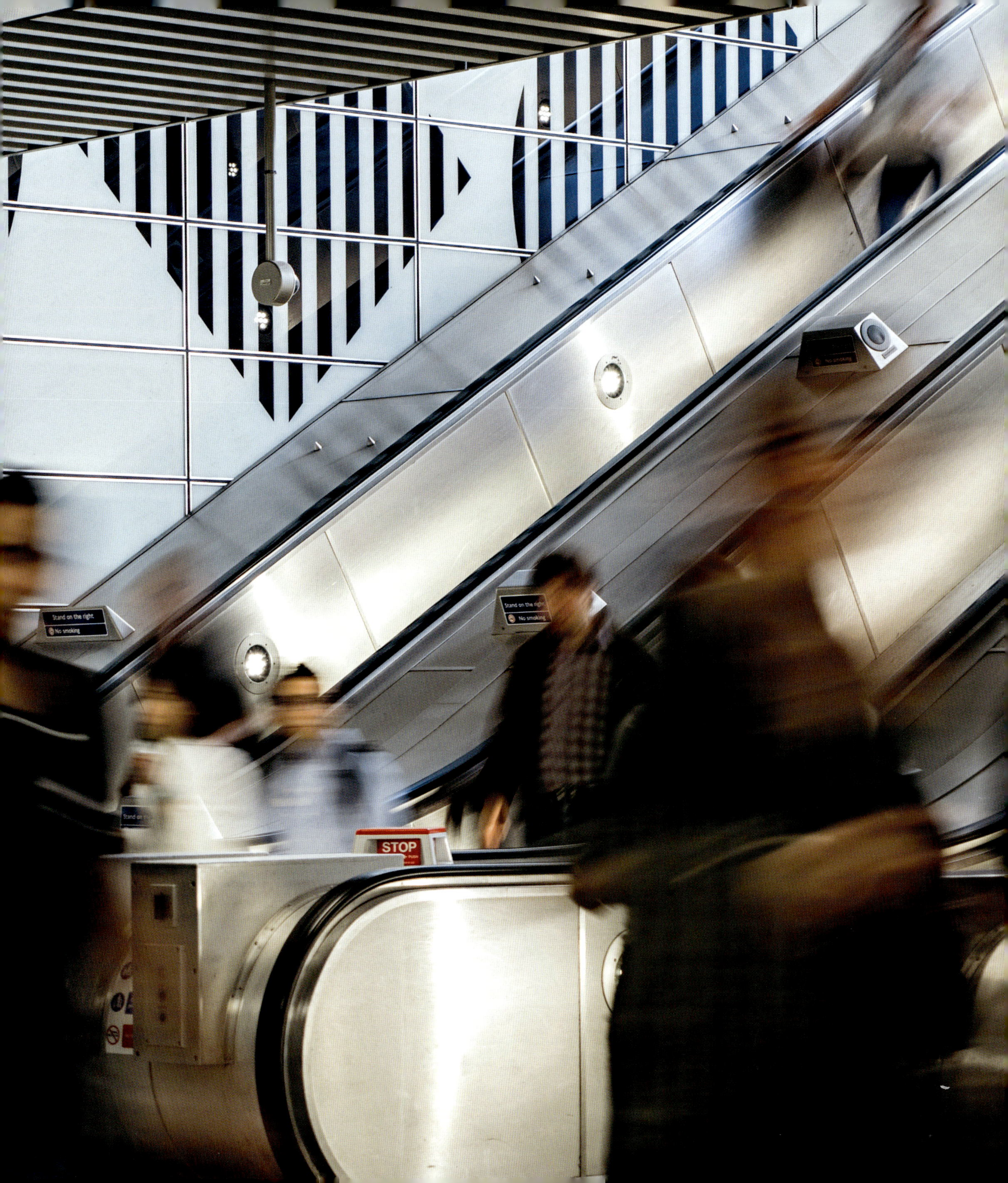
Stand on the right
No smoking
Stand on the right
No smoking
STOP

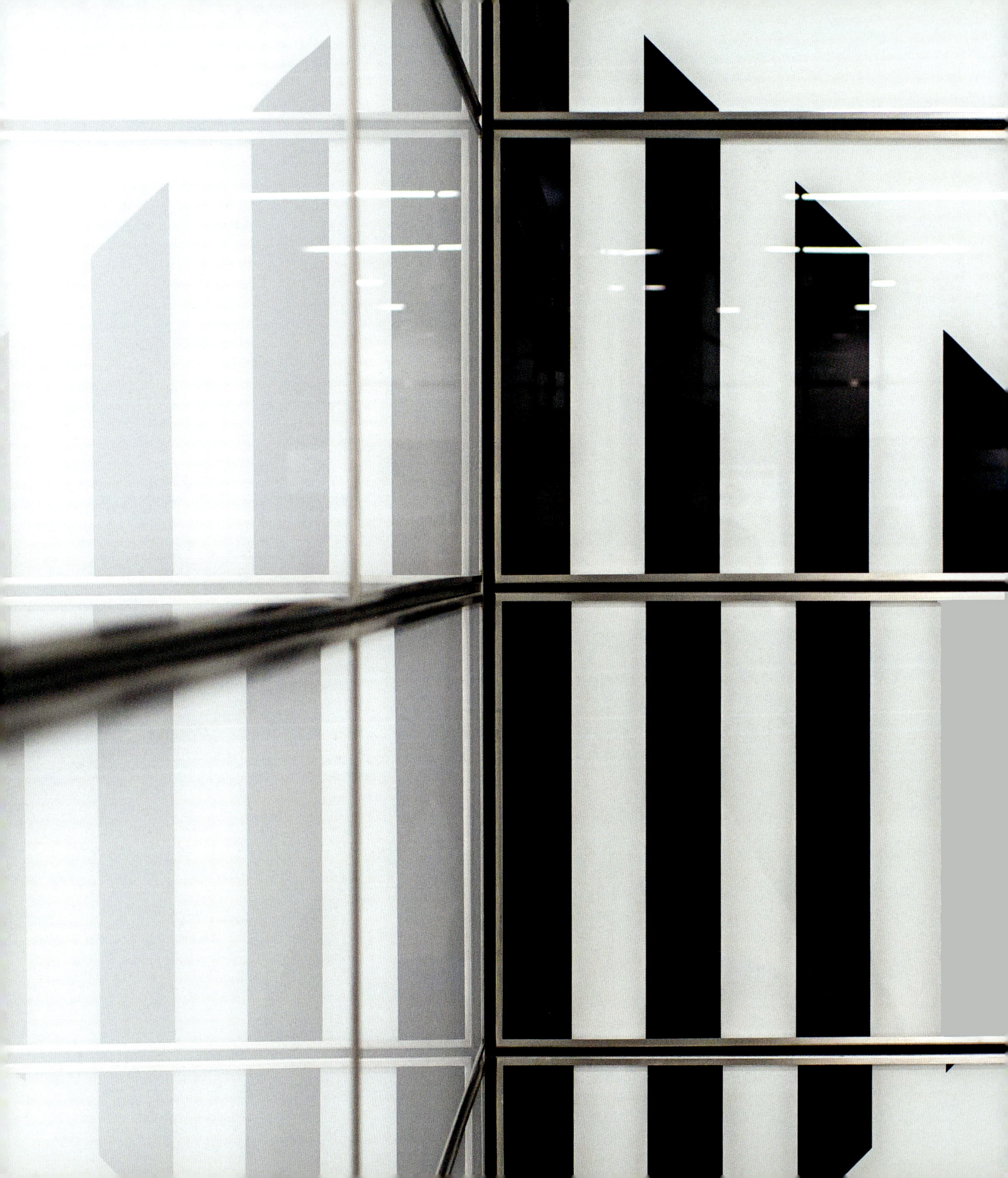

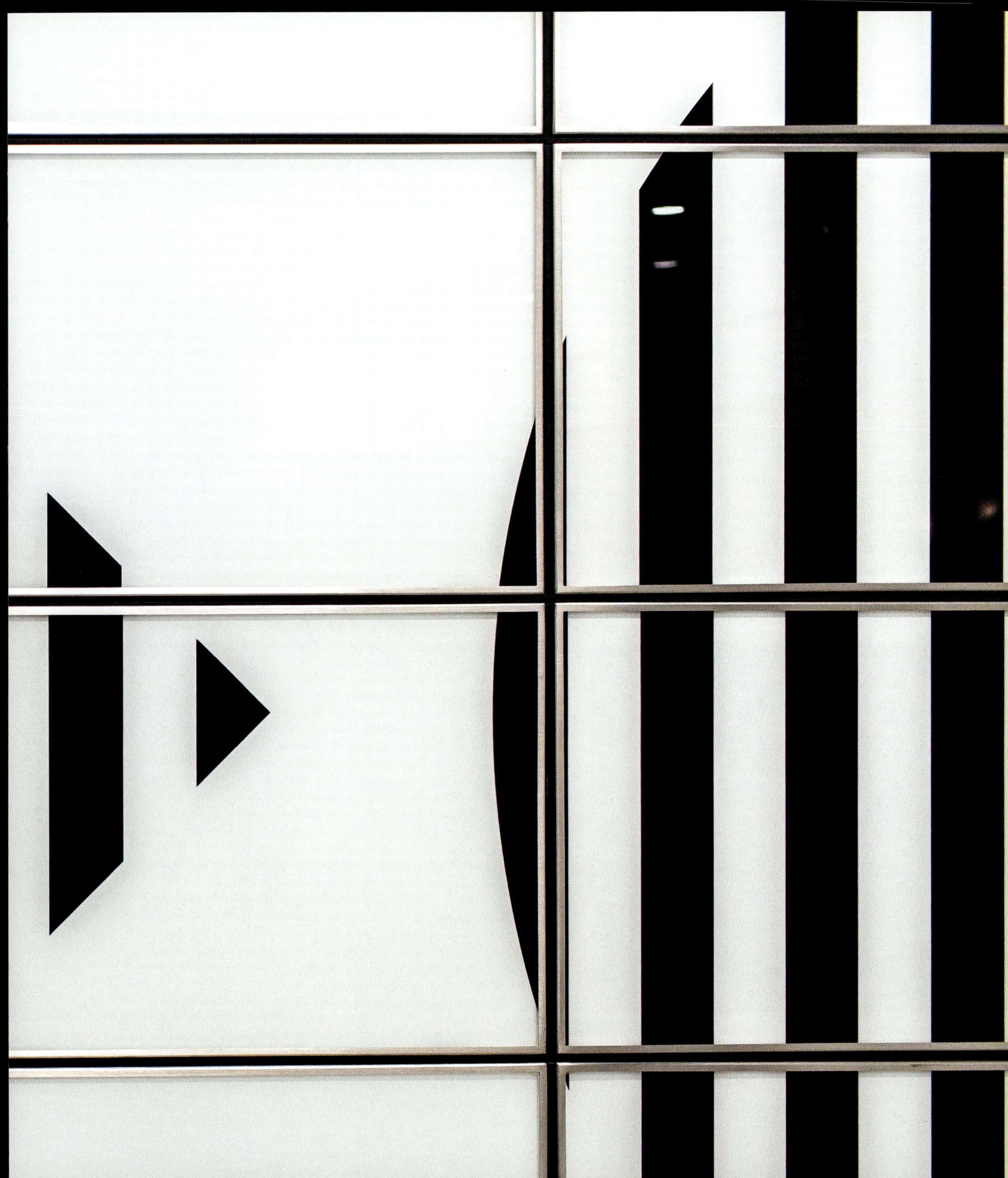

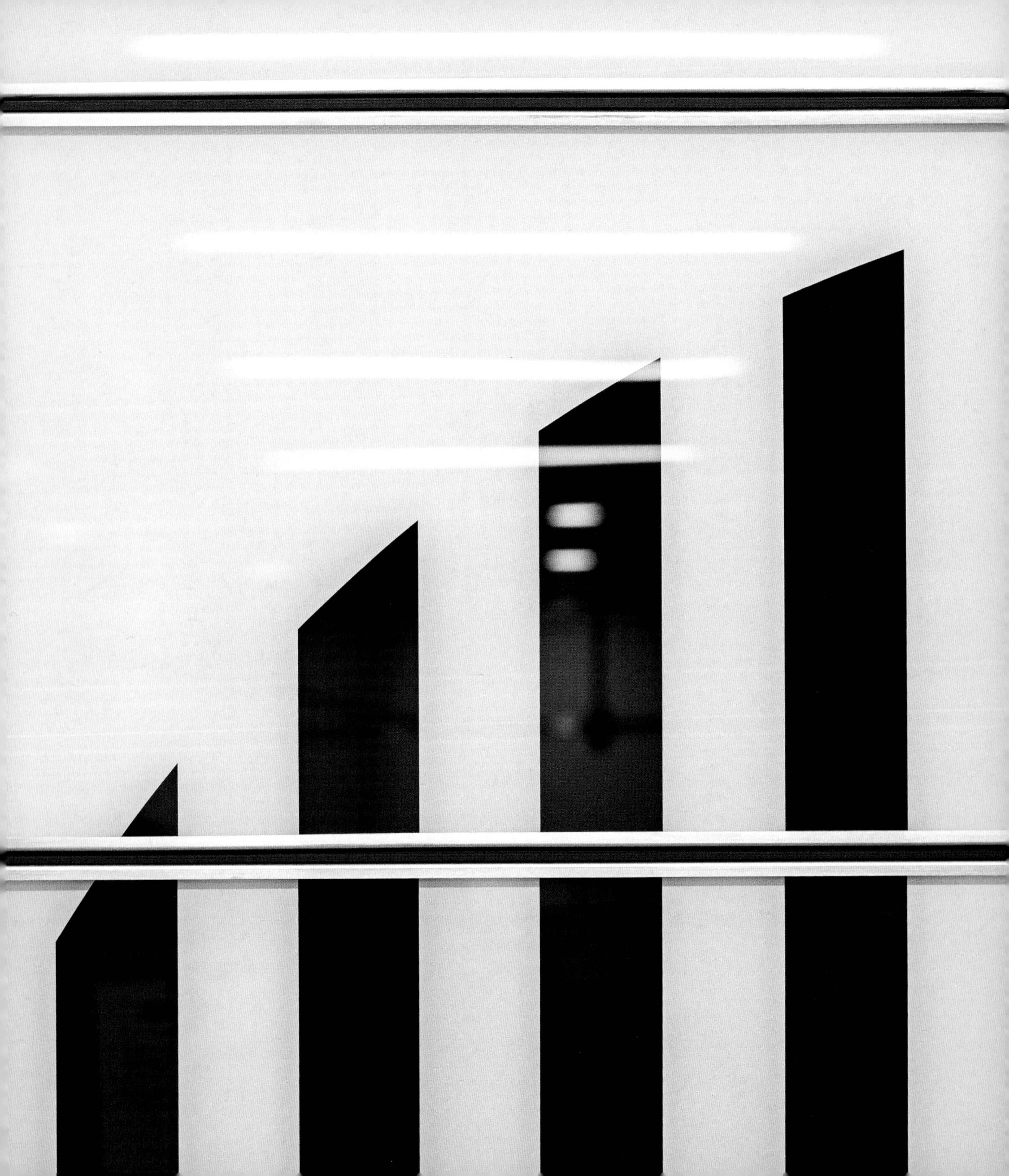

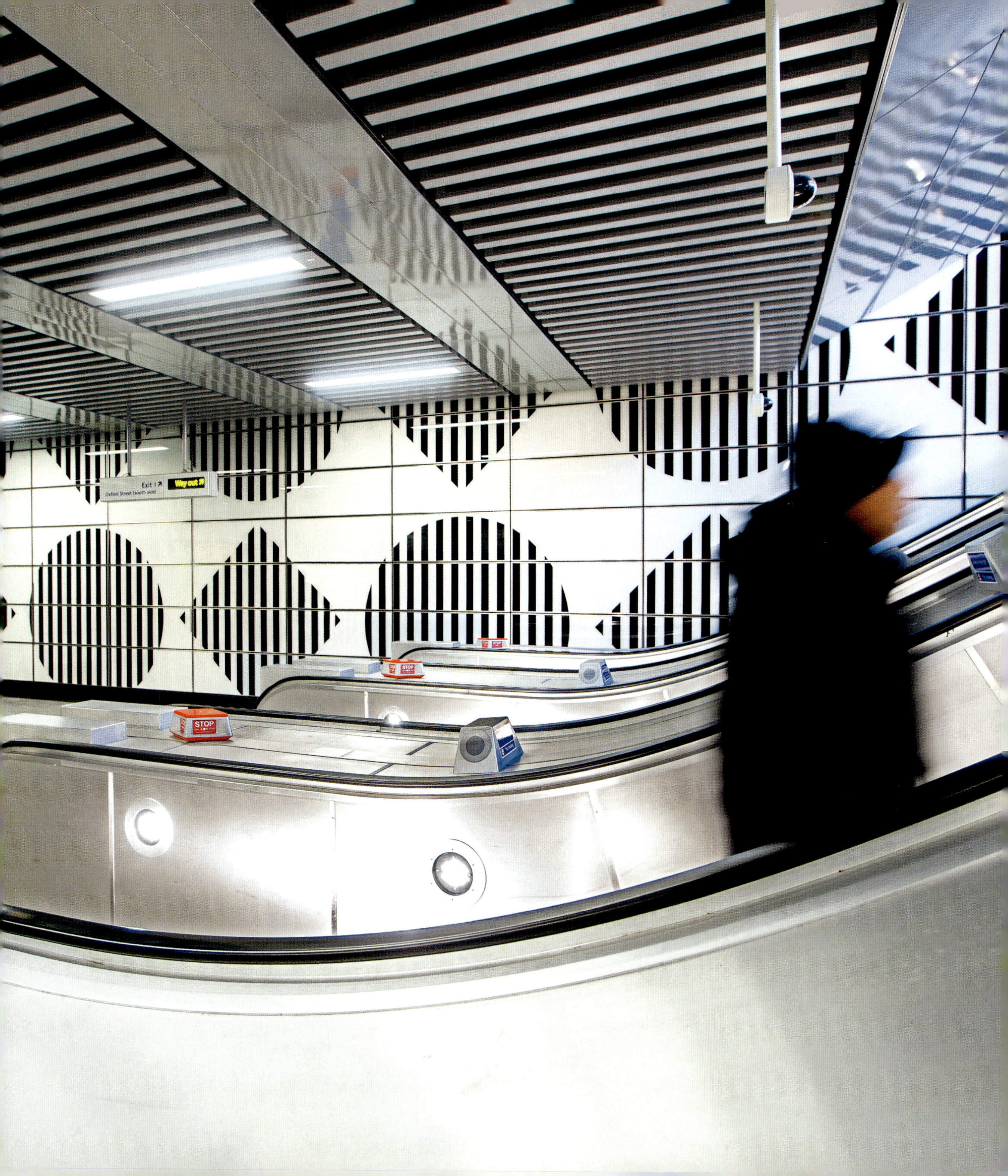

Exit 1 ↗
Oxford Street (south side)
Way out ↗
STOP
STOP

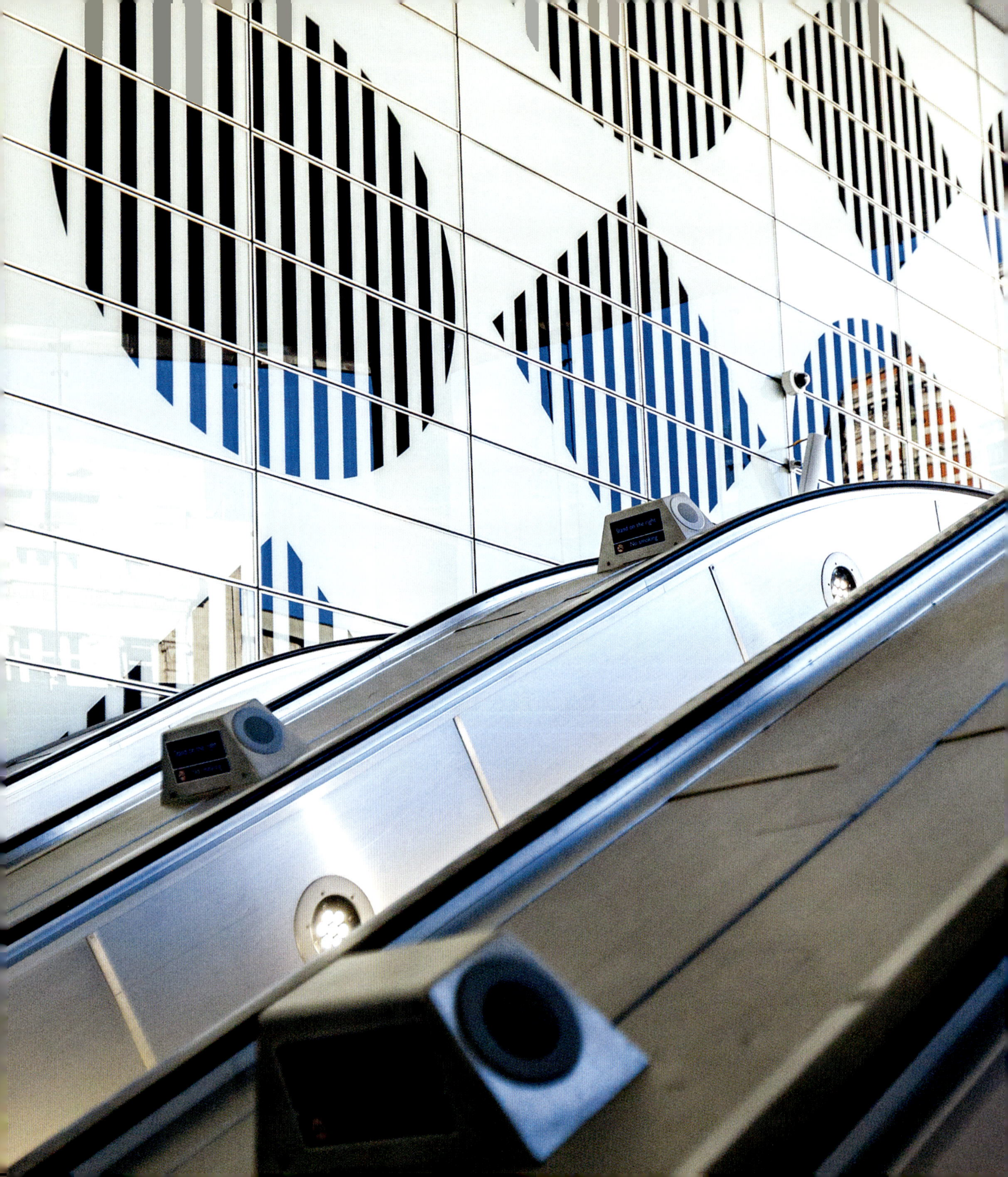

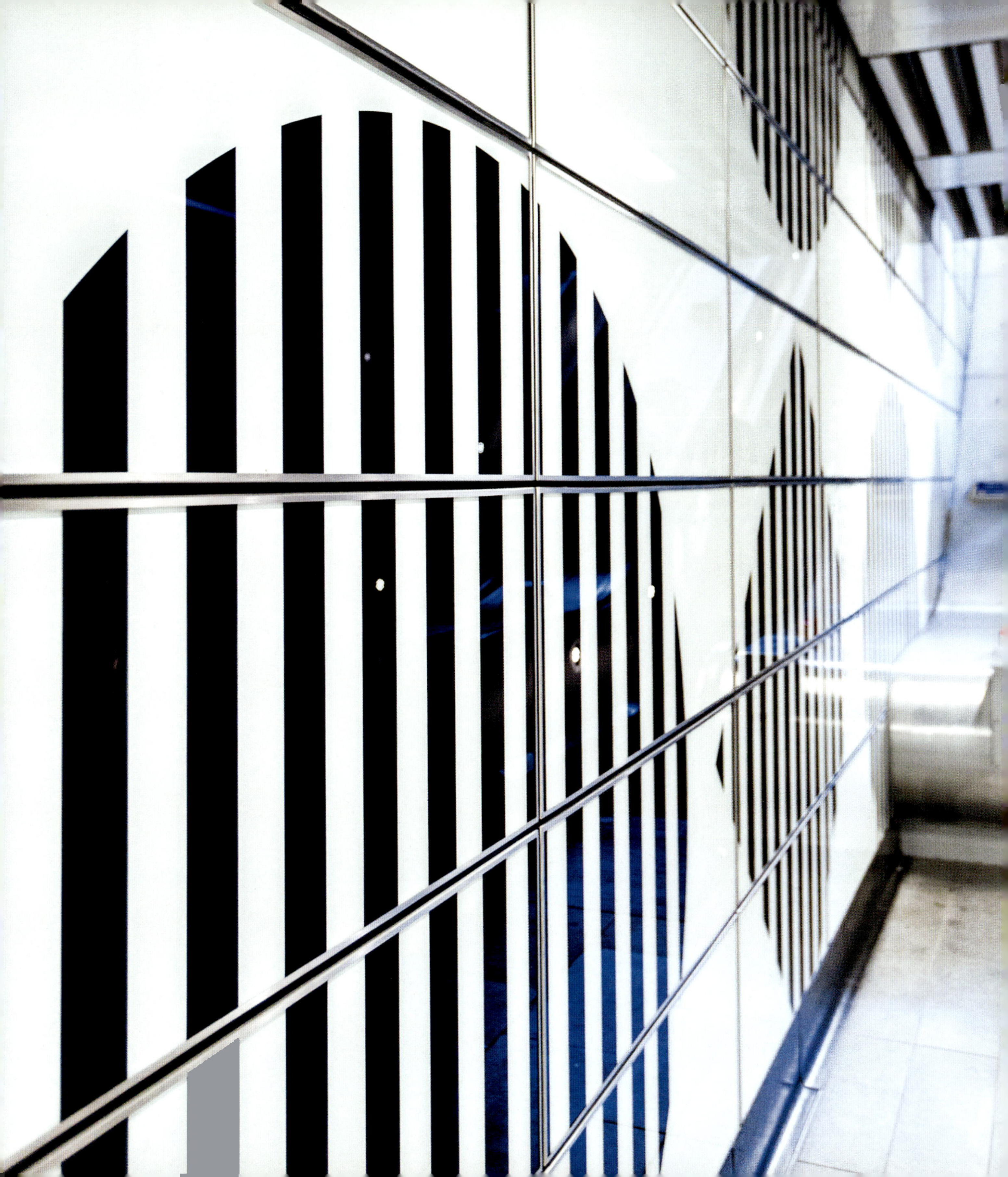

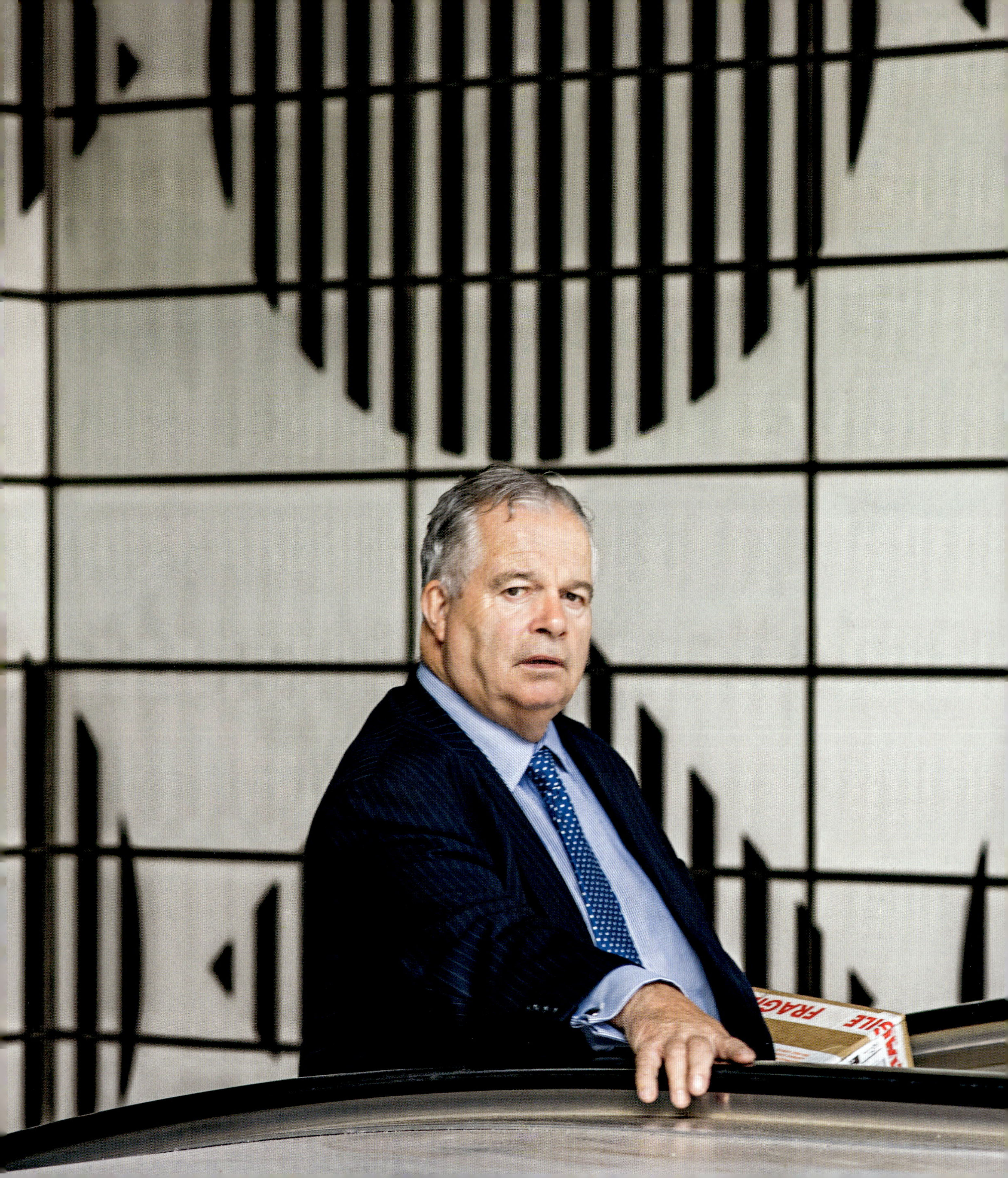

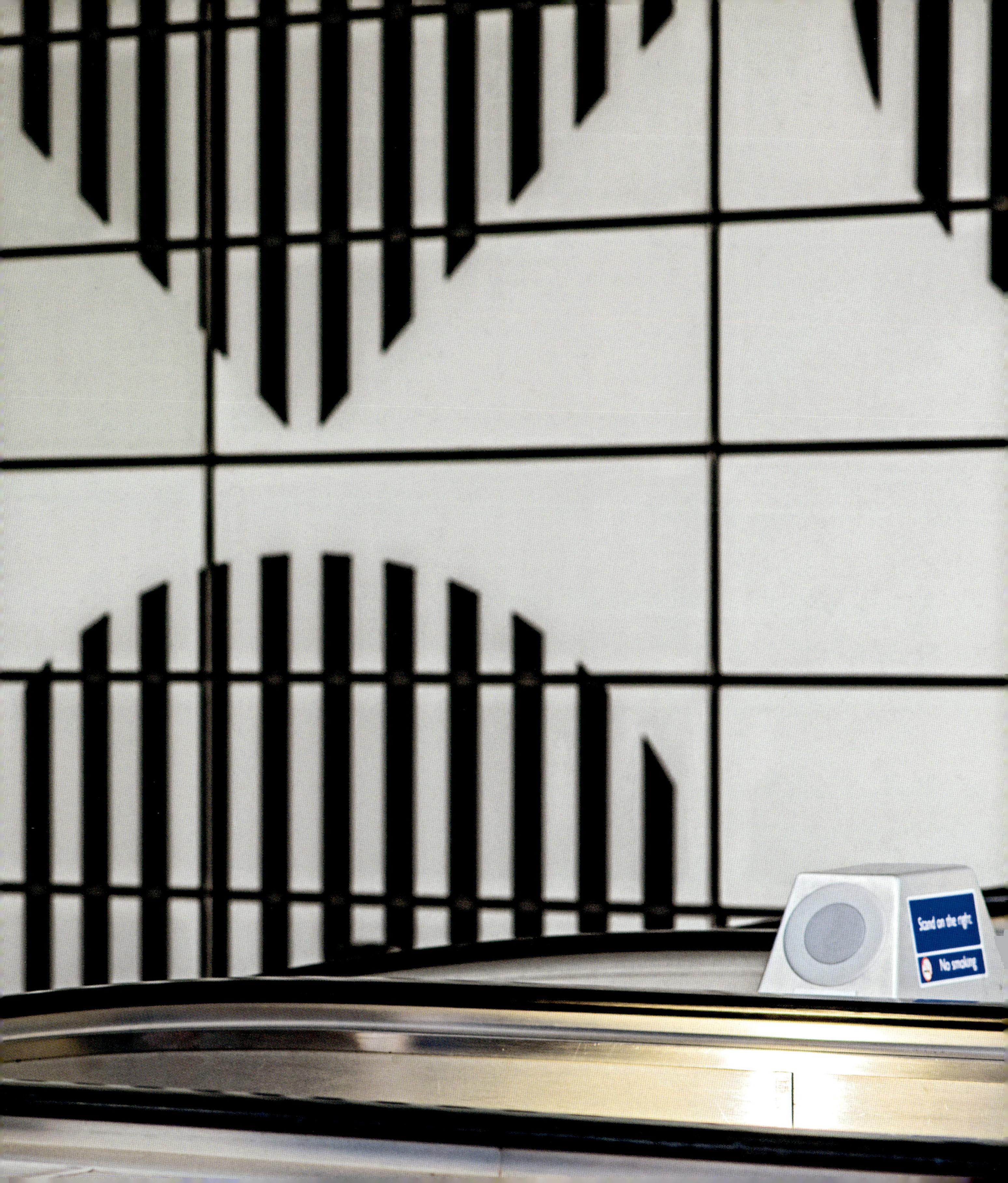
Stand on the right
No smoking

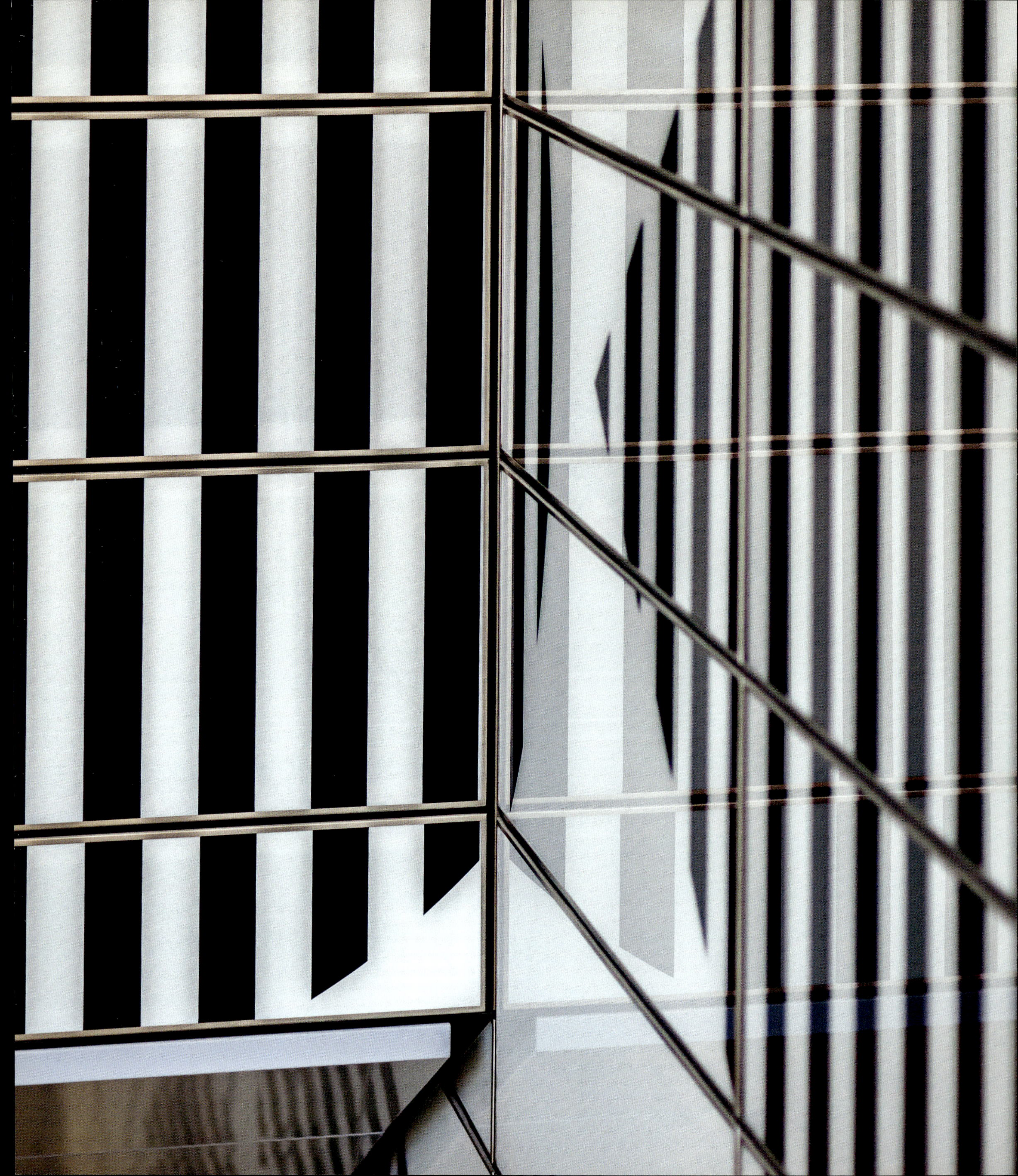

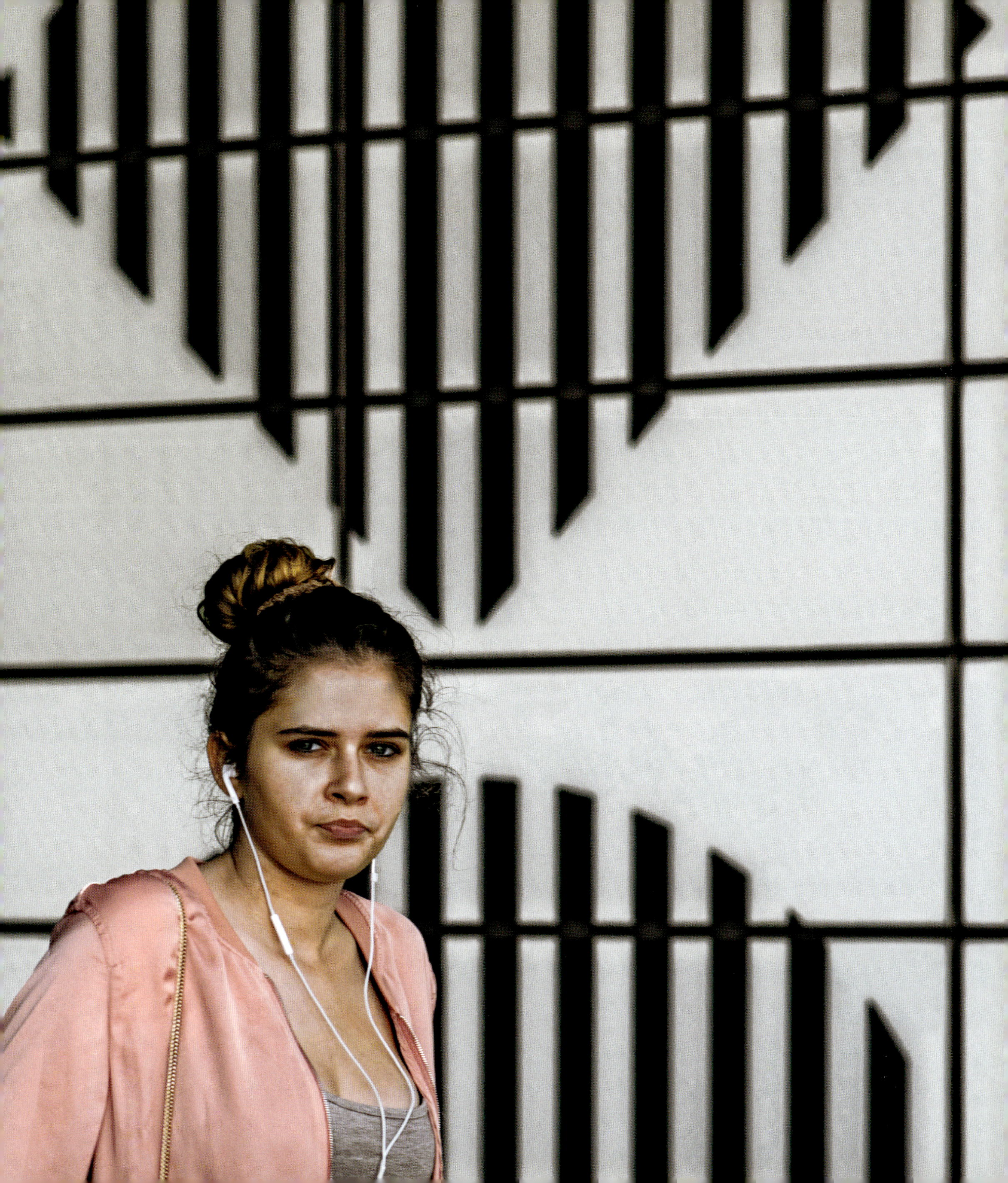

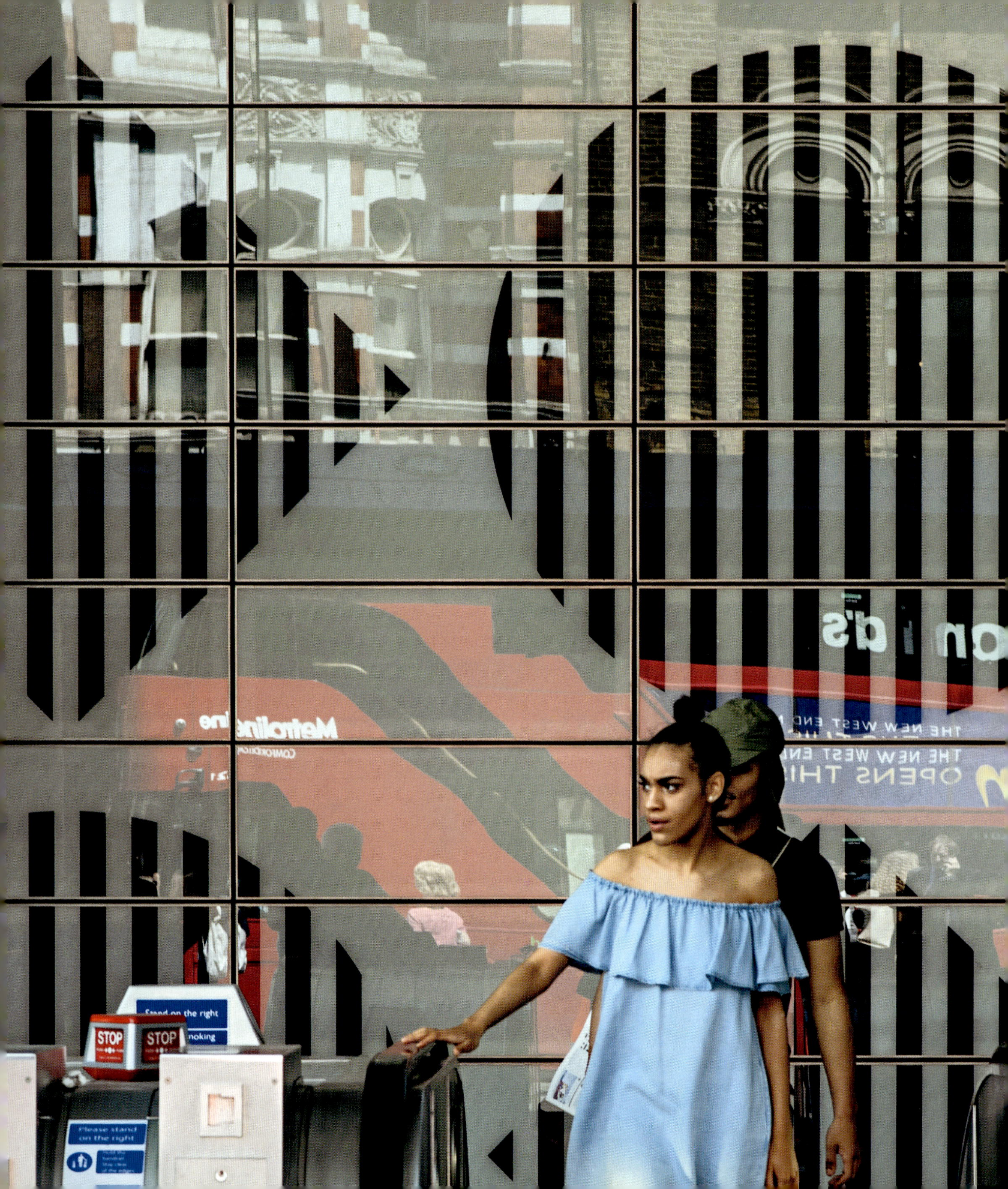

Metroline
THE NEW WEST END
THE NEW WEST END
OPENS THIS
on d's
STOP
STOP
Stand on the right
noking
Please stand
on the right

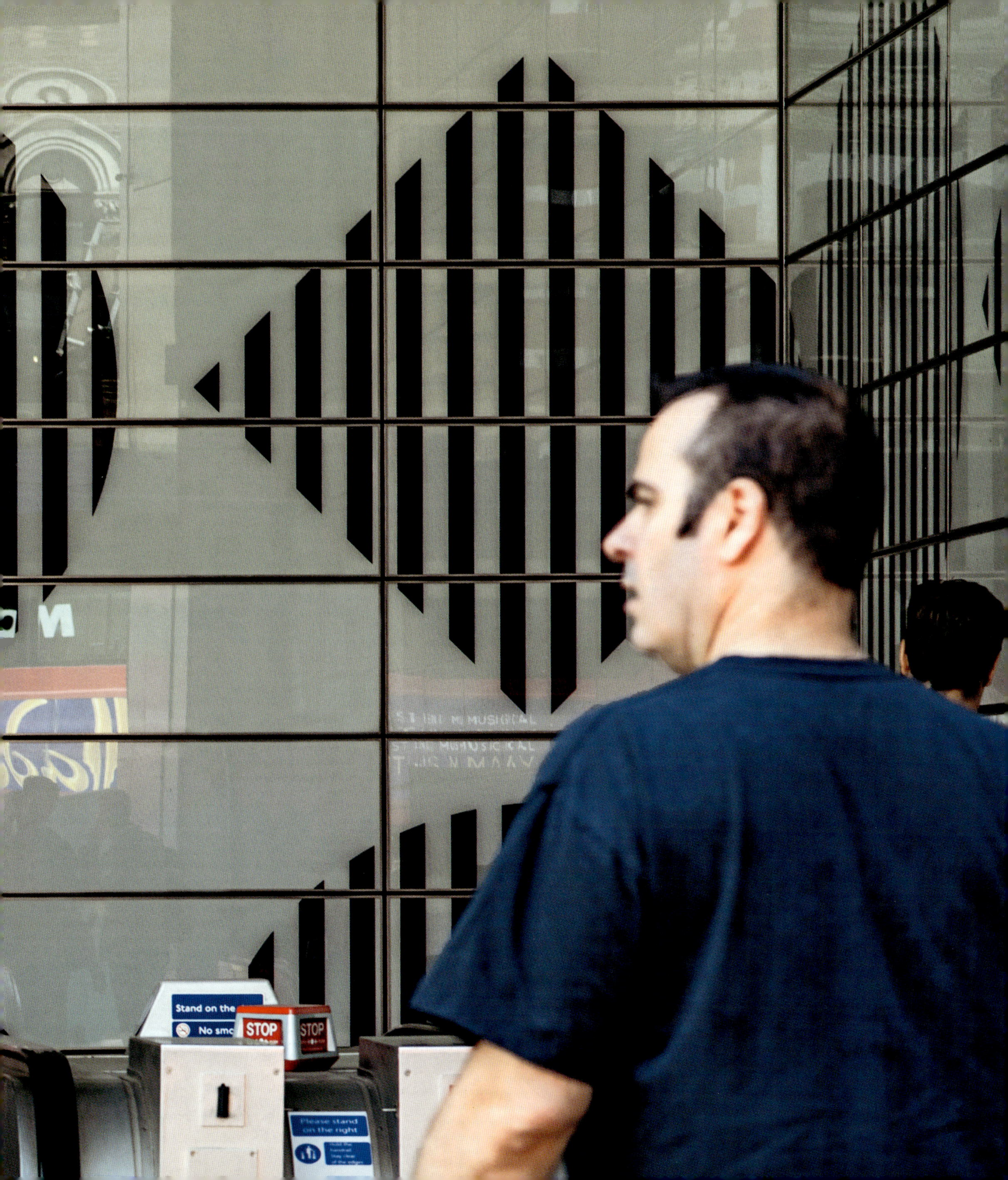
Stand on the
No smc
STOP
STOP
Please stand
on the right

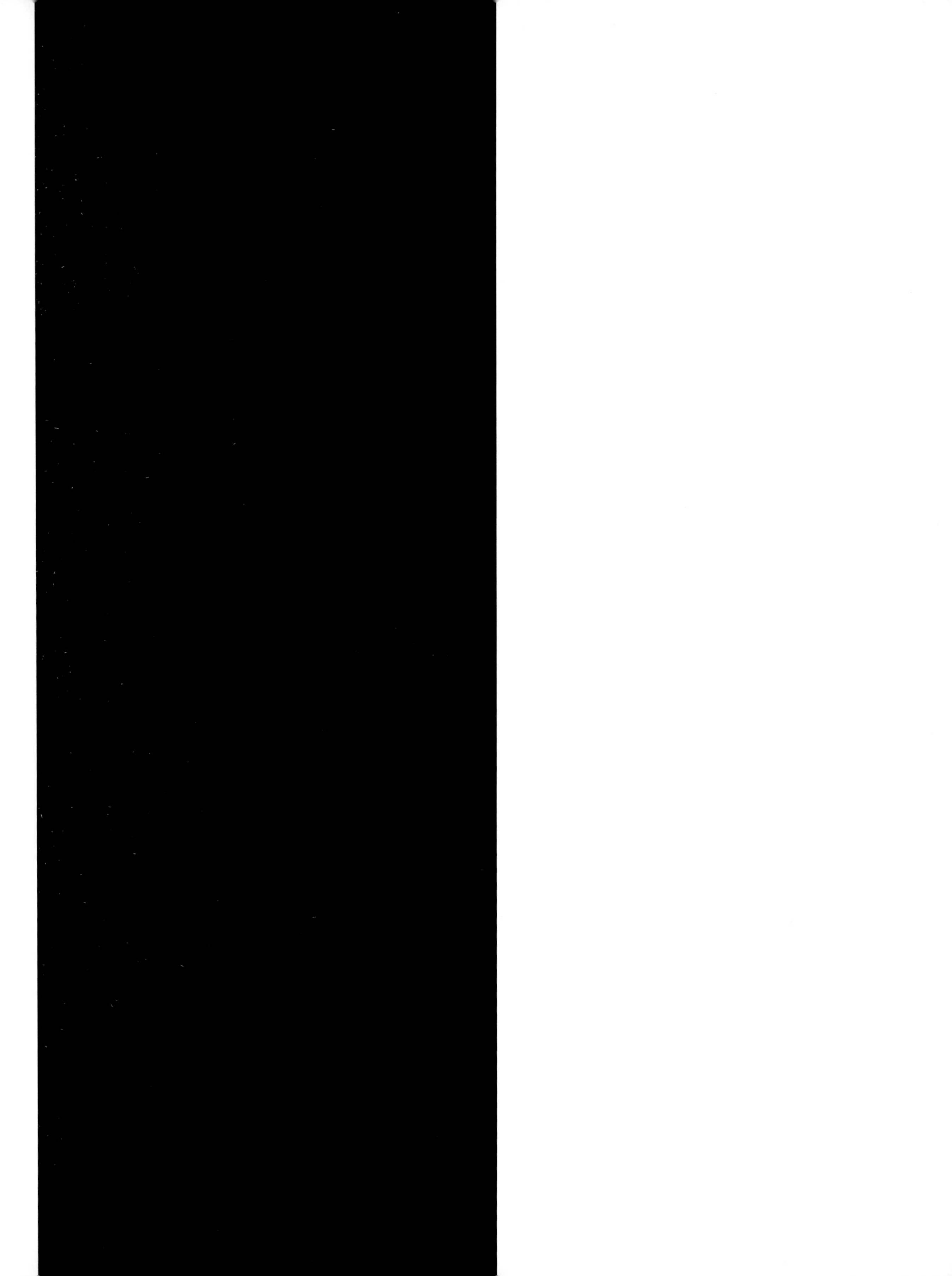

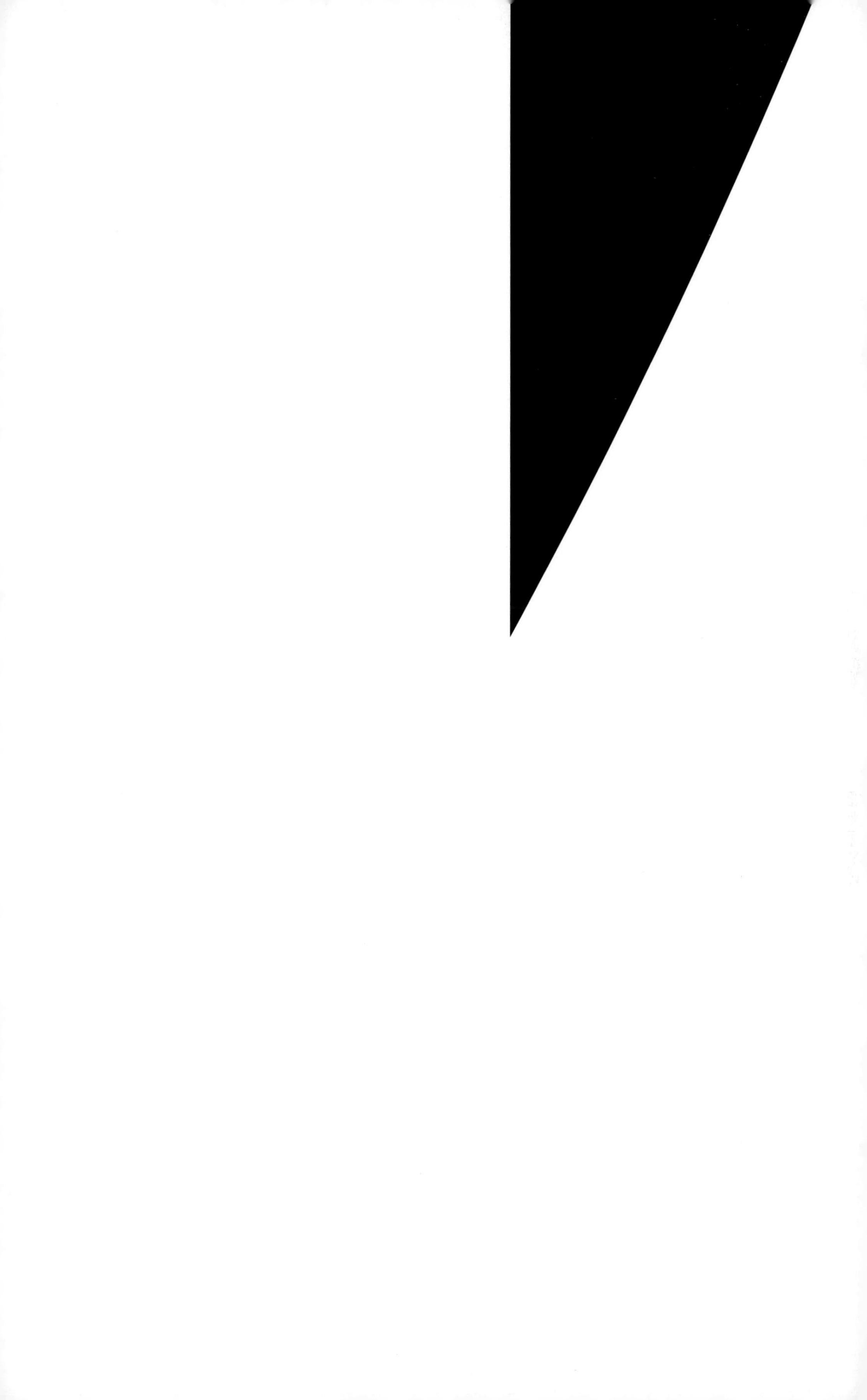

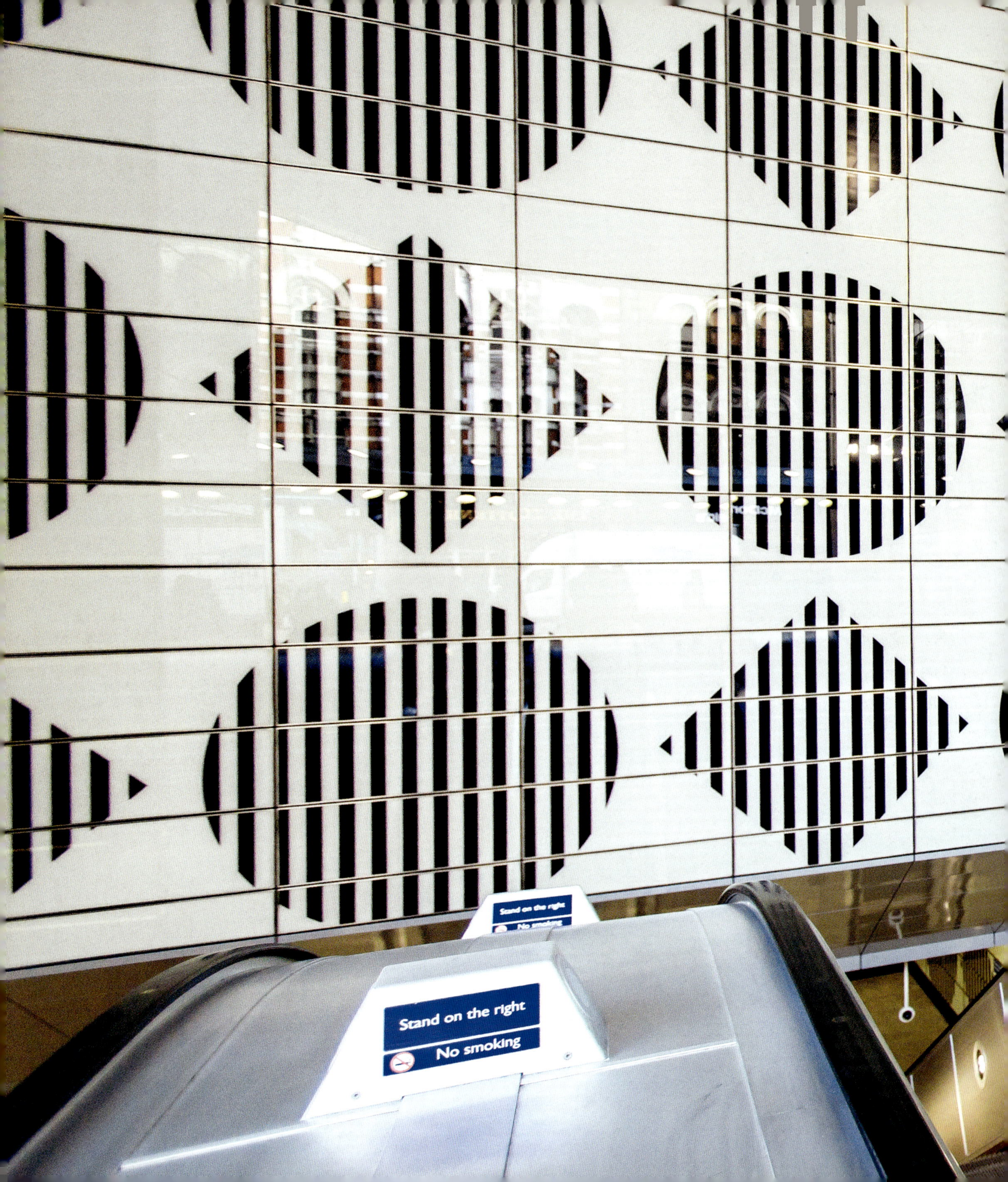

Stand on the right
No smoking
Stand on the right
No smoking

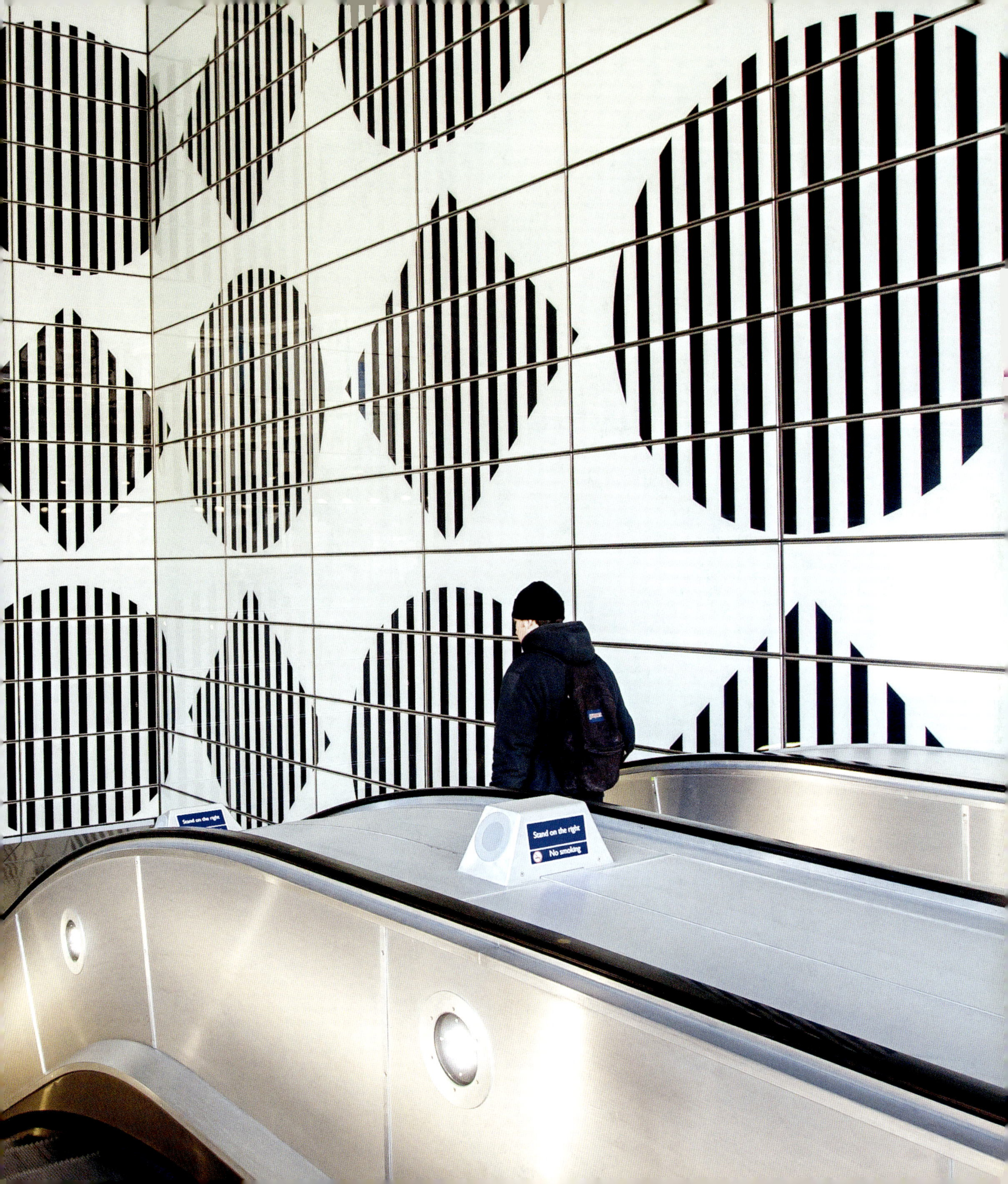

Stand on the right
No smoking
Stand on the right

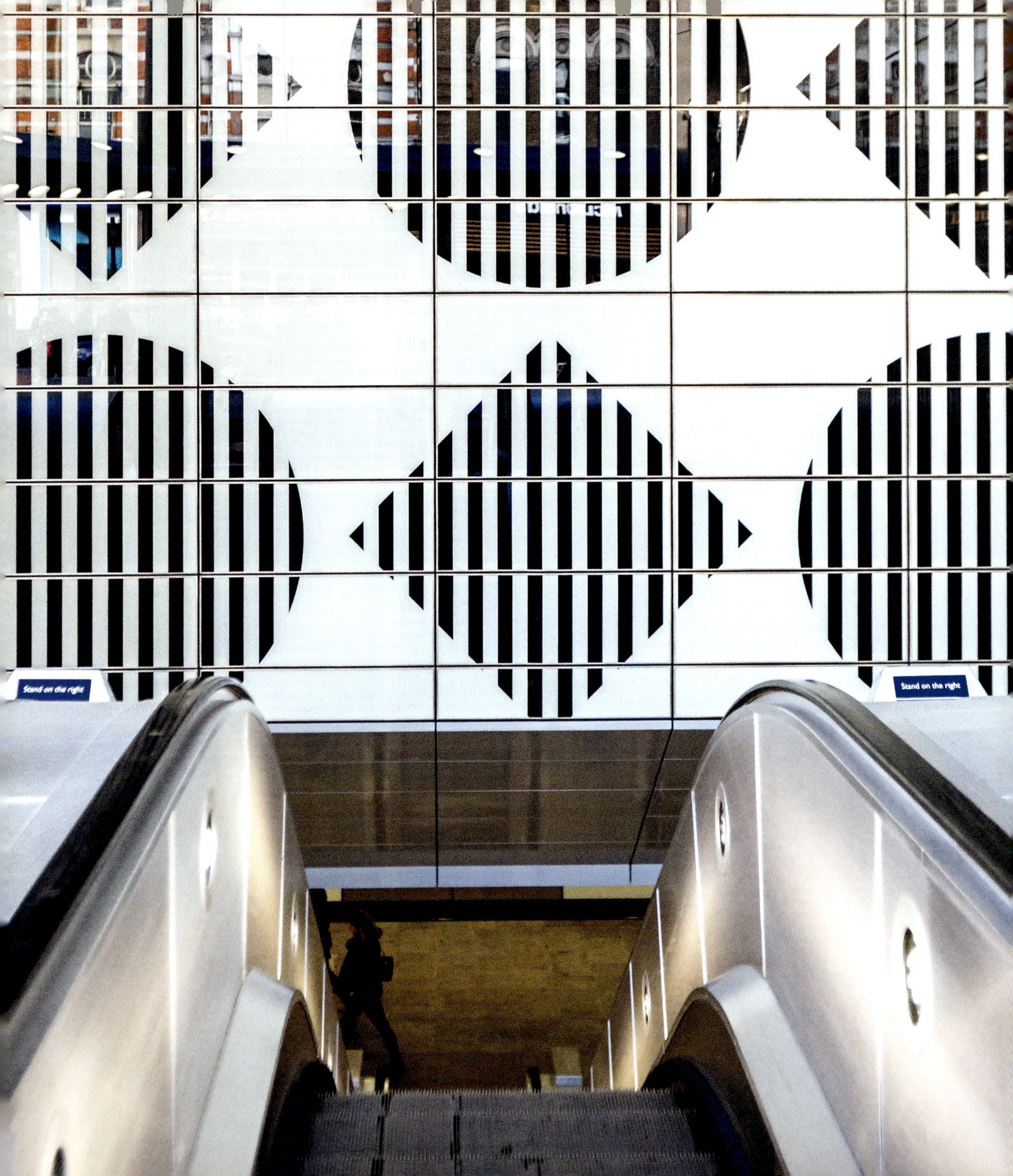

Stand on the right
Stand on the right

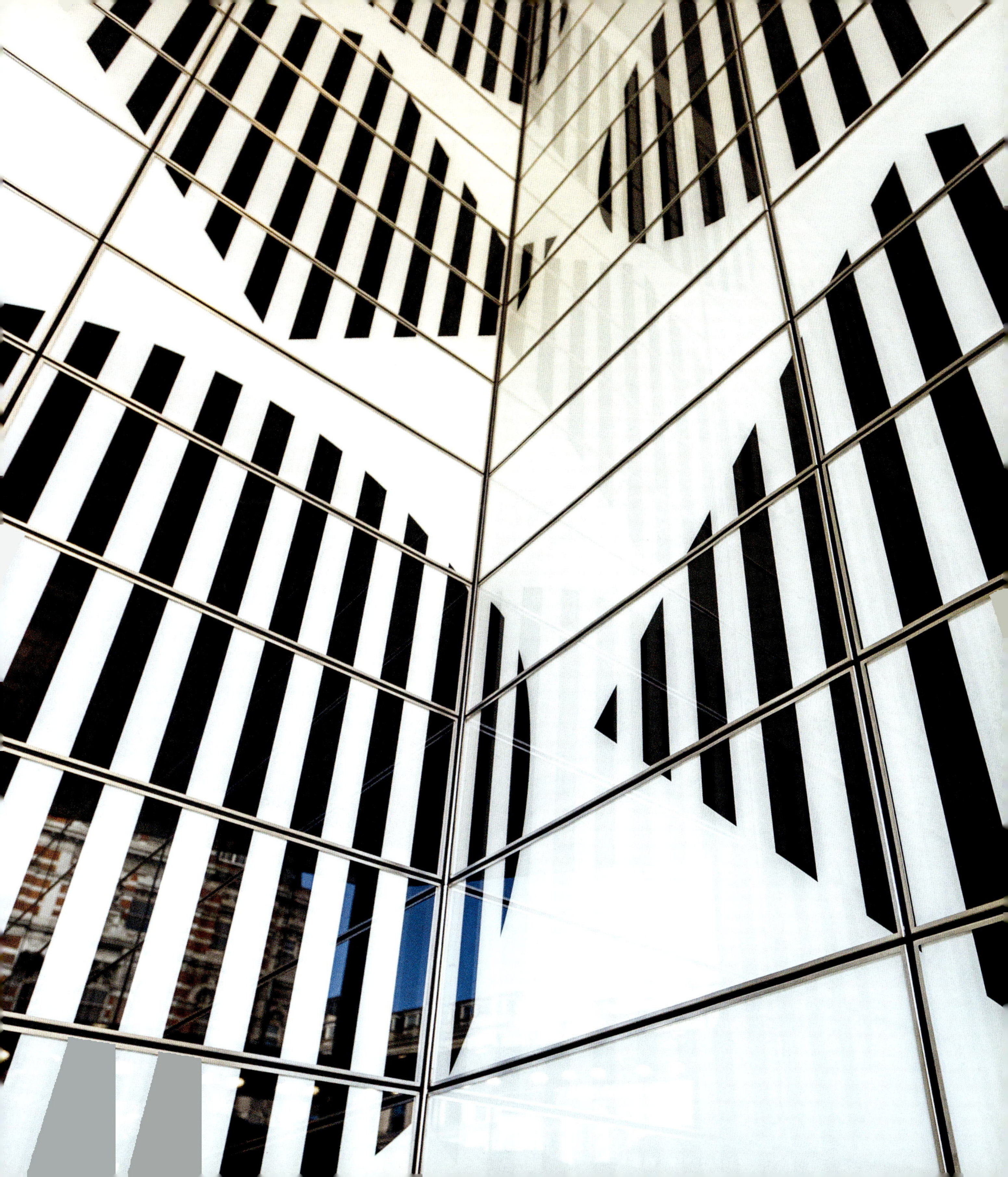

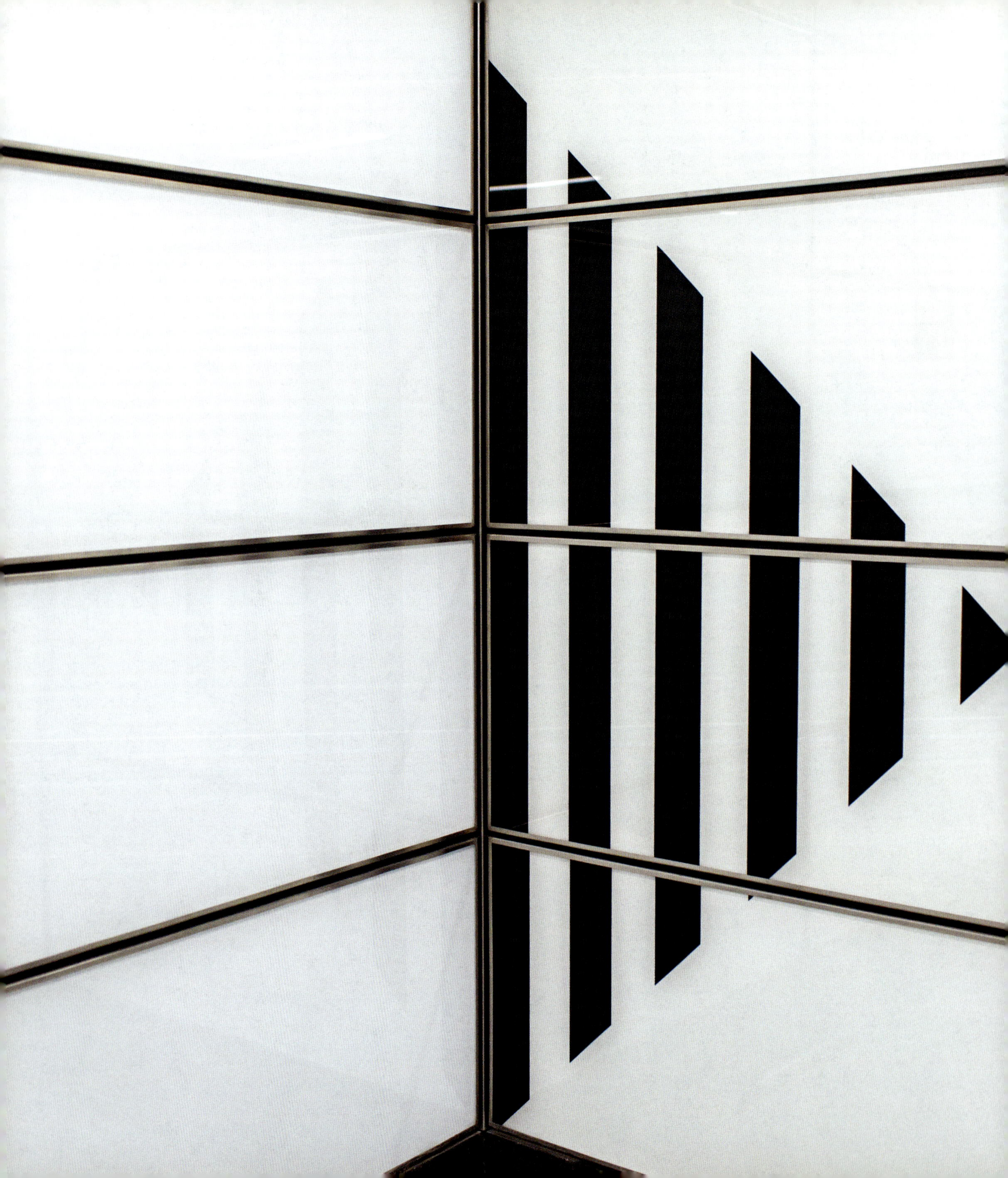

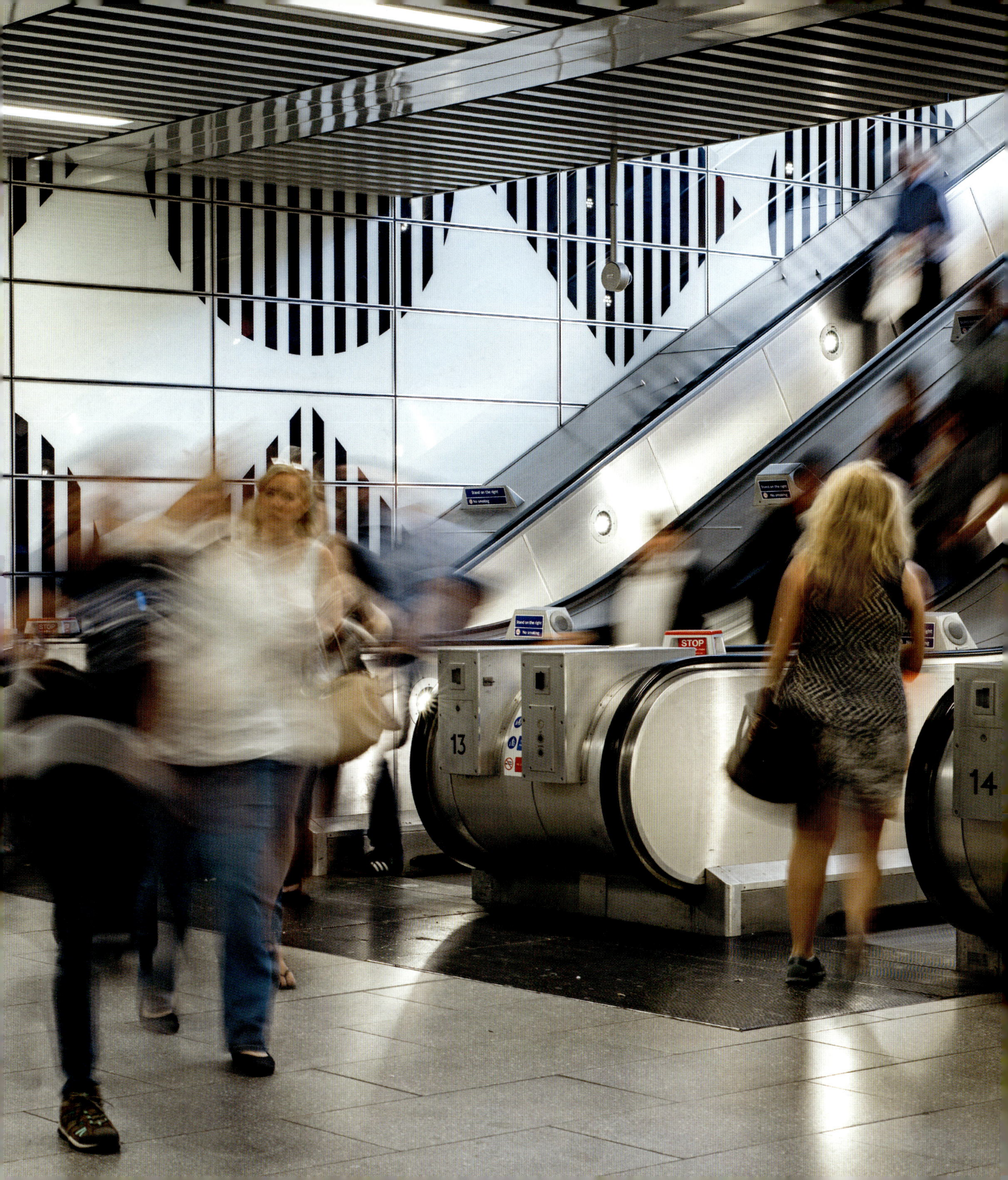

STOP
STOP
Stand on the right
No smoking
Stand on the right
No smoking
13
14

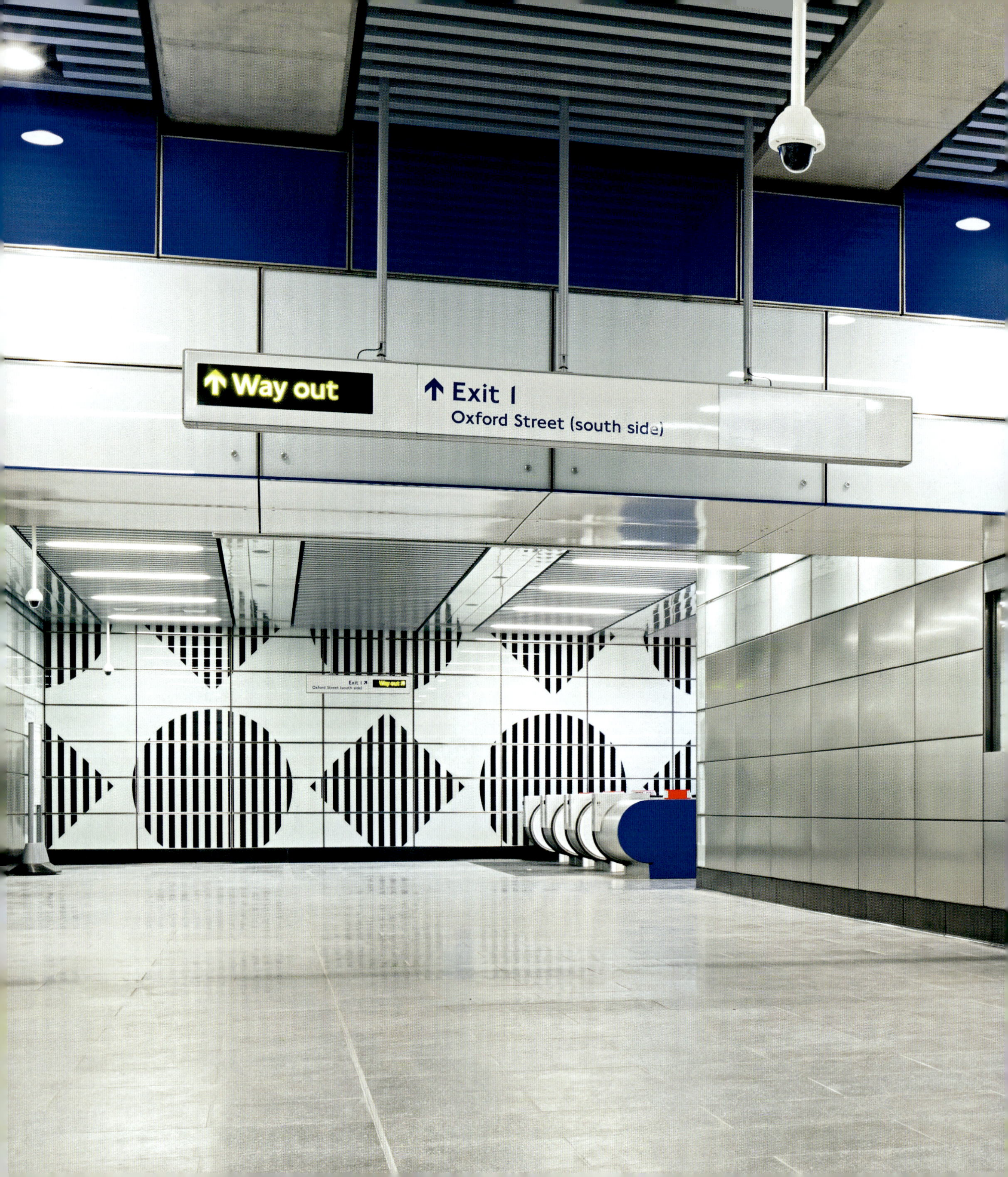

↑ Way out
↑ Exit 1
Oxford Street (south side)

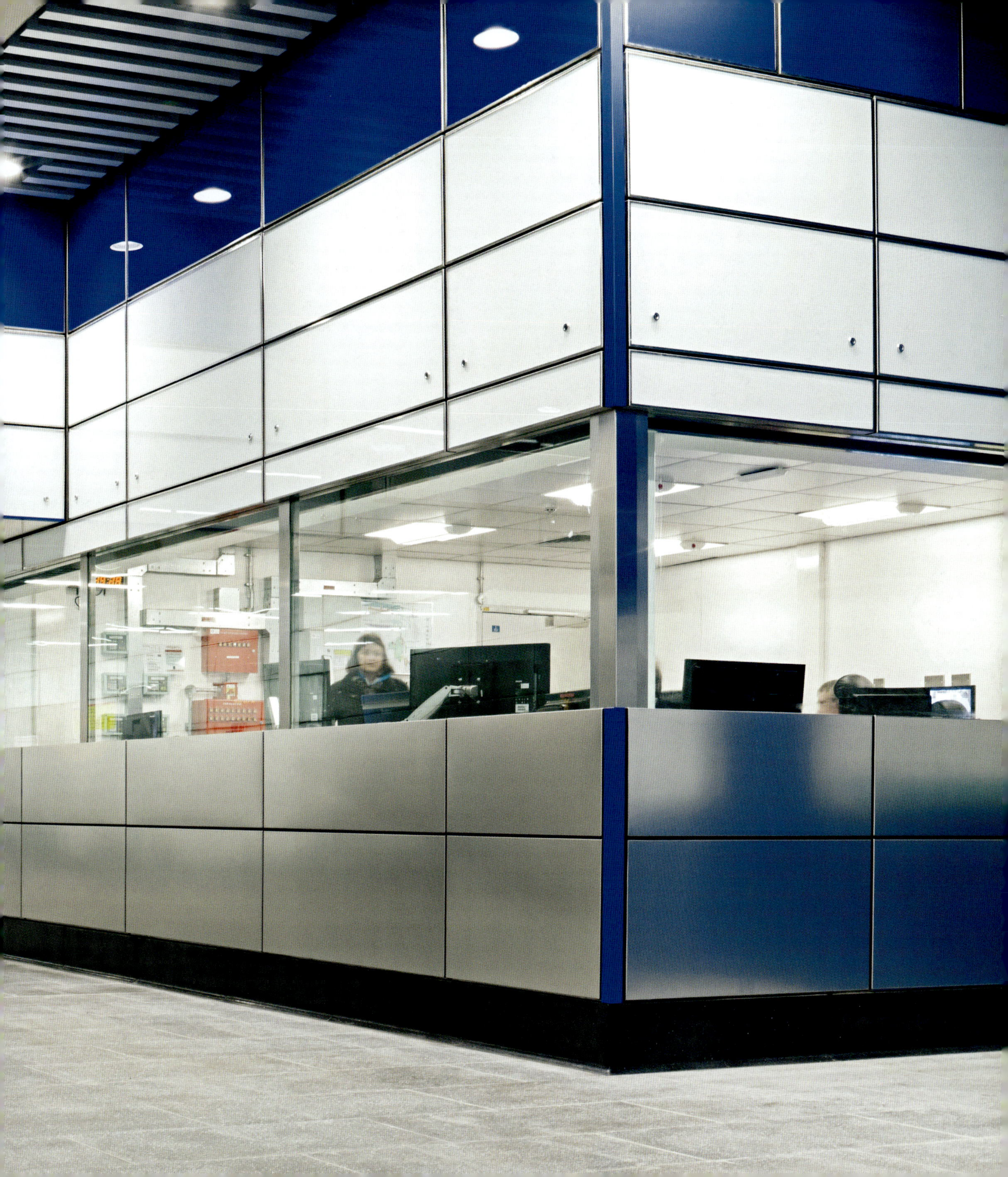

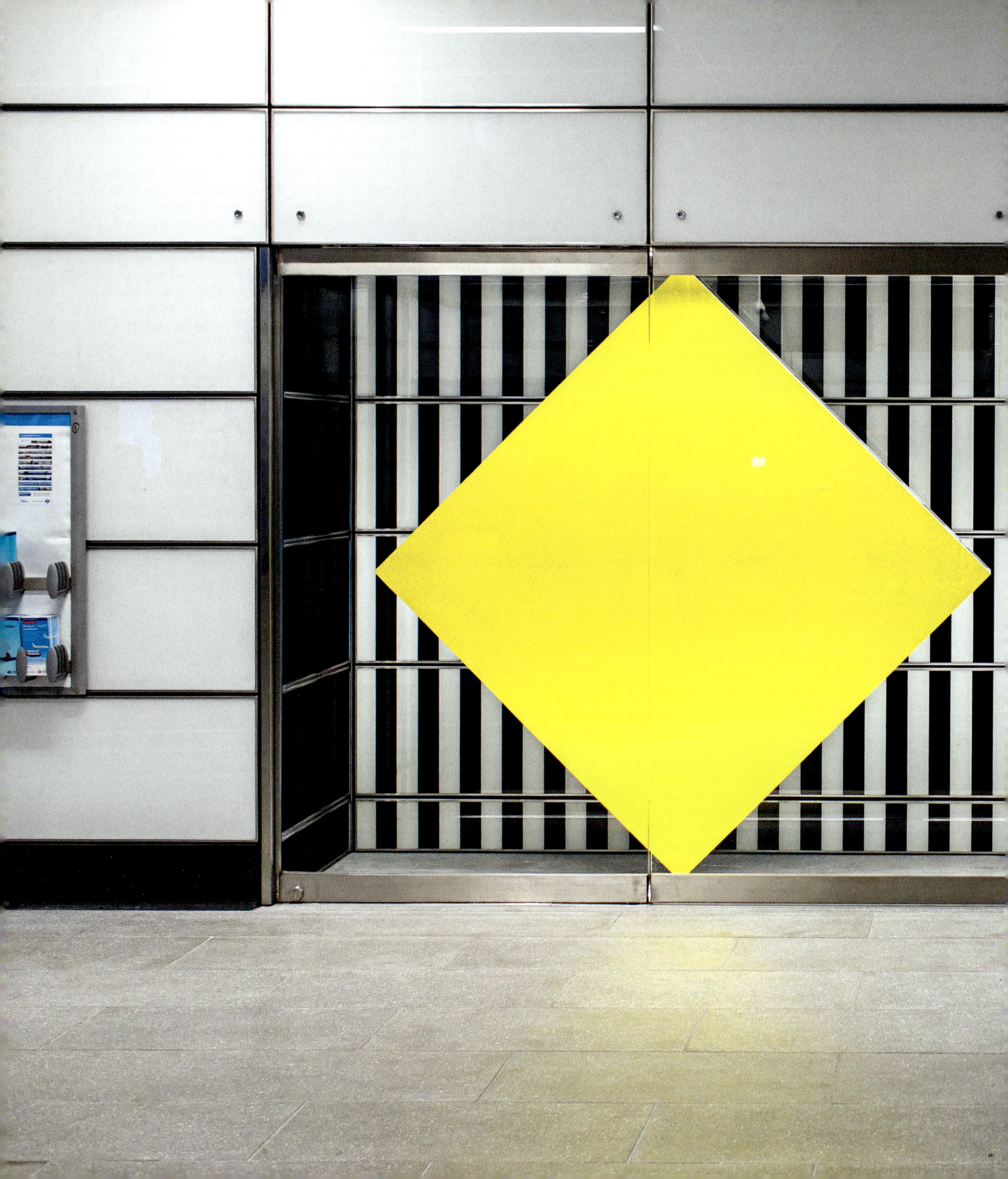

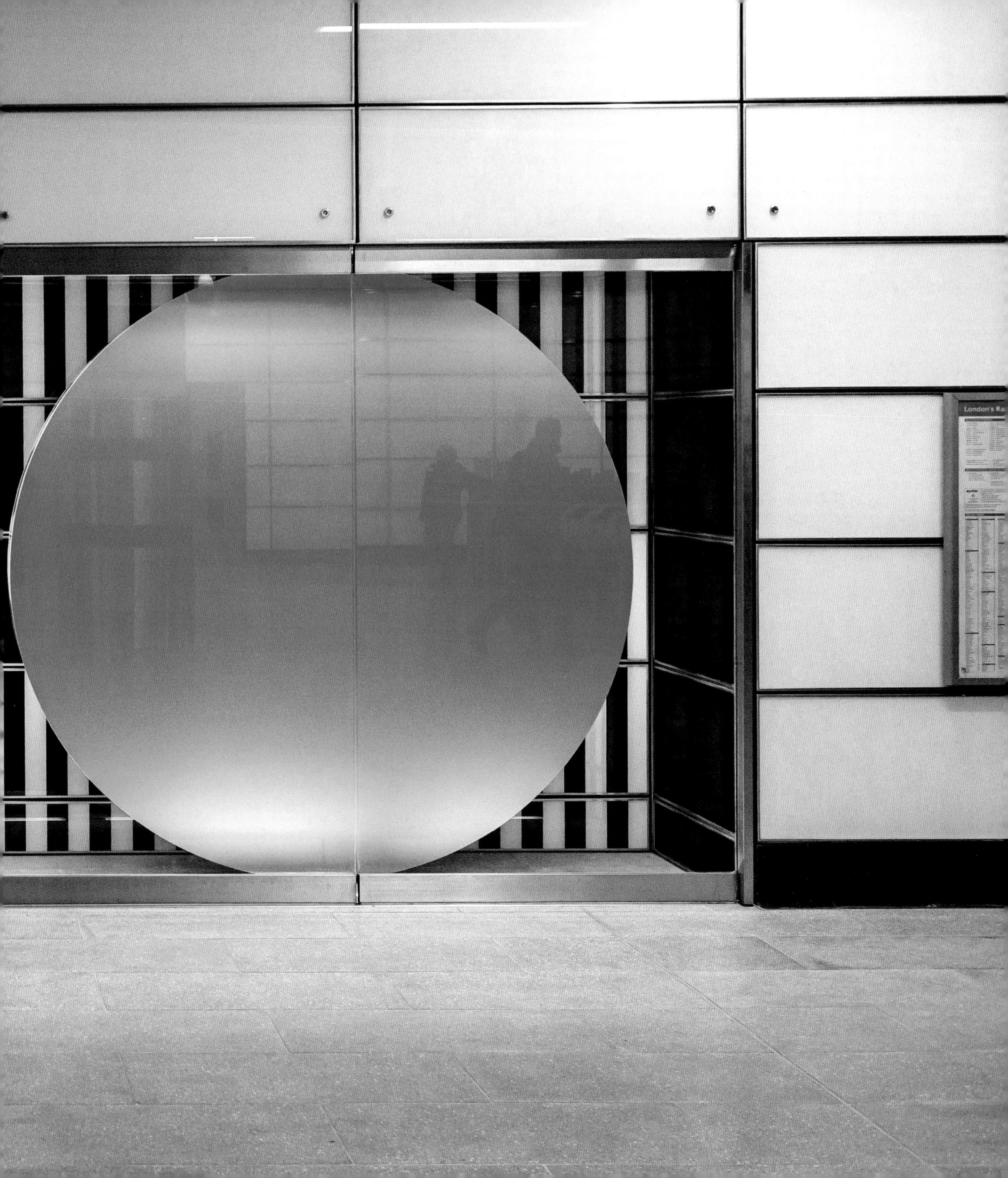

London's Ra

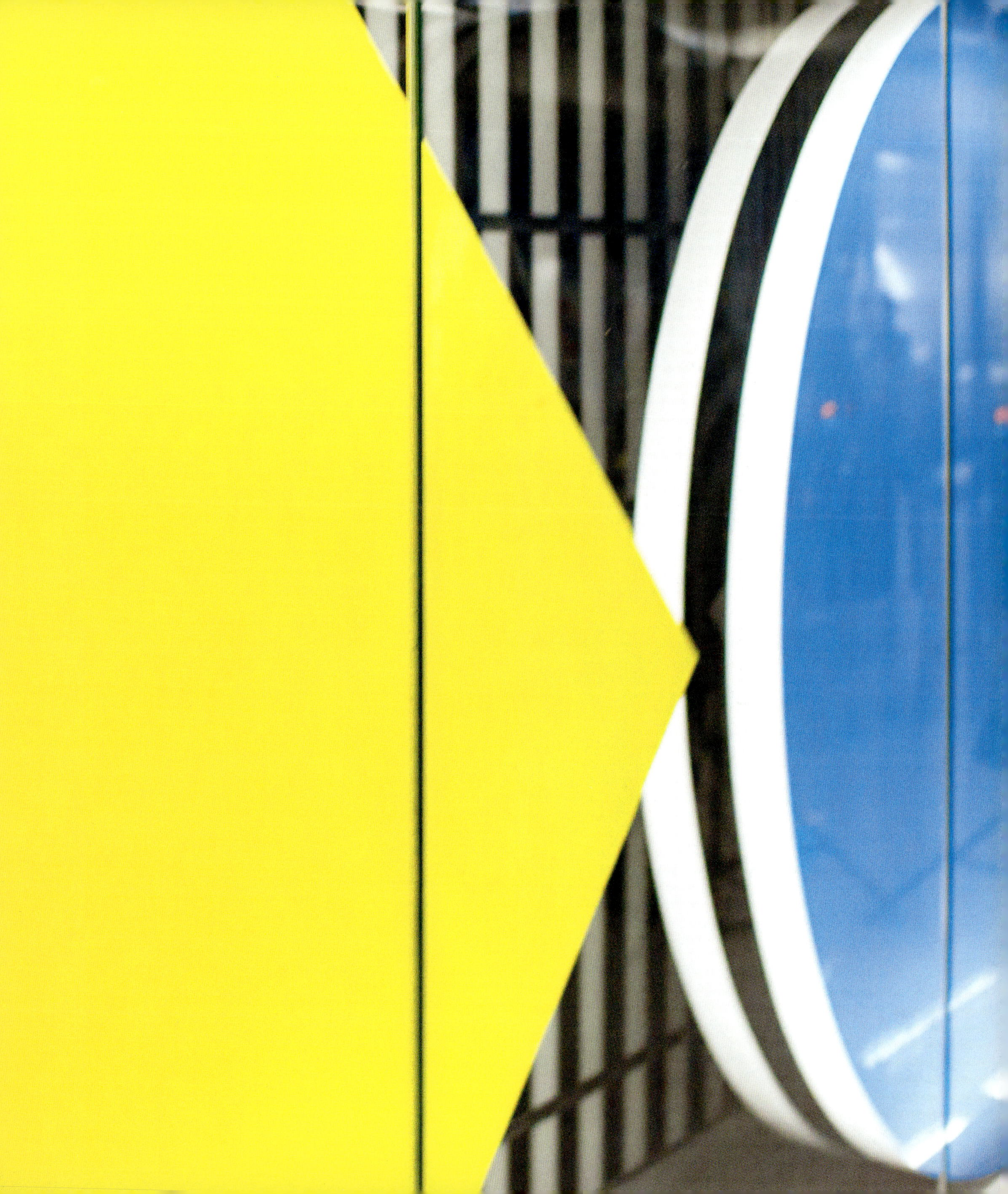

I have always used colour, even when it was completely rejected, and I got a lot of criticism for the vivid colours I was using. I have always thought that colour in visual art is the only thing that is totally impossible to describe and replace with words. I think it is the only way in art to speak without speaking. Everything else you can describe….
For me, colour is pure thought, and therefore completely inexpressible, every bit as abstract as a mathematical formula or a philosophical concept.

Daniel Buren

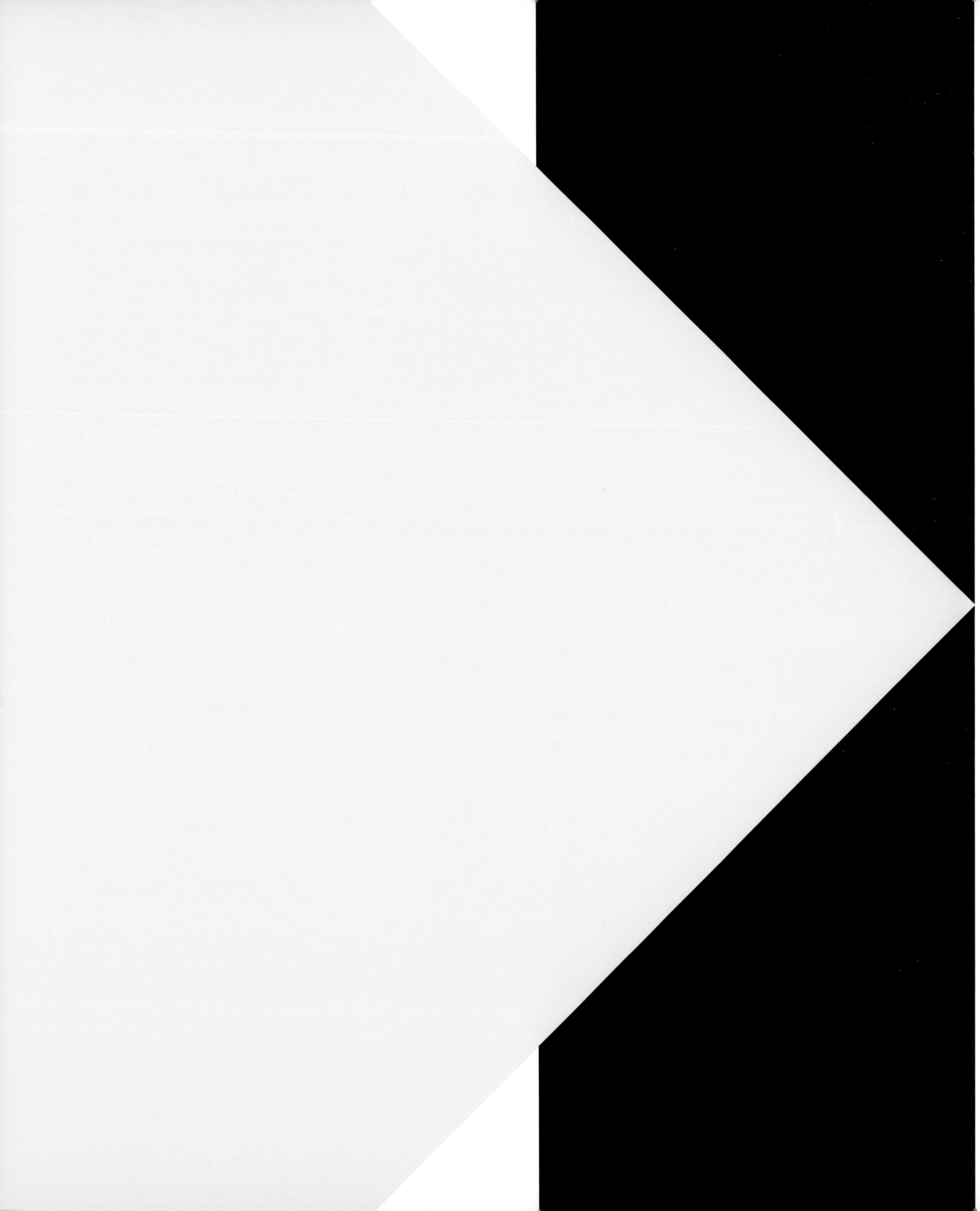

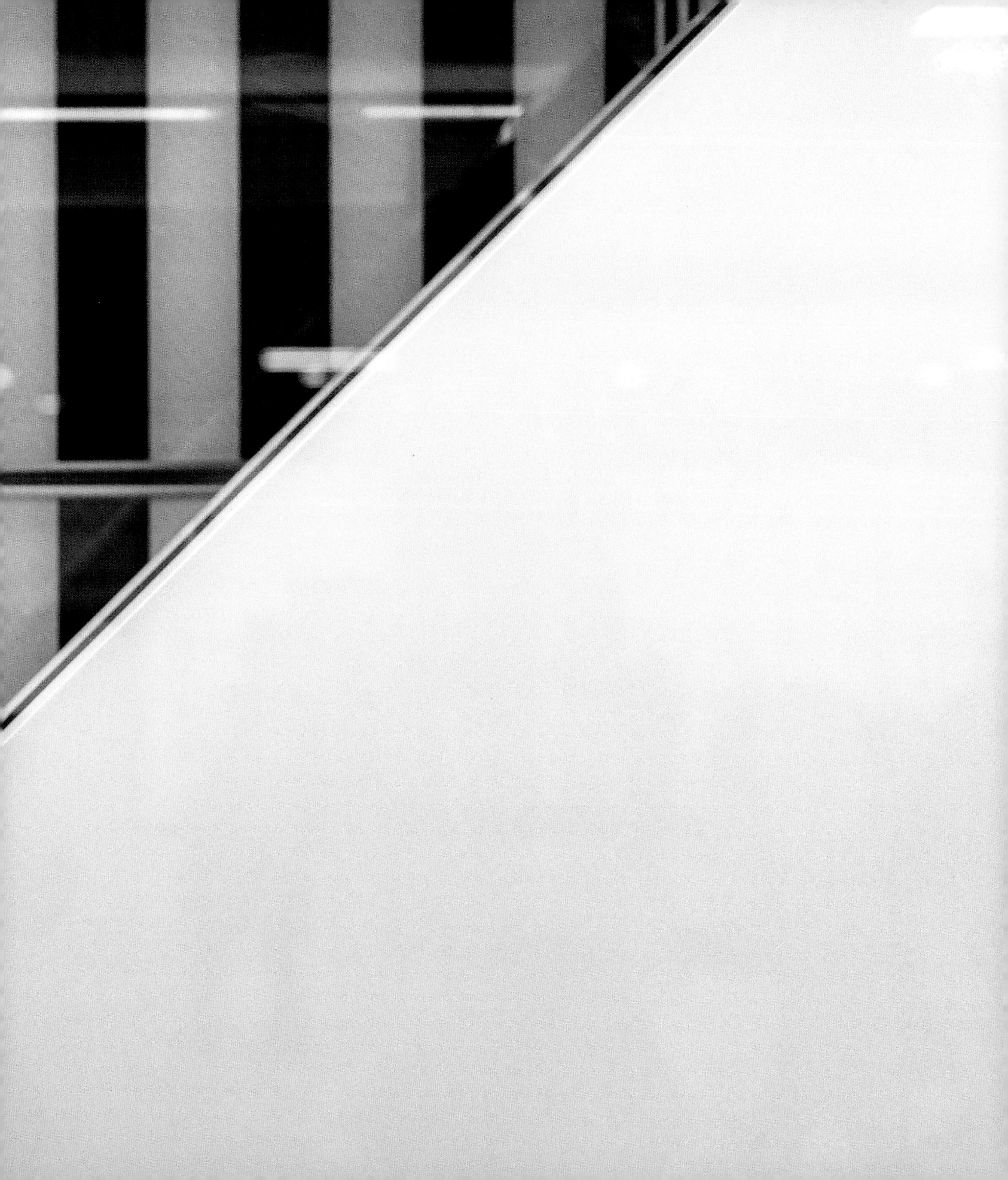

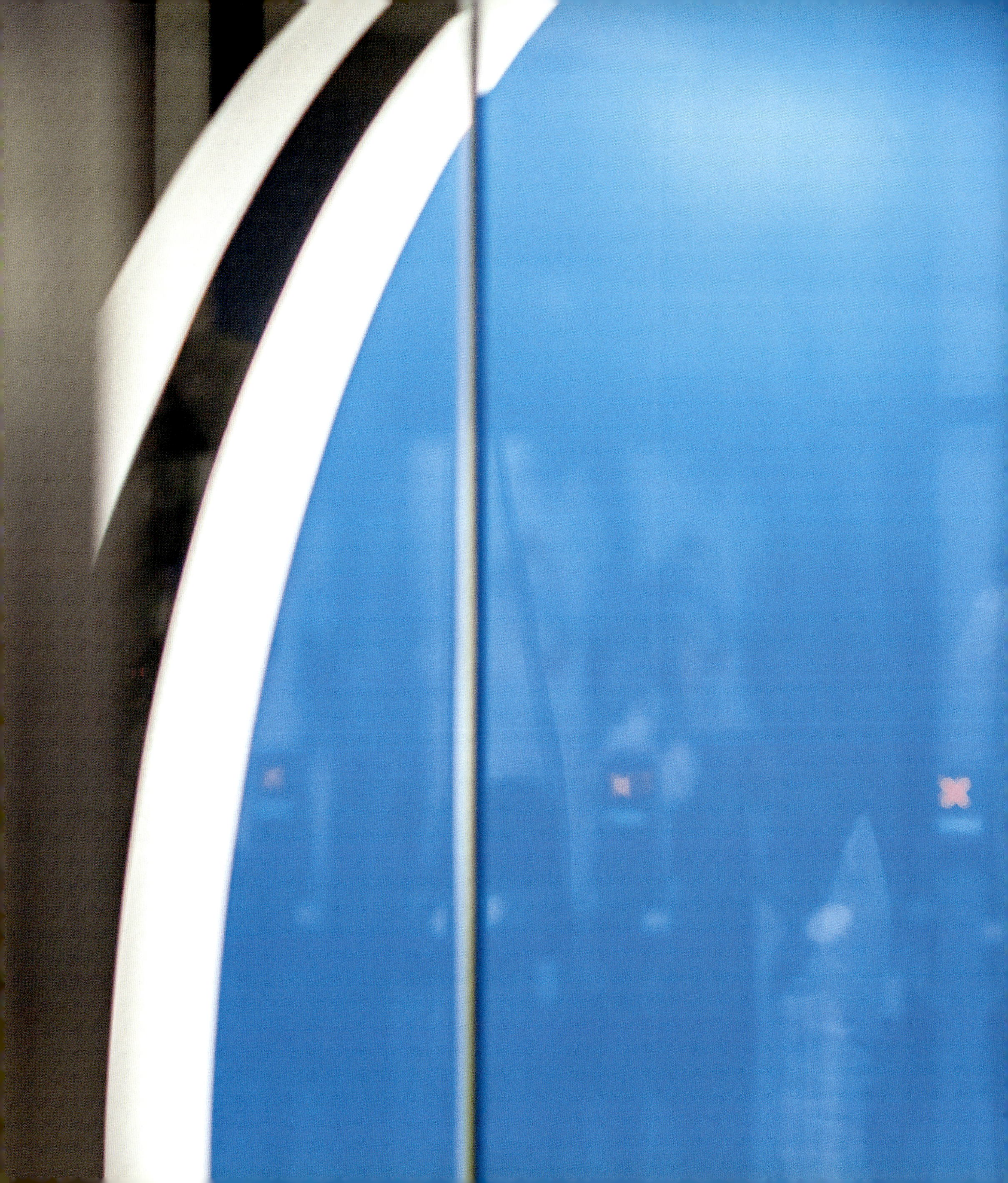

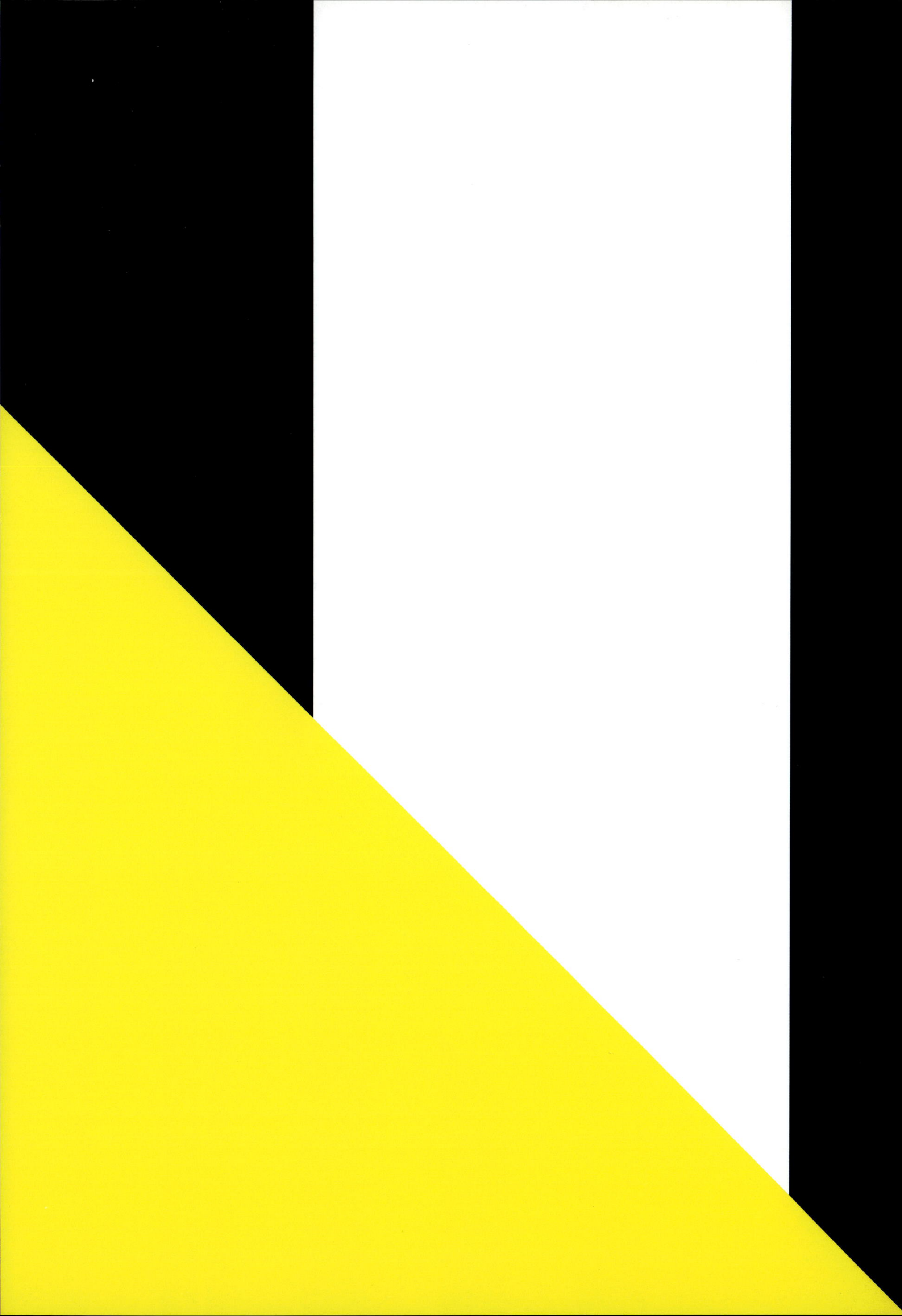

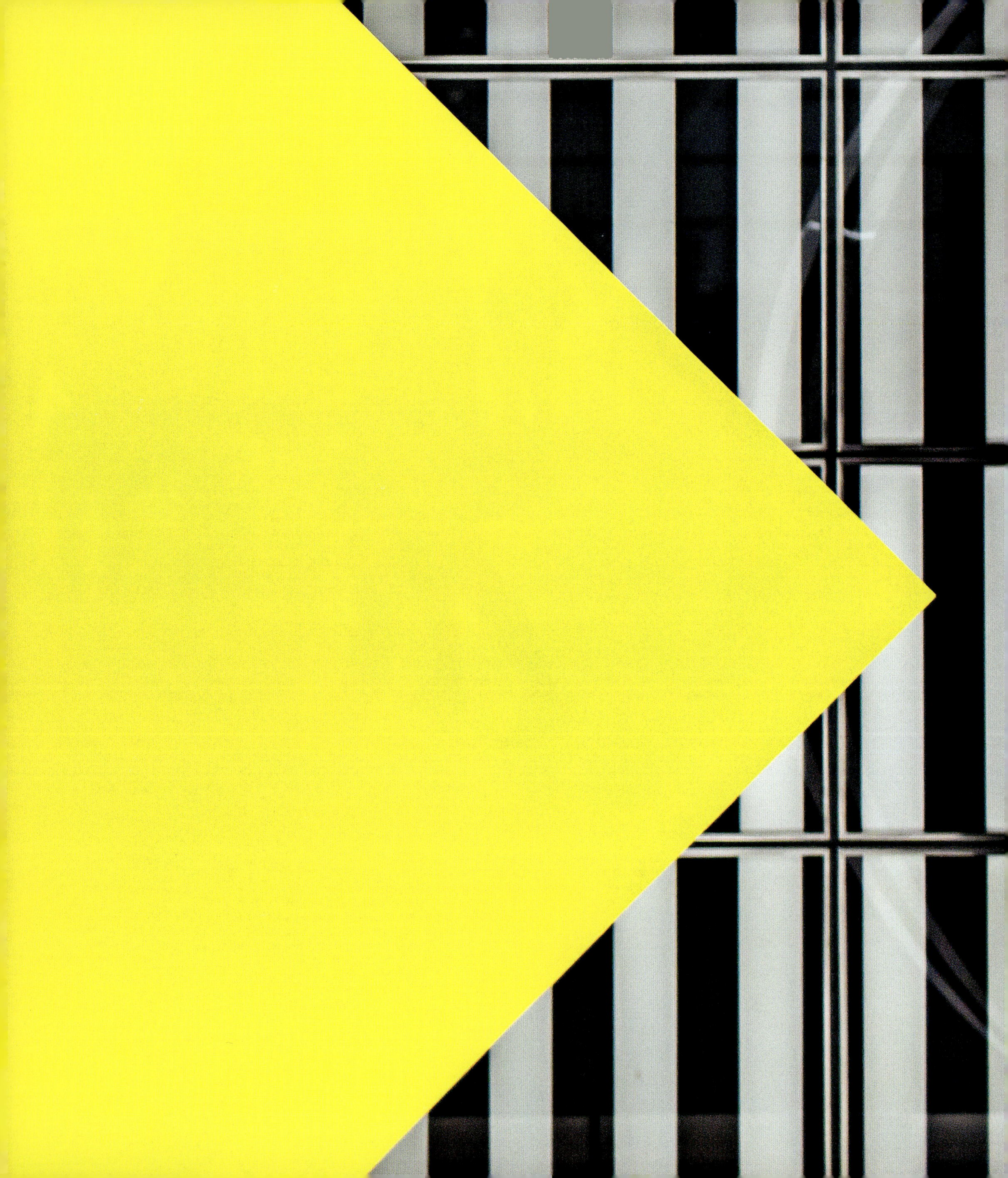

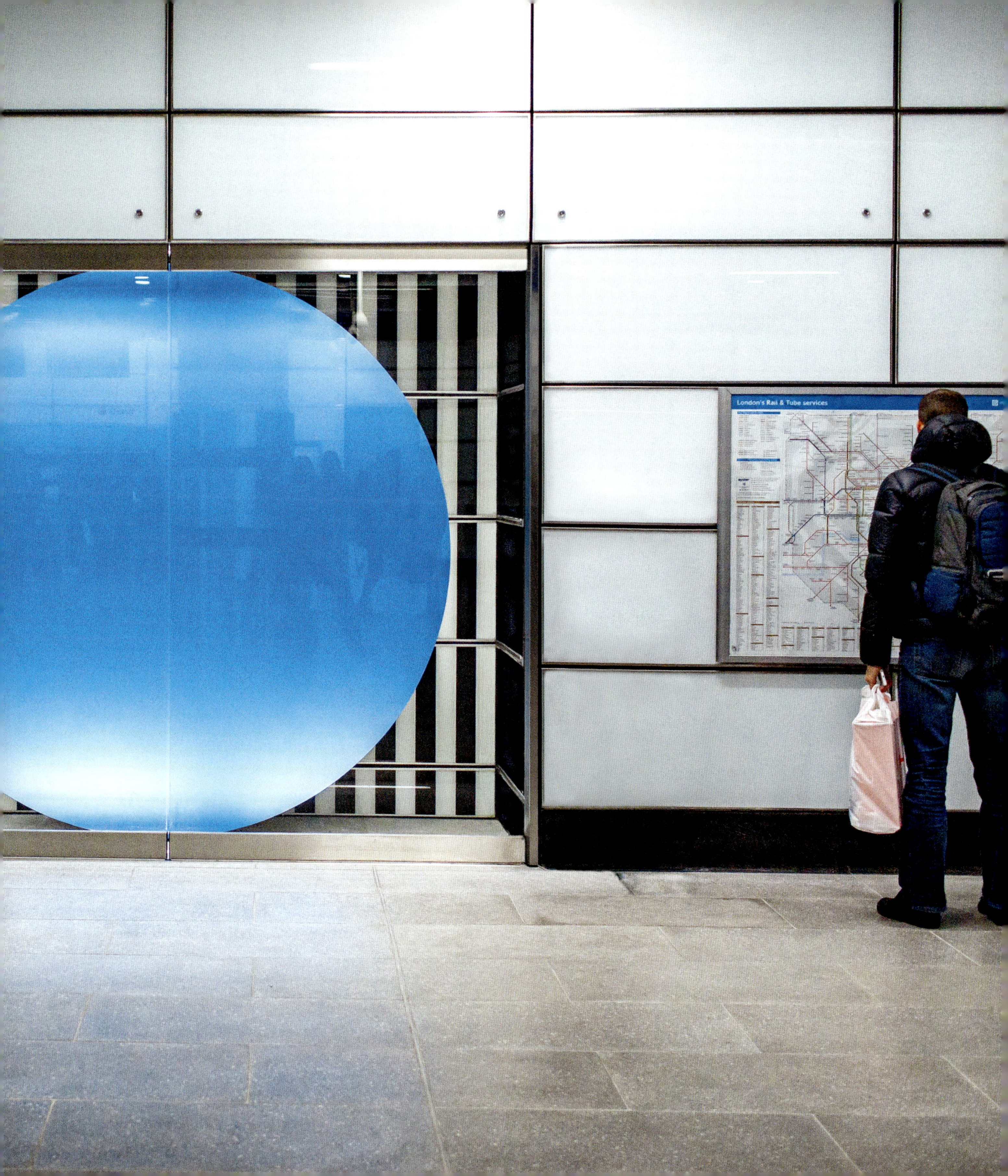
London's Rail & Tube services

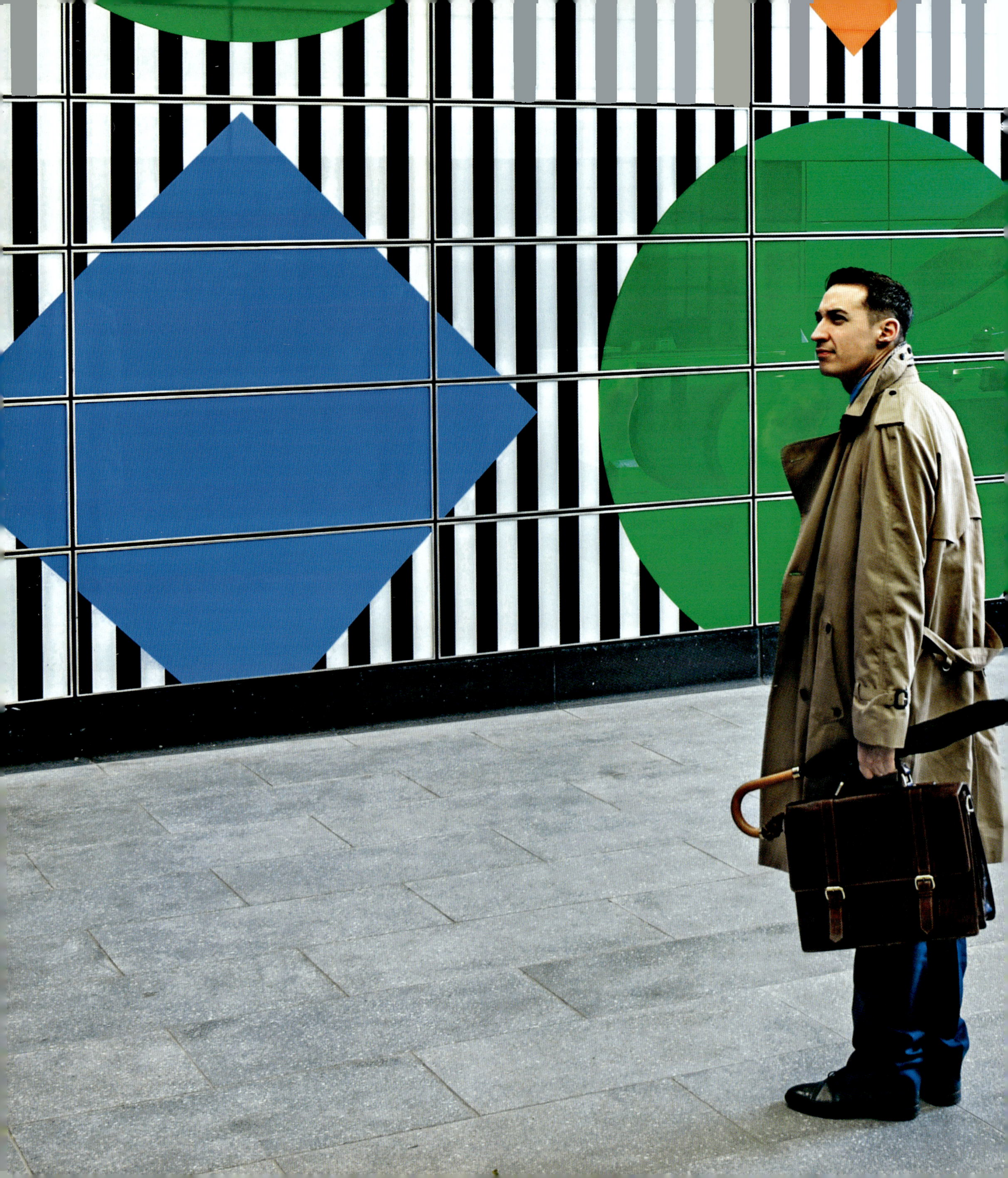

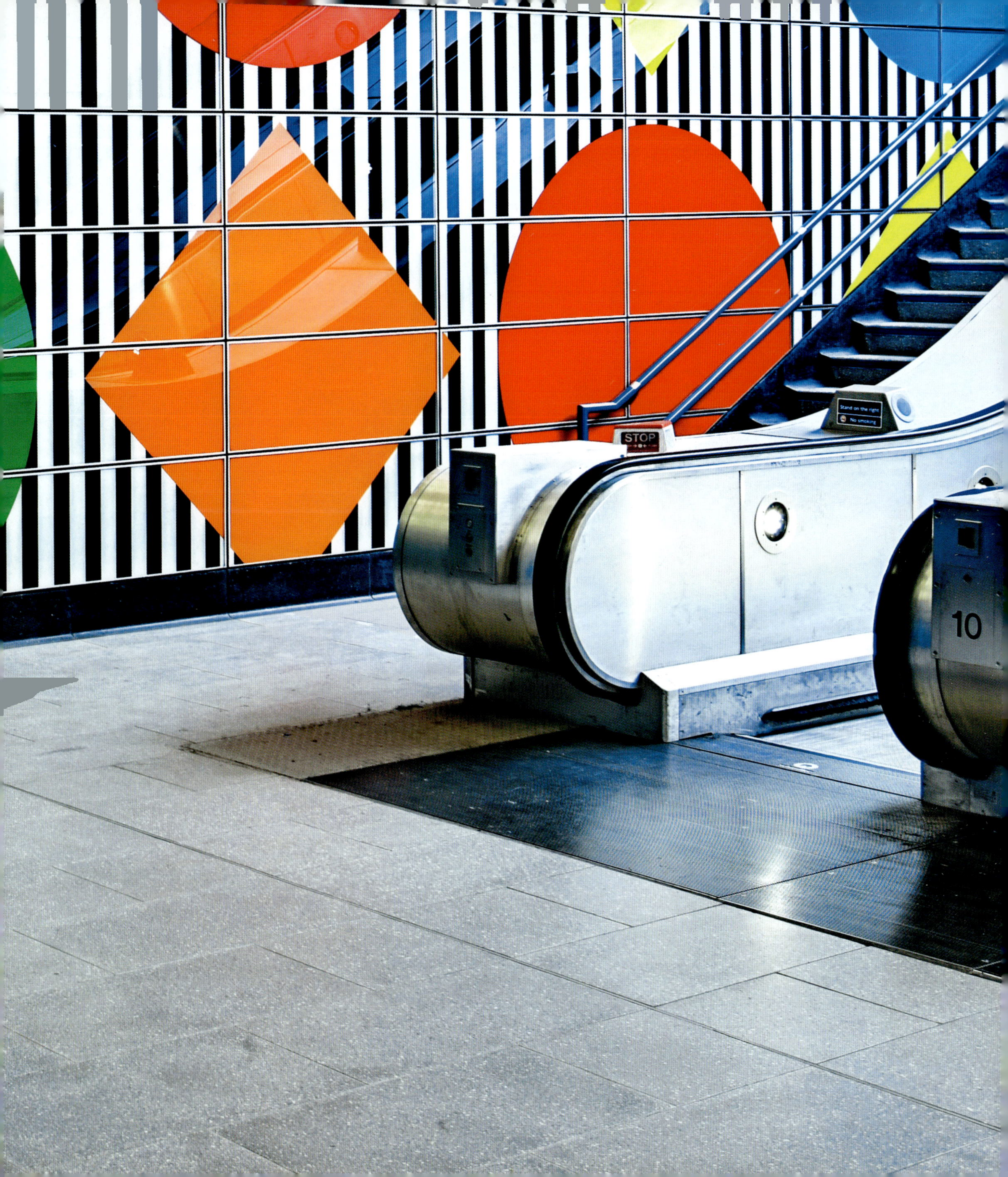
STOP
Stand on the right
No smoking
10

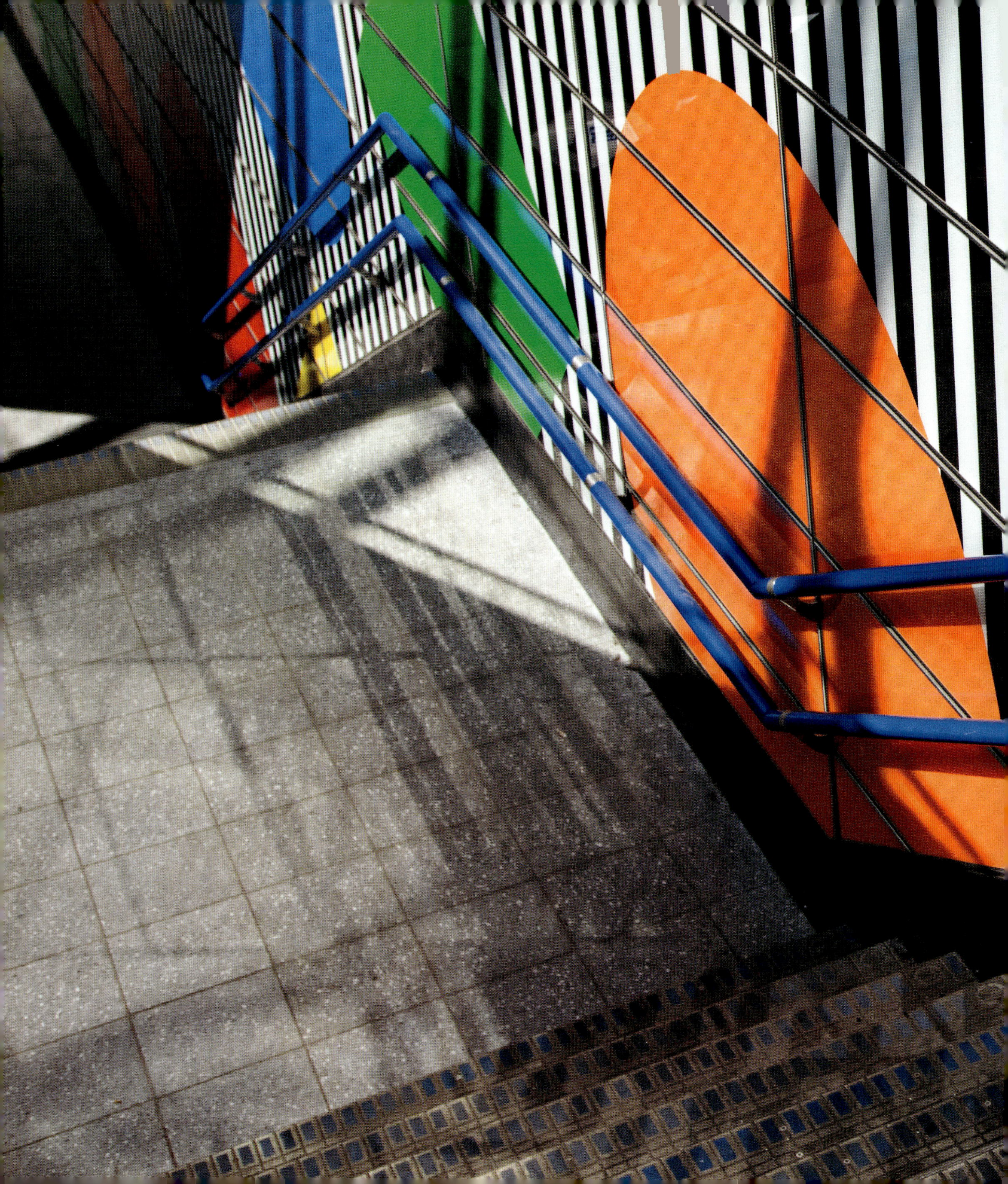

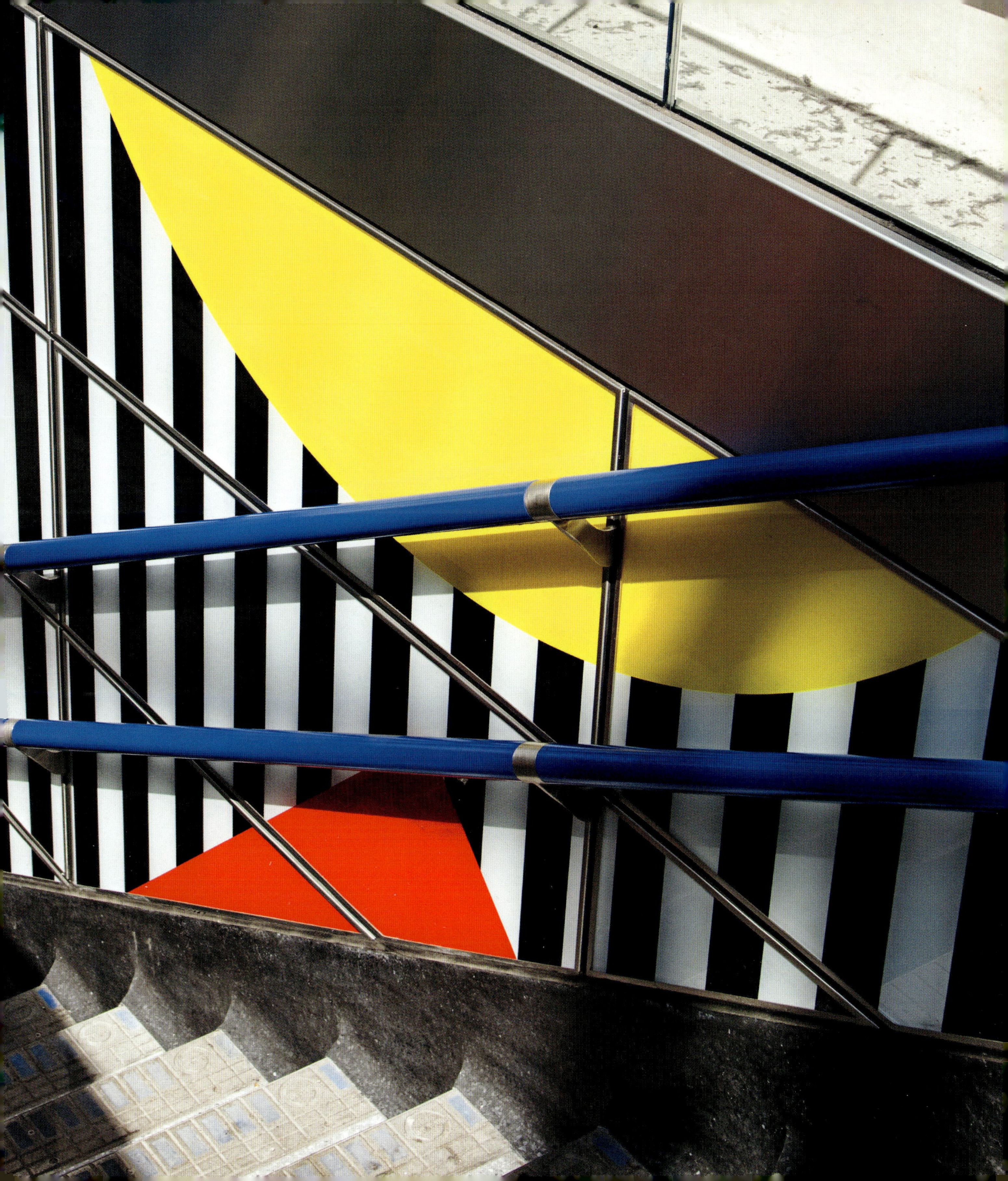

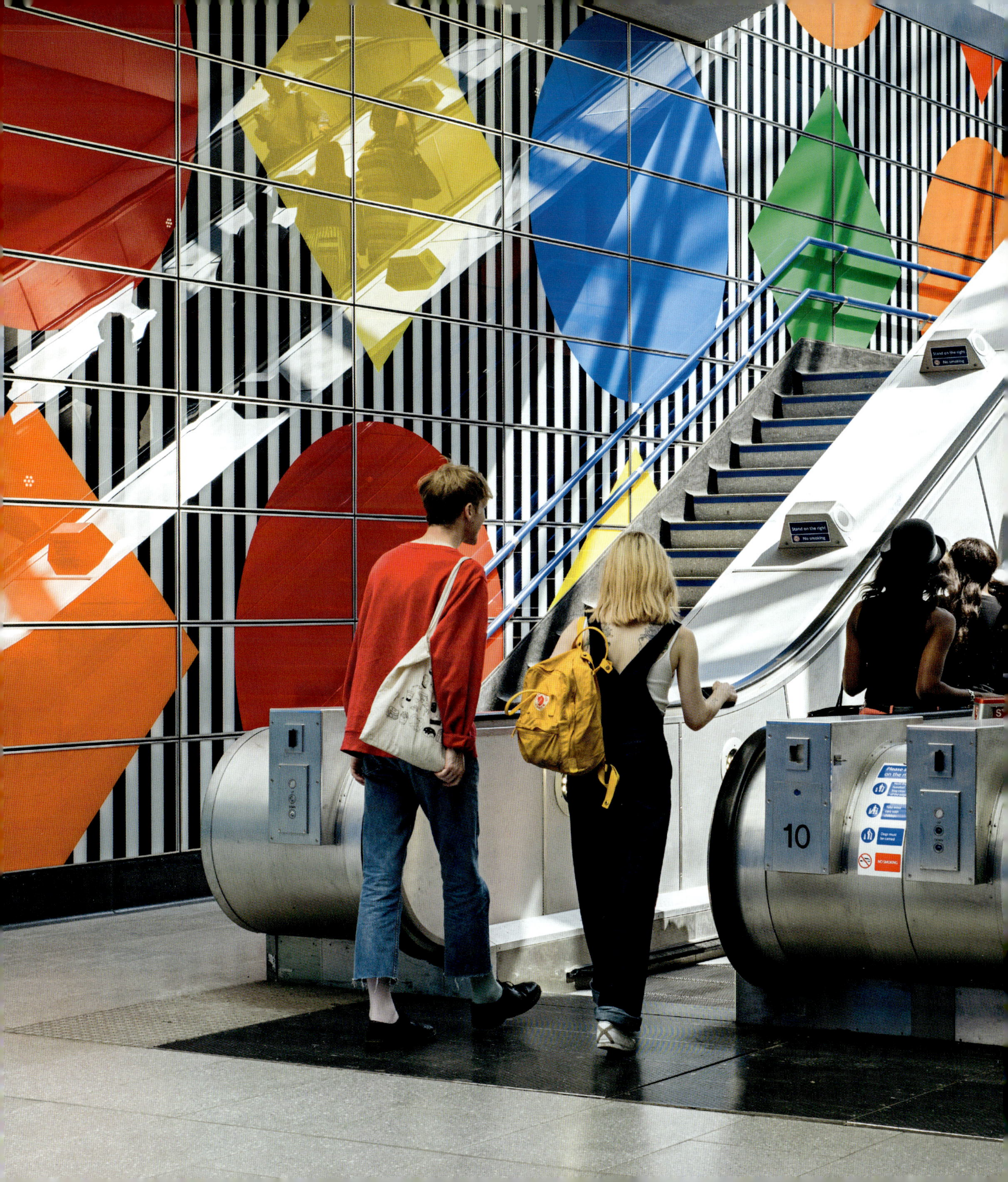

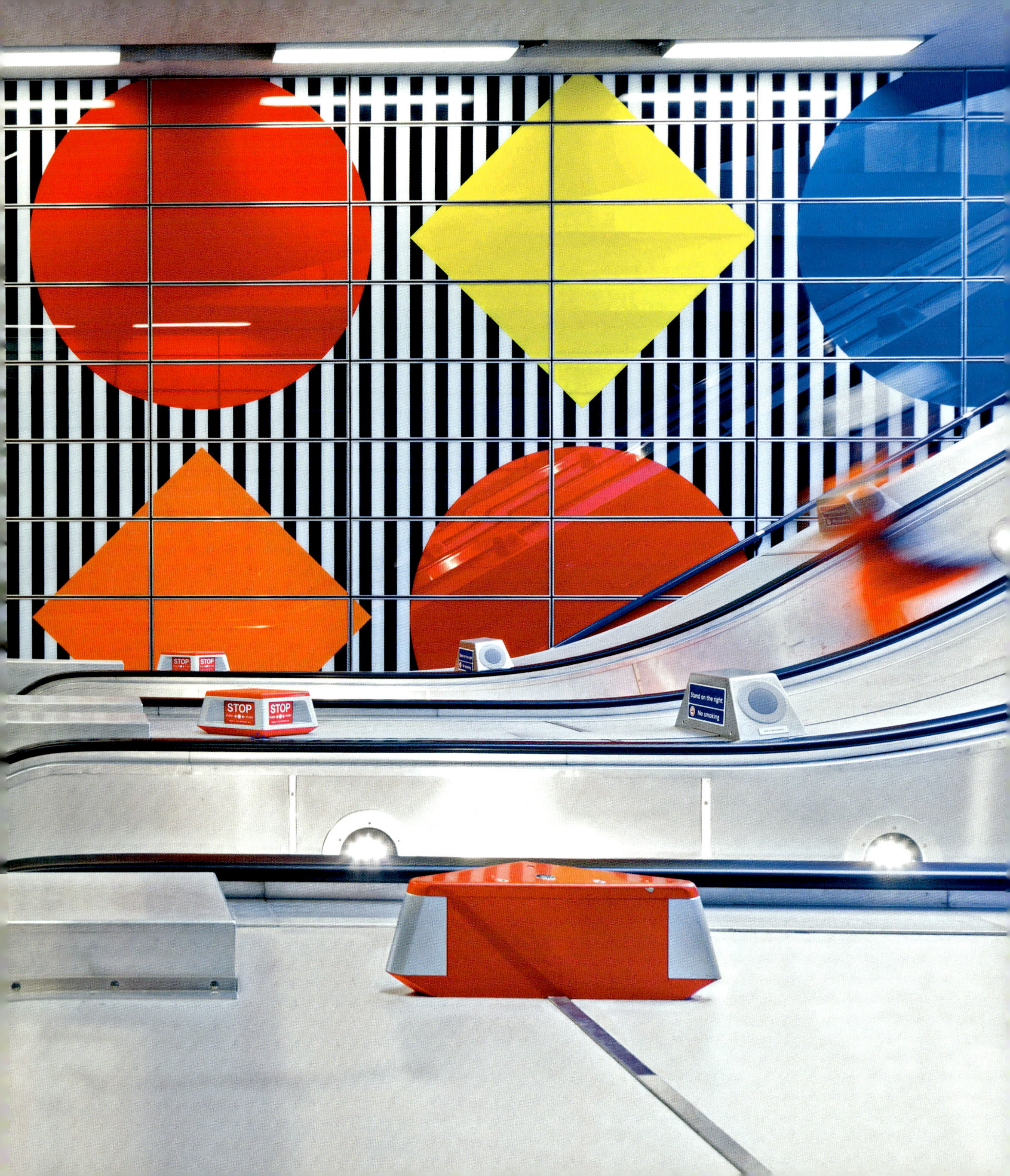

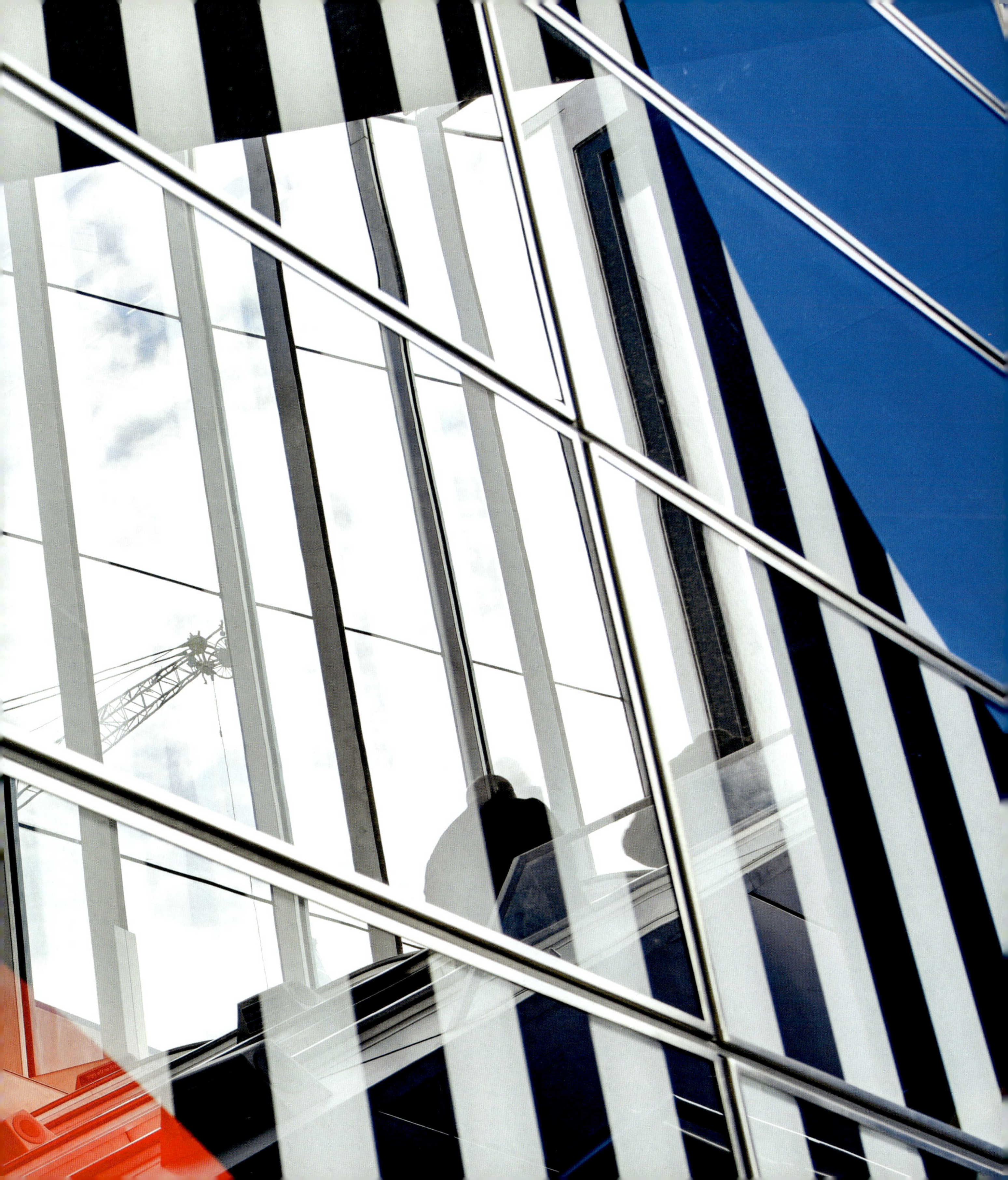

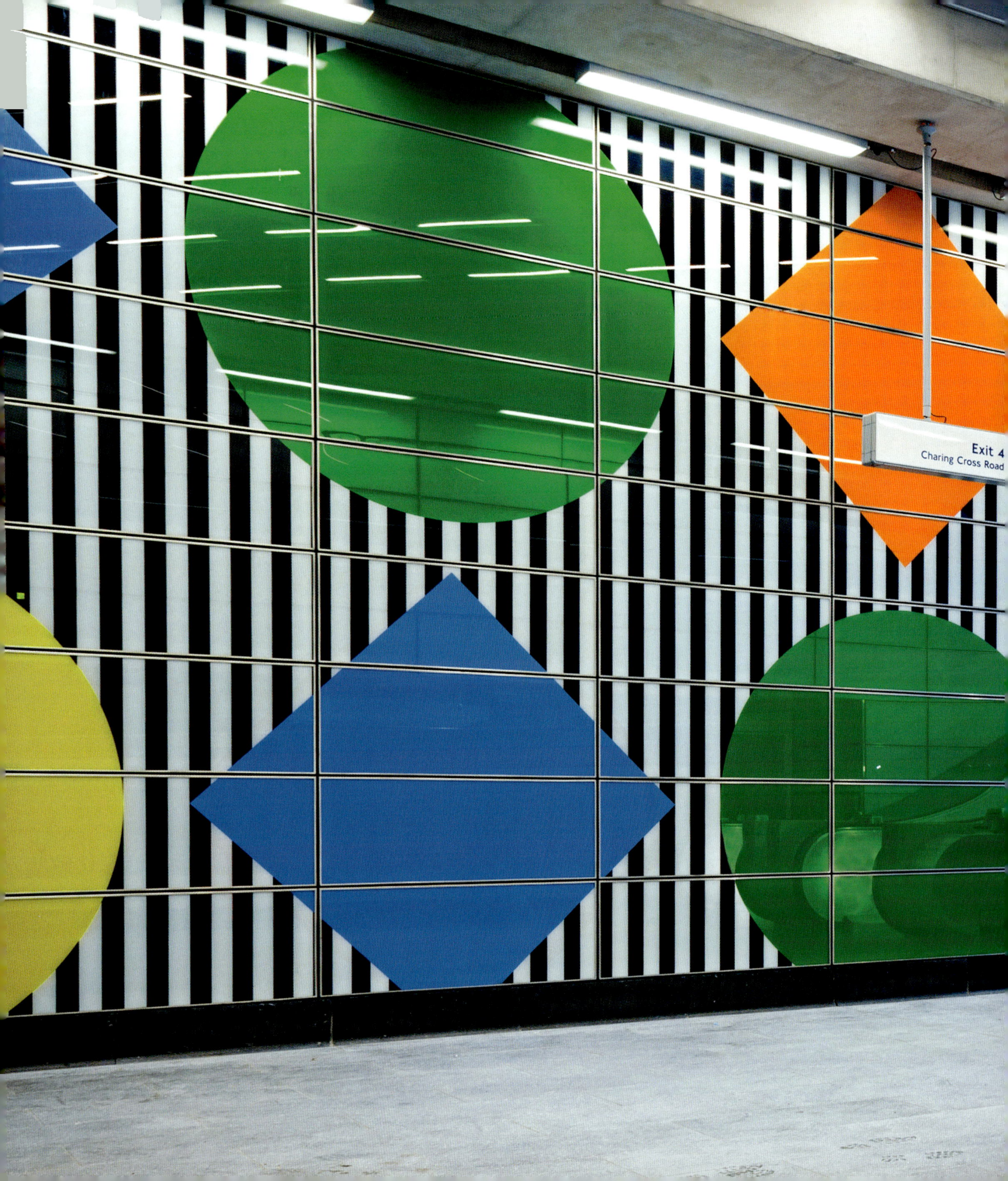

Exit 4
Charing Cross Road

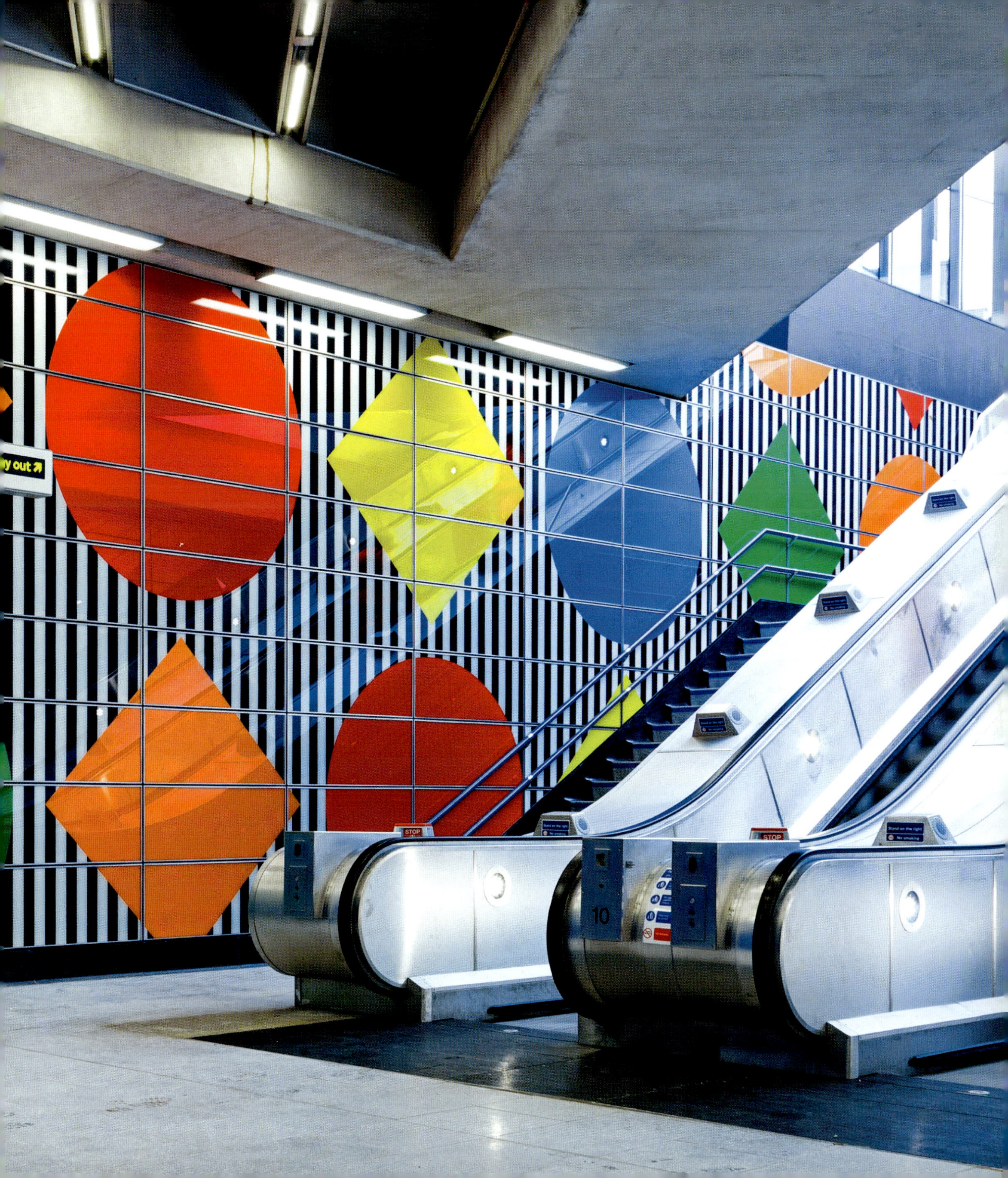

ay out
STOP
Stand on the right
No smoking
STOP
Stand on the right
No smoking
10

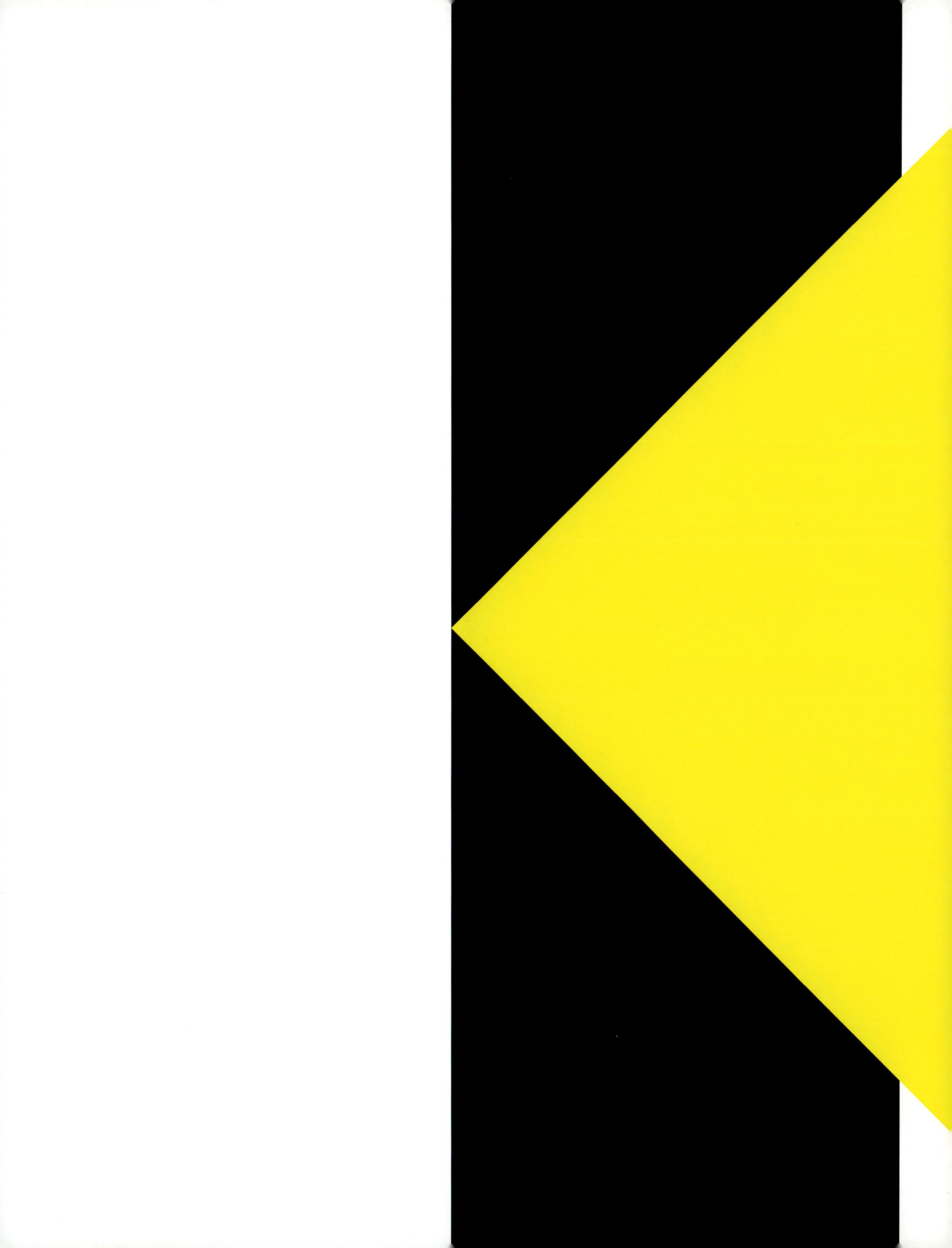

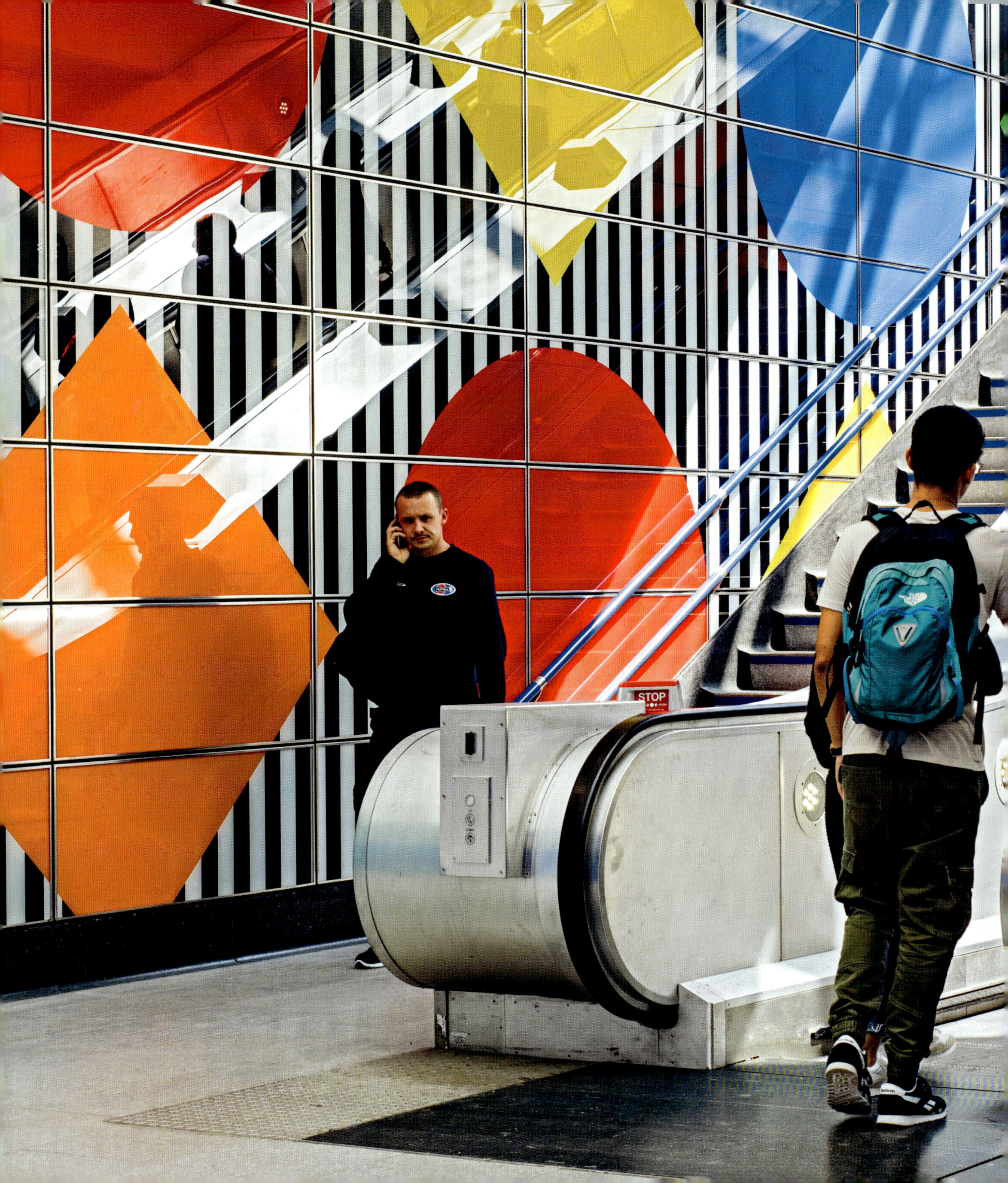

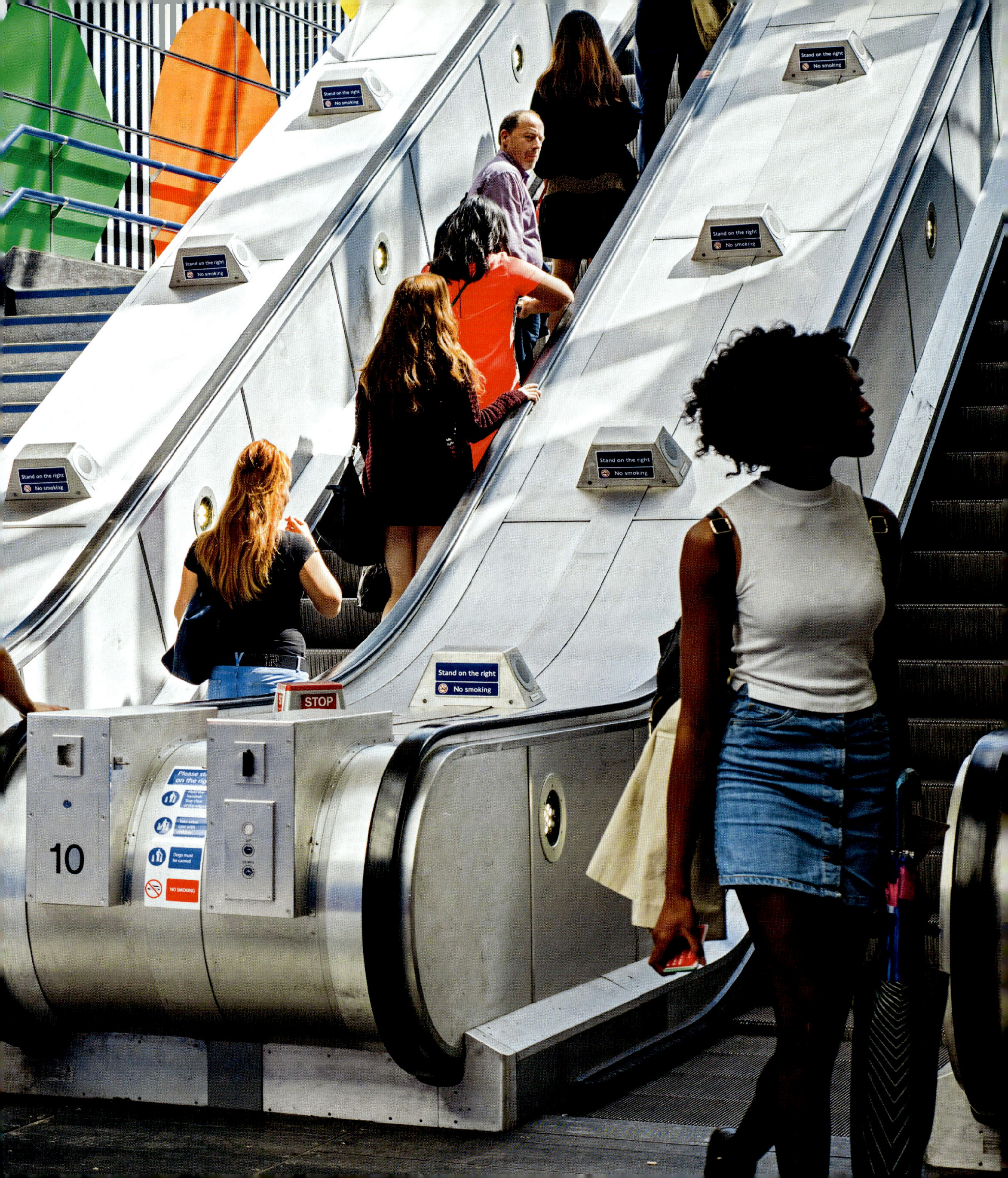

Stand on the right
No smoking
Stand on the right
No smoking
Stand on the right
No smoking
Stand on the right
No smoking
Stand on the right
No smoking
Stand on the right
No smoking
STOP
Please stand
on the right
Dogs must
be carried
NO SMOKING
10

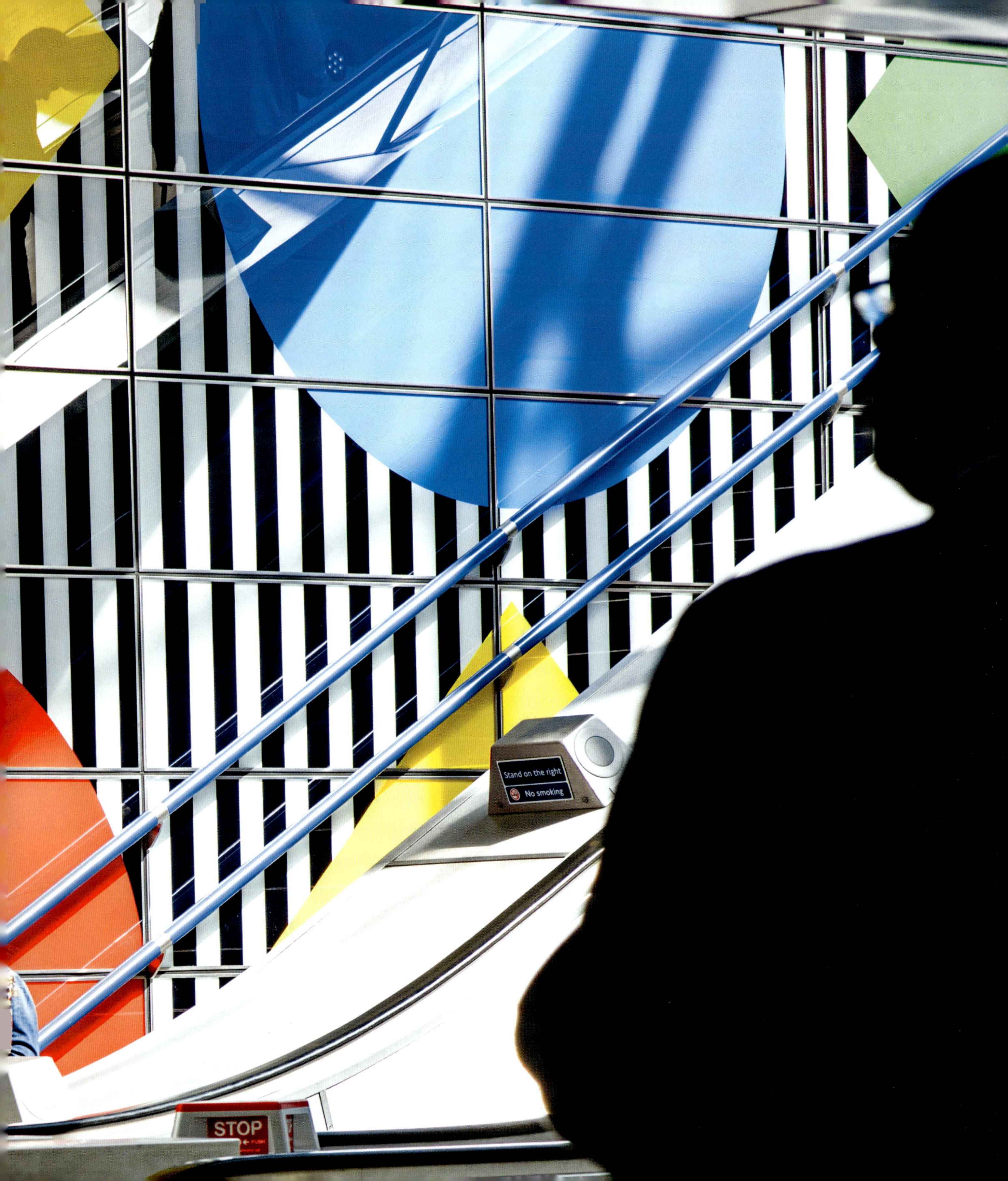

Stand on the right
No smoking
STOP

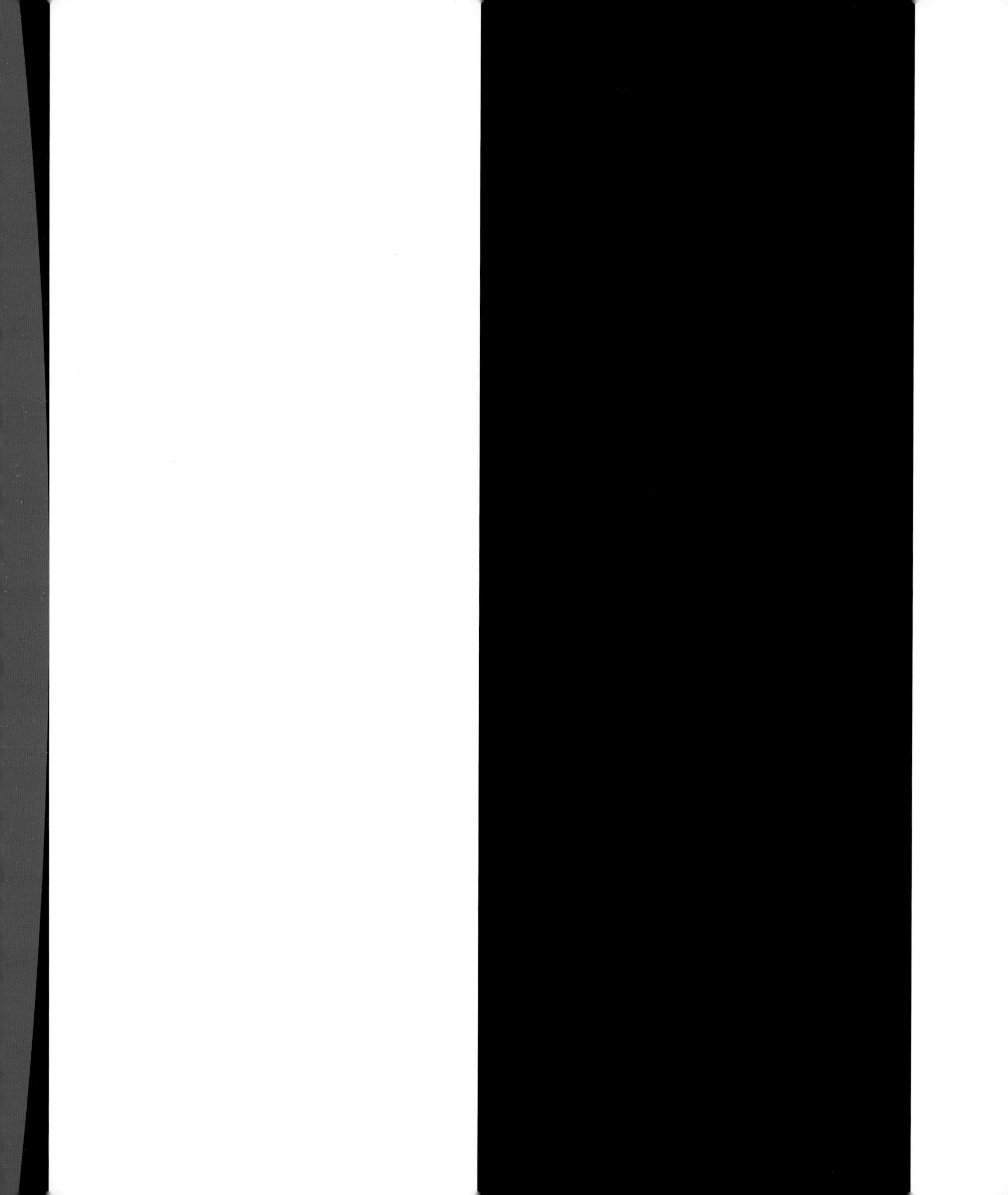

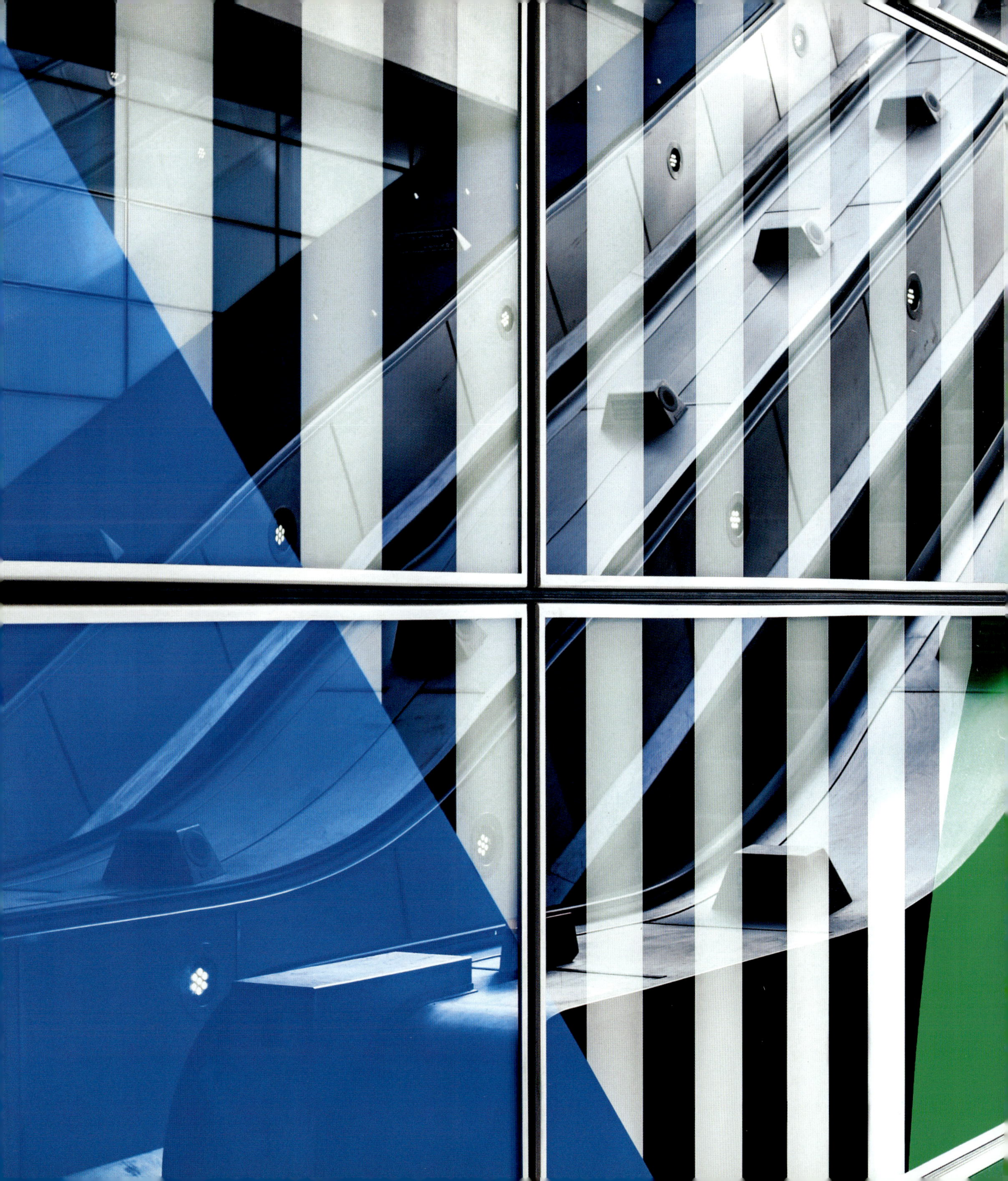

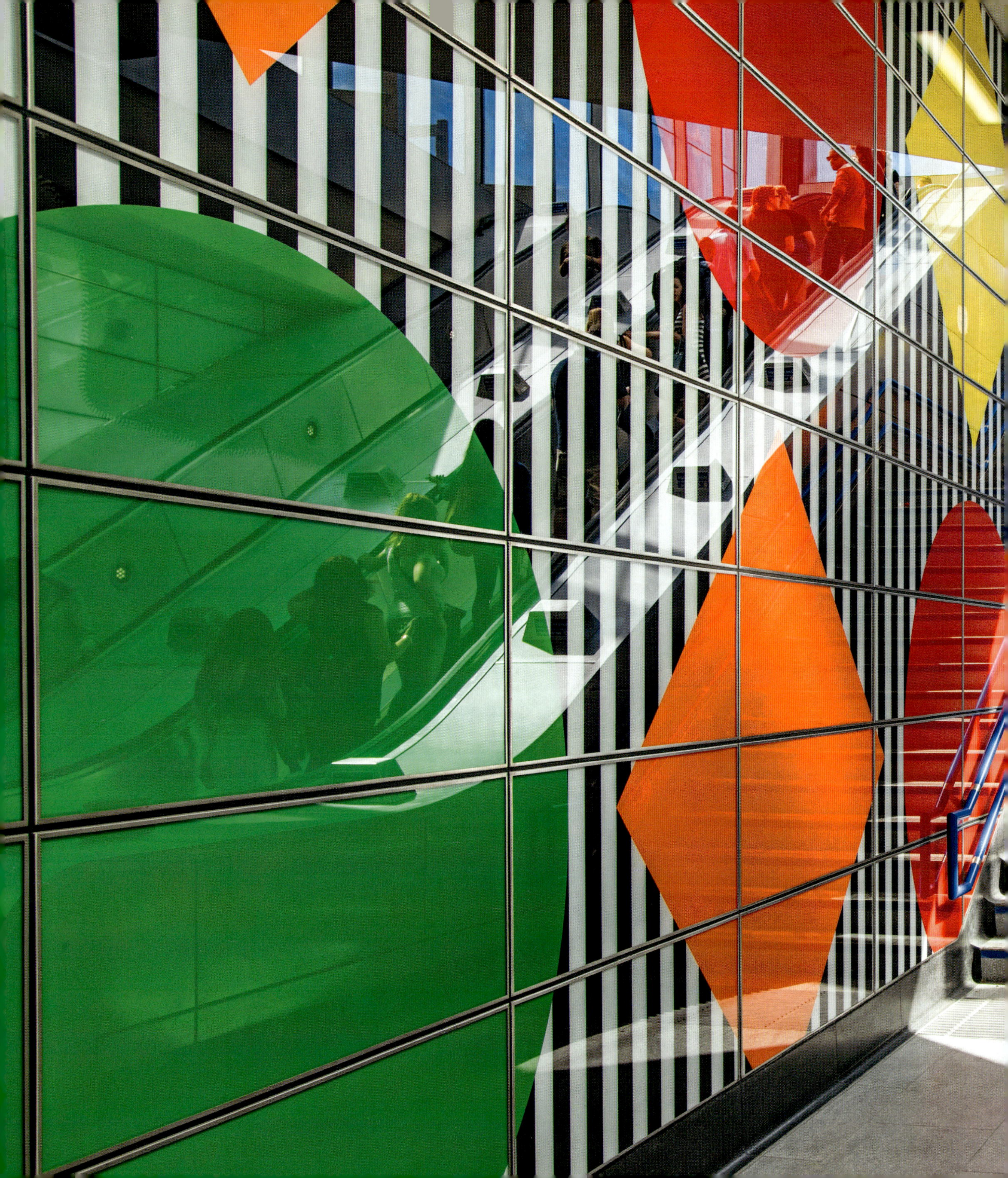

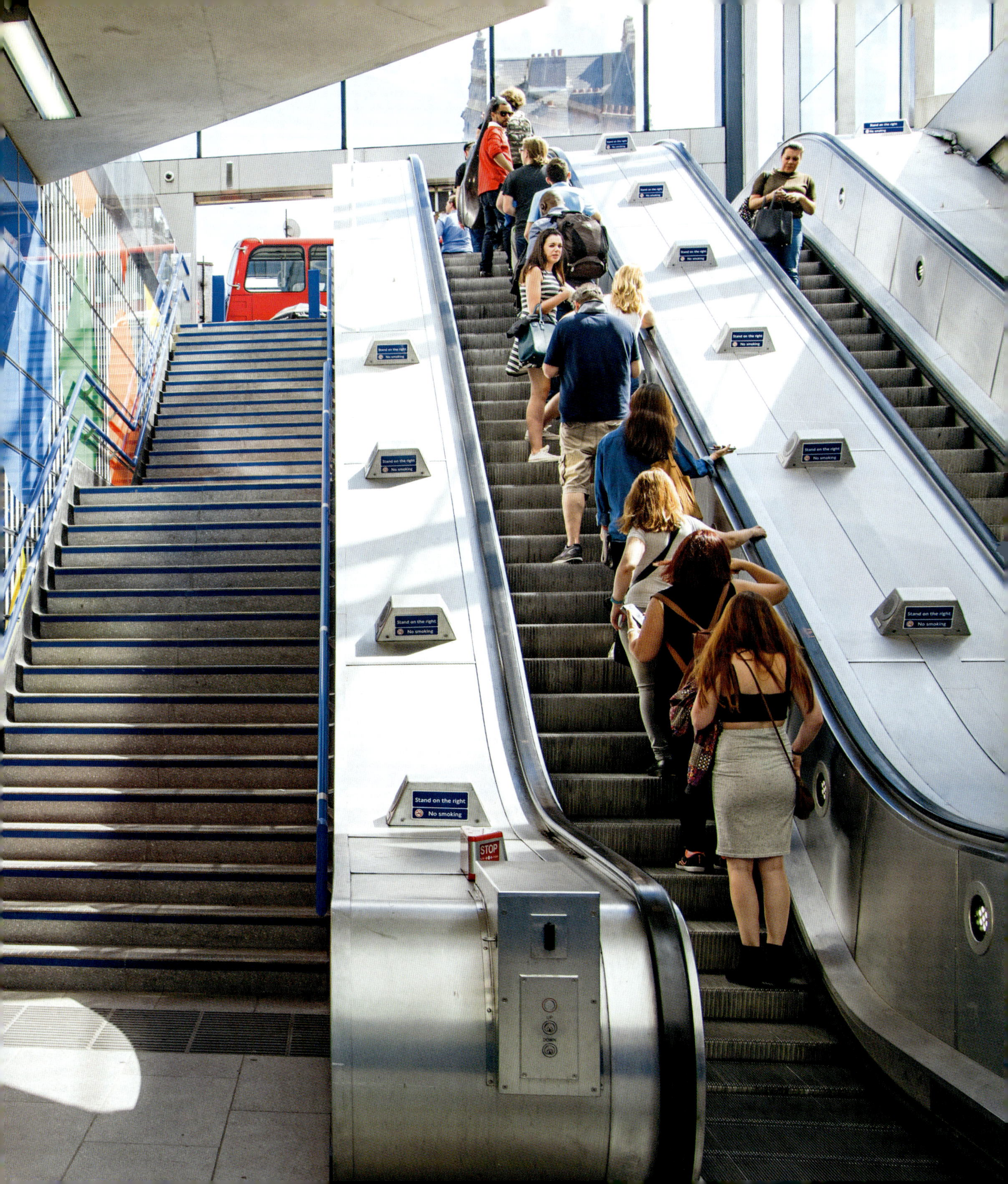

Stand on the right
No smoking
STOP
DOWN

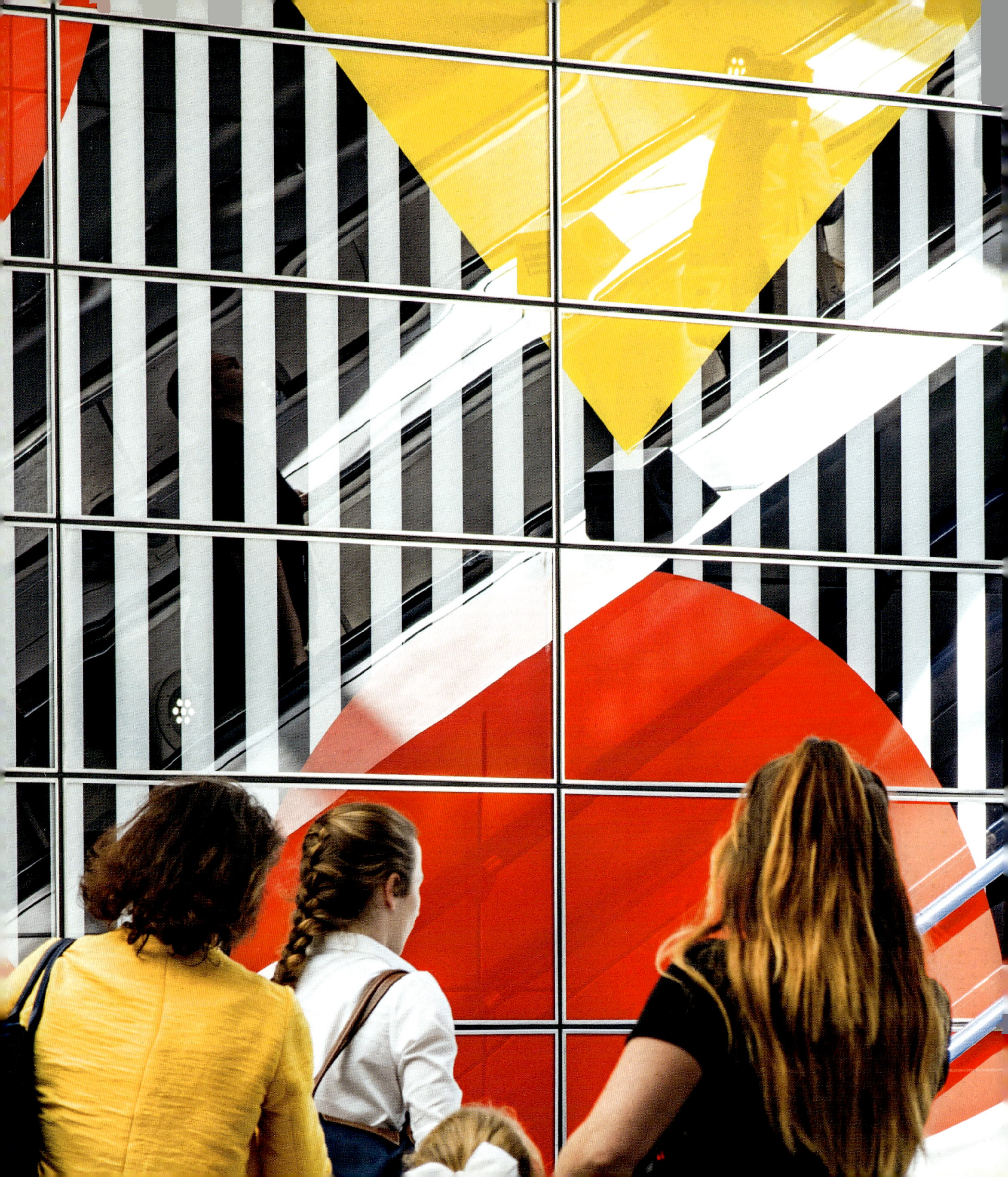

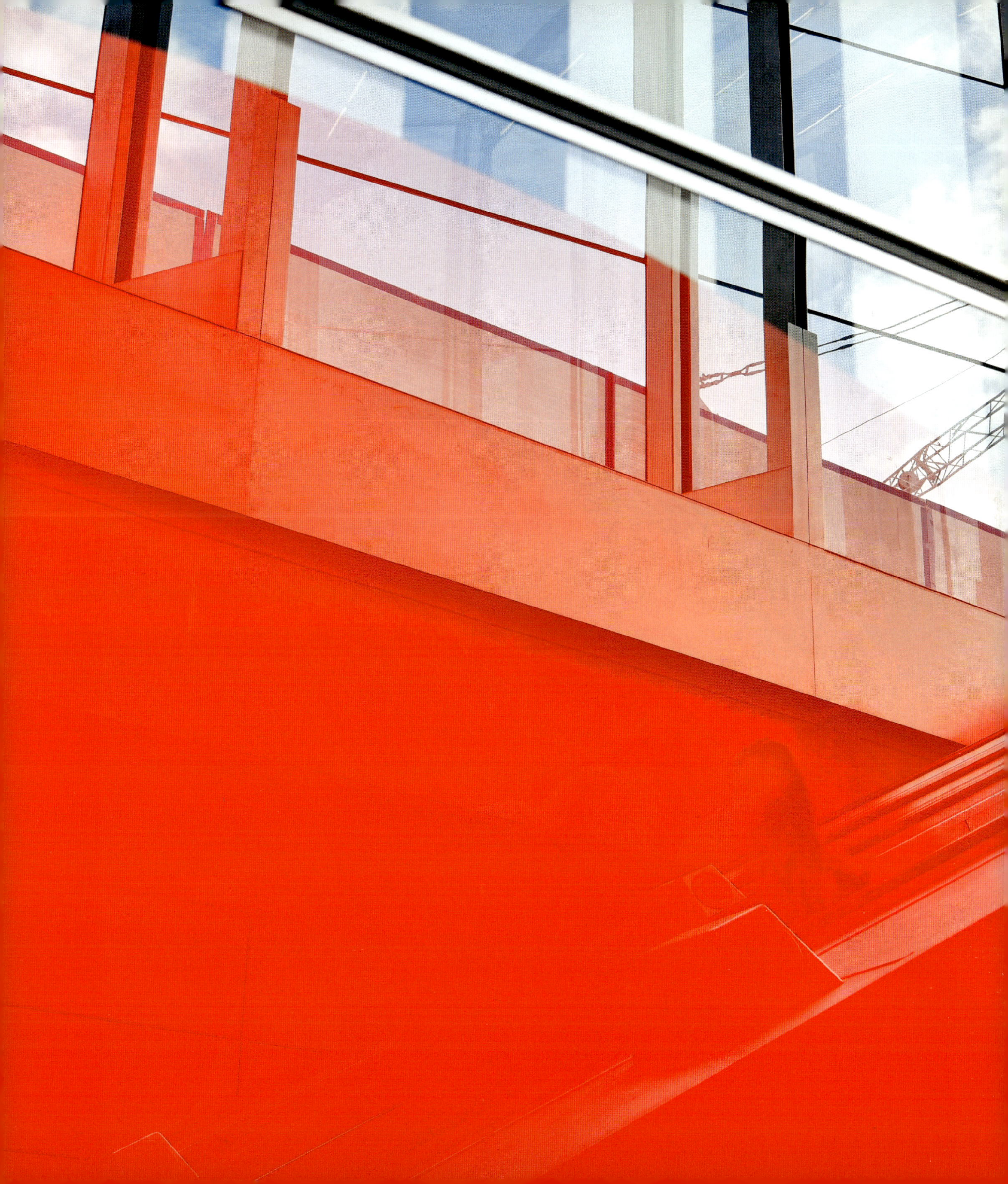

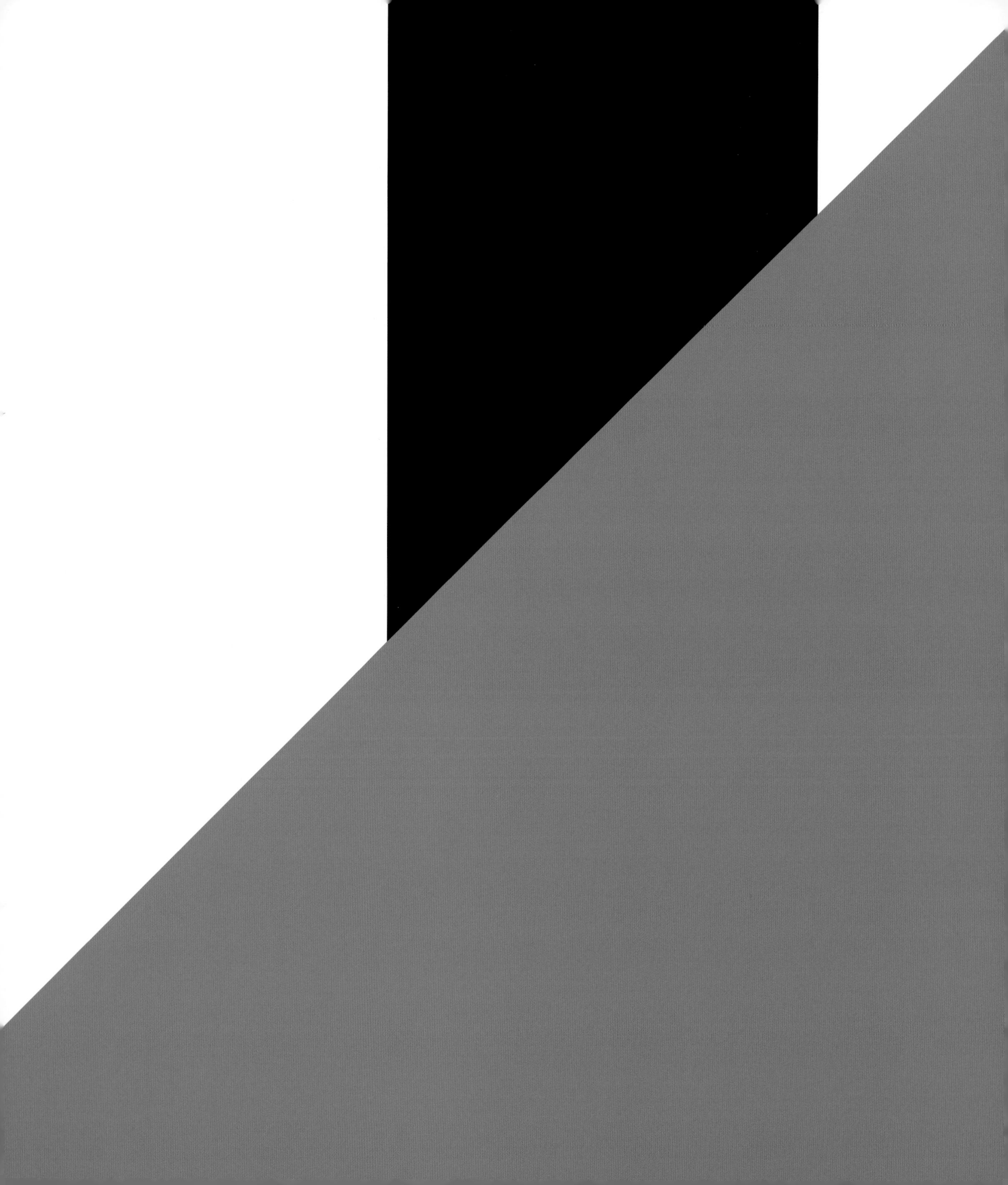

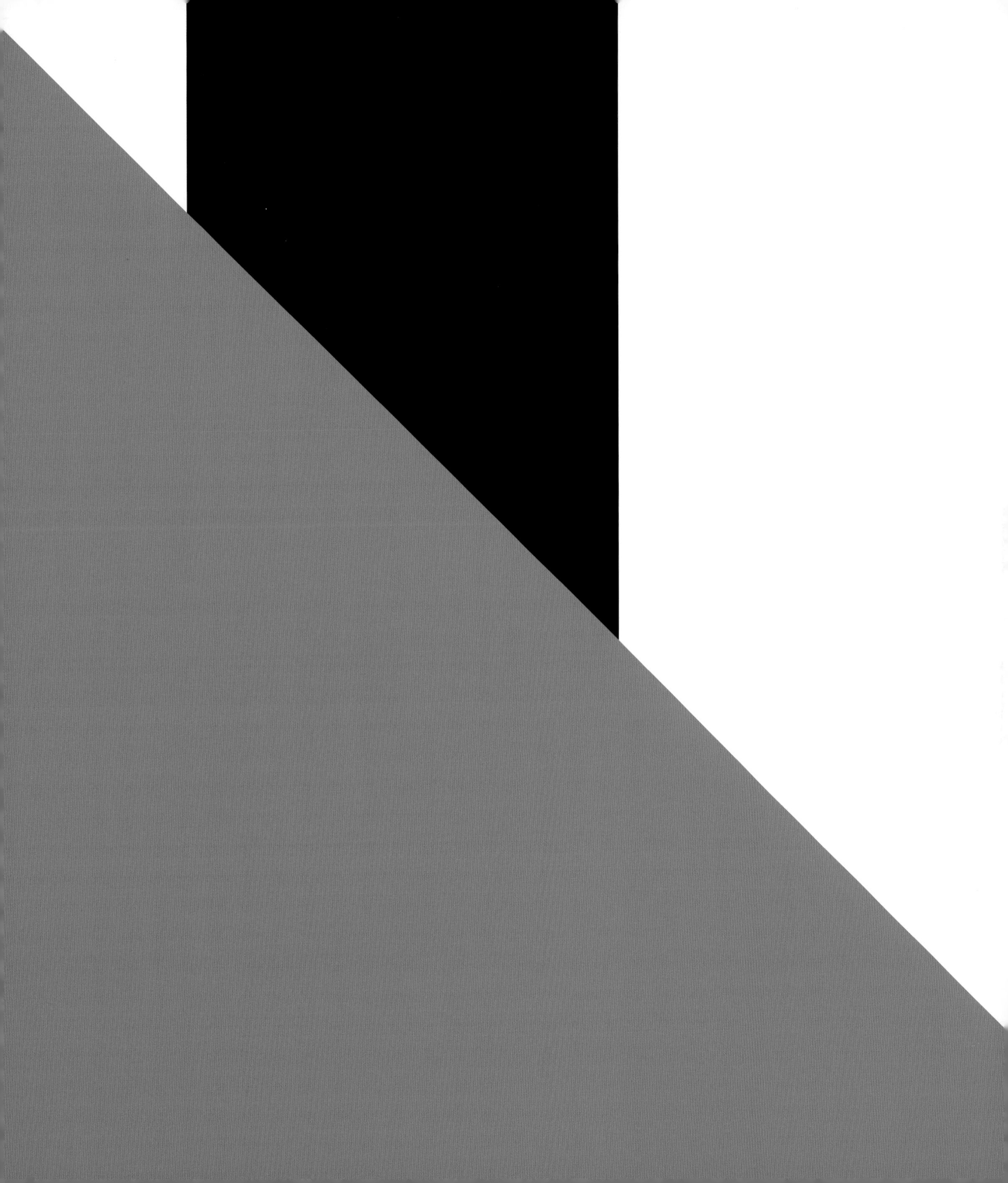

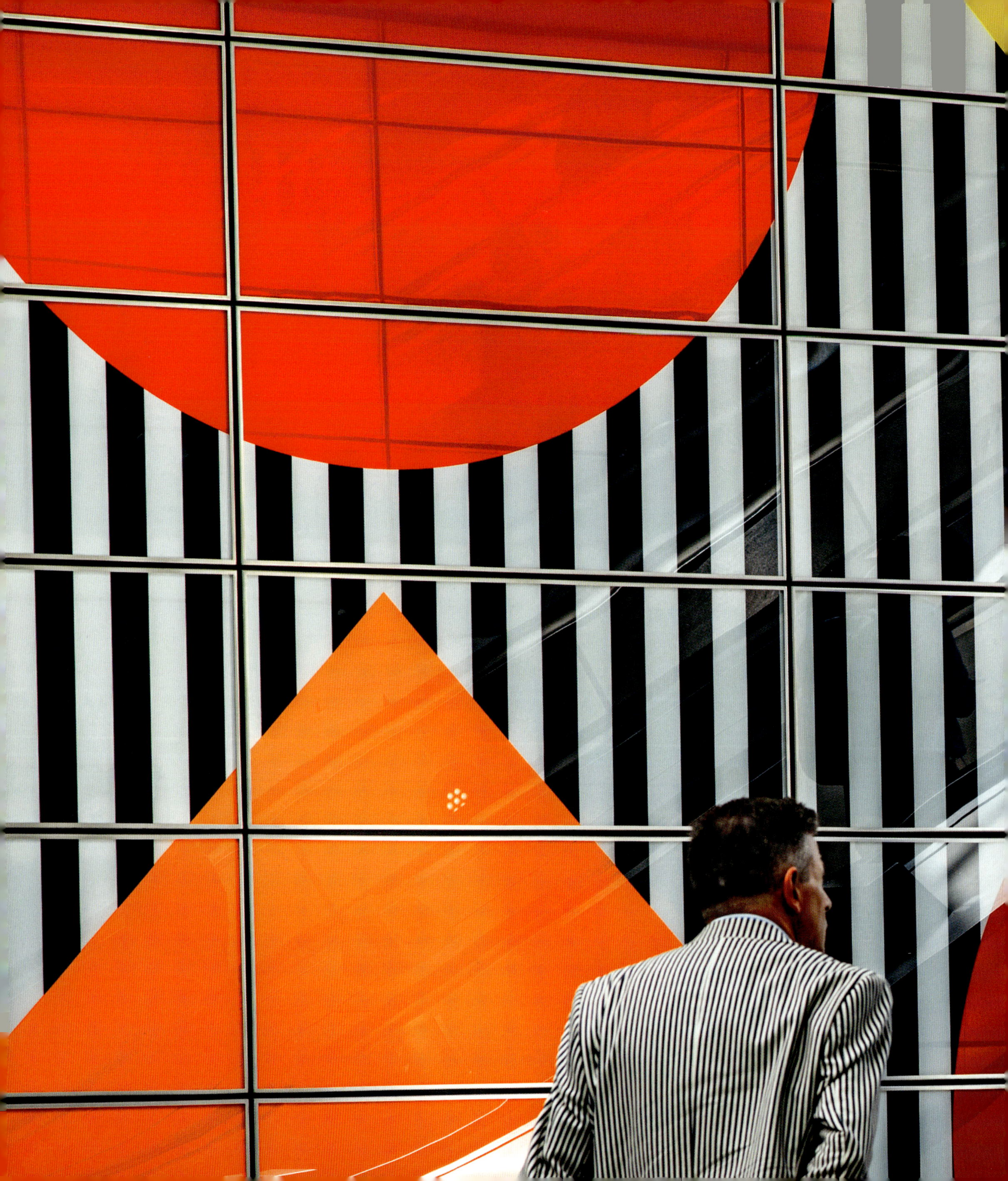

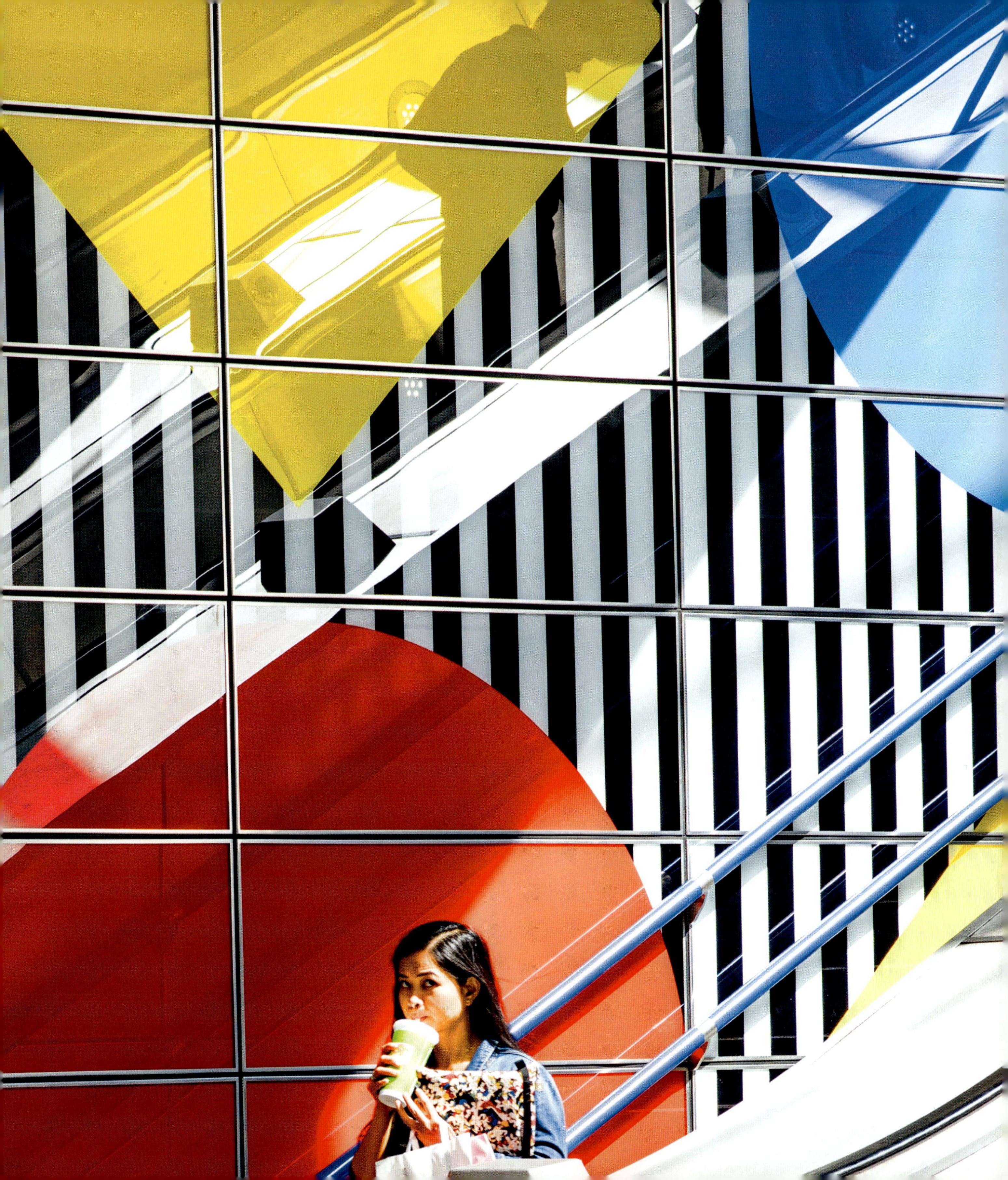

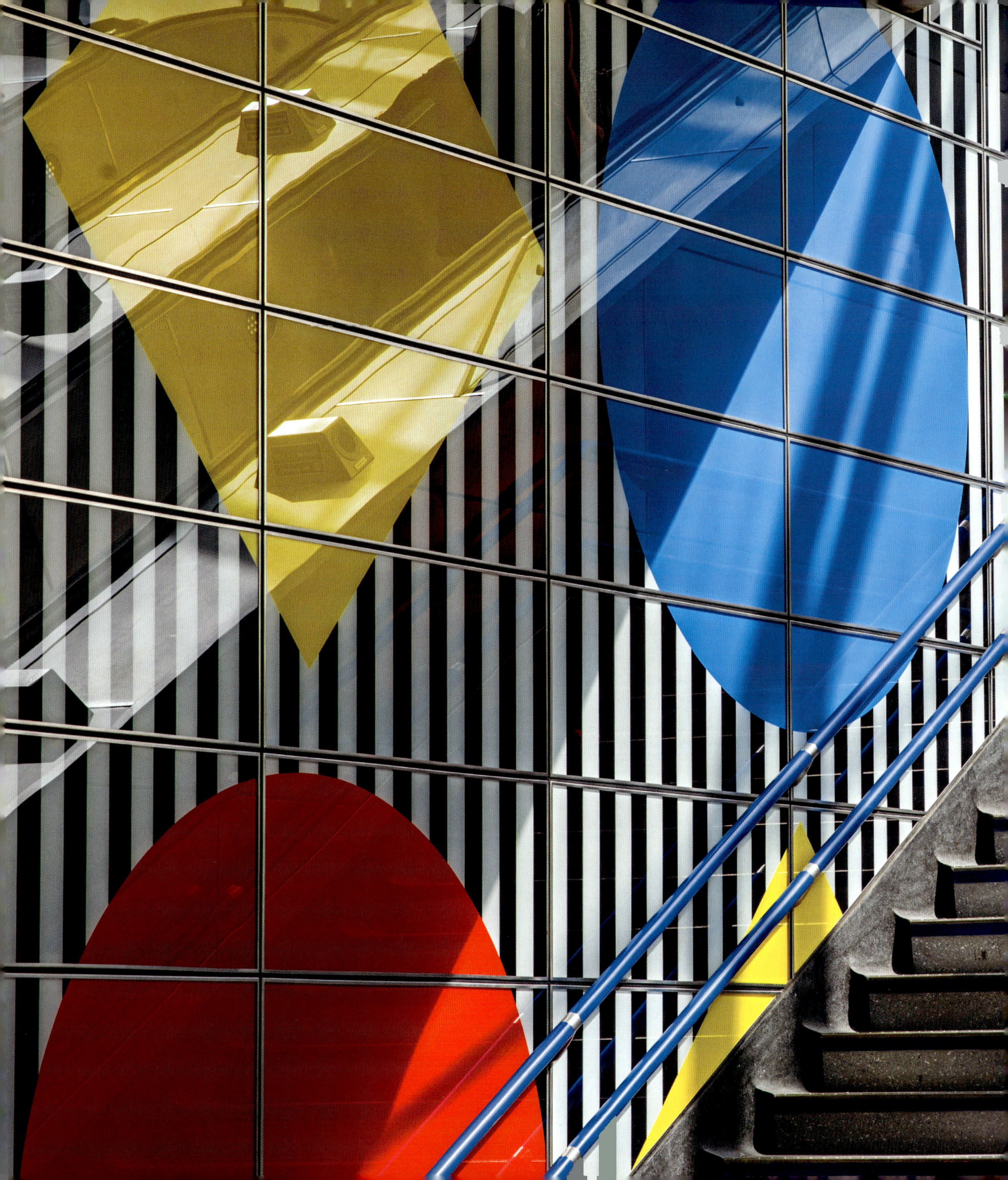

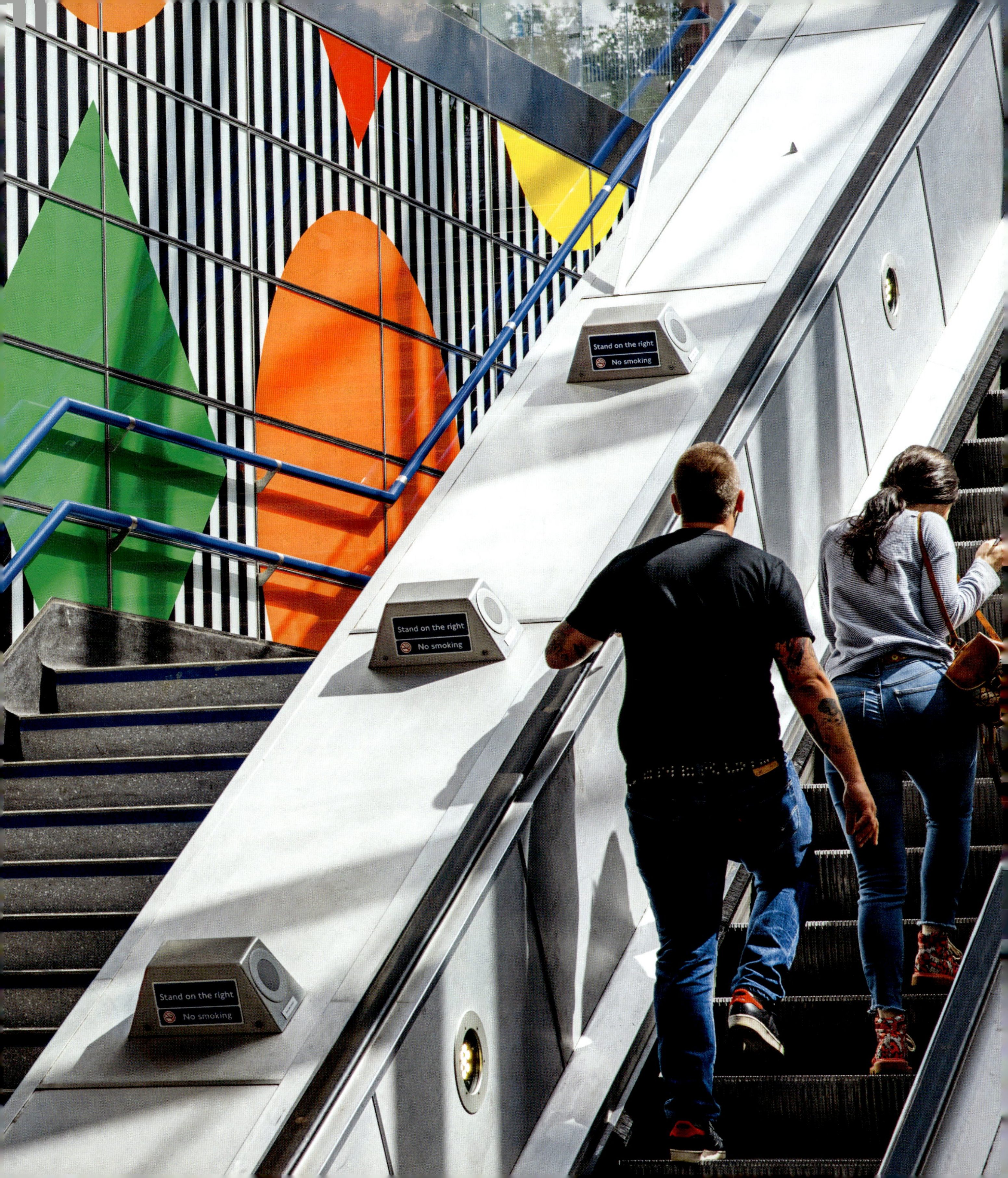

Stand on the right
No smoking
Stand on the right
No smoking
Stand on the right
No smoking

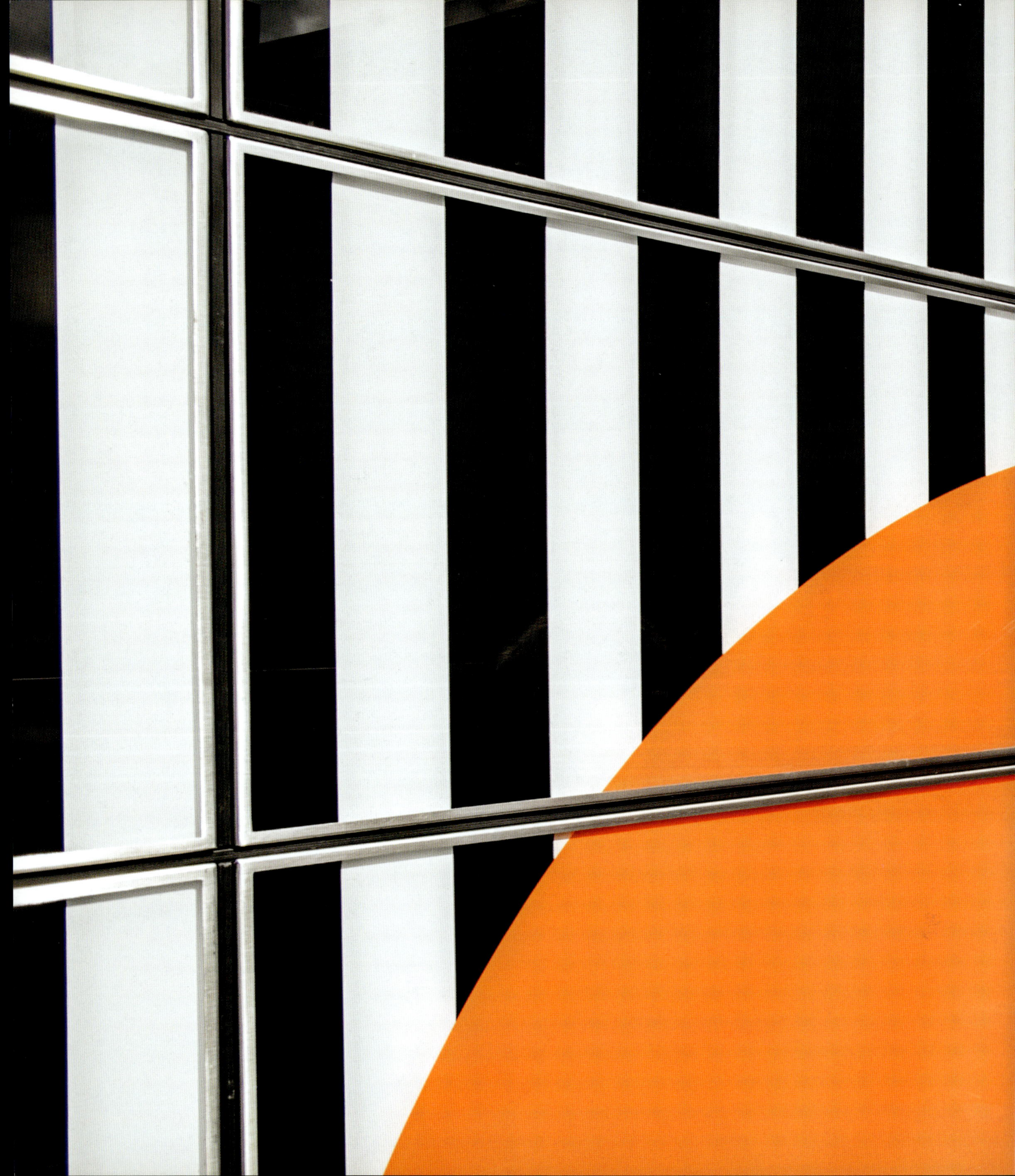

A public work is interesting for me because
you can develop the place, the people who
use the space, and connections between
all of these things…. Museums attract only
a portion of the population. The public in
the Tube station is everyone, and there is a
constant flux of people running both ways.
I want to offer them a beautiful balloon of
oxygen for the spirit.

Daniel Buren

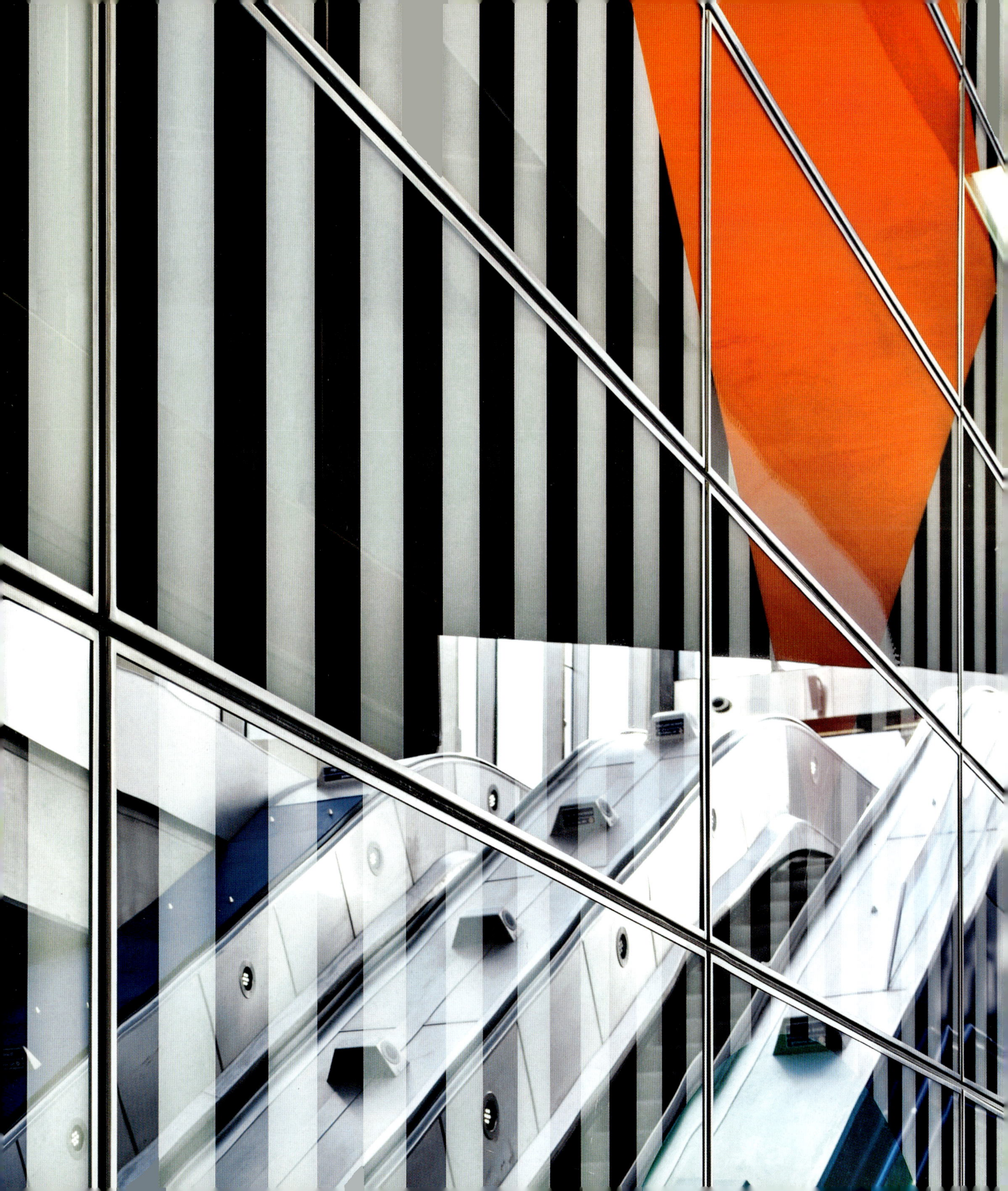

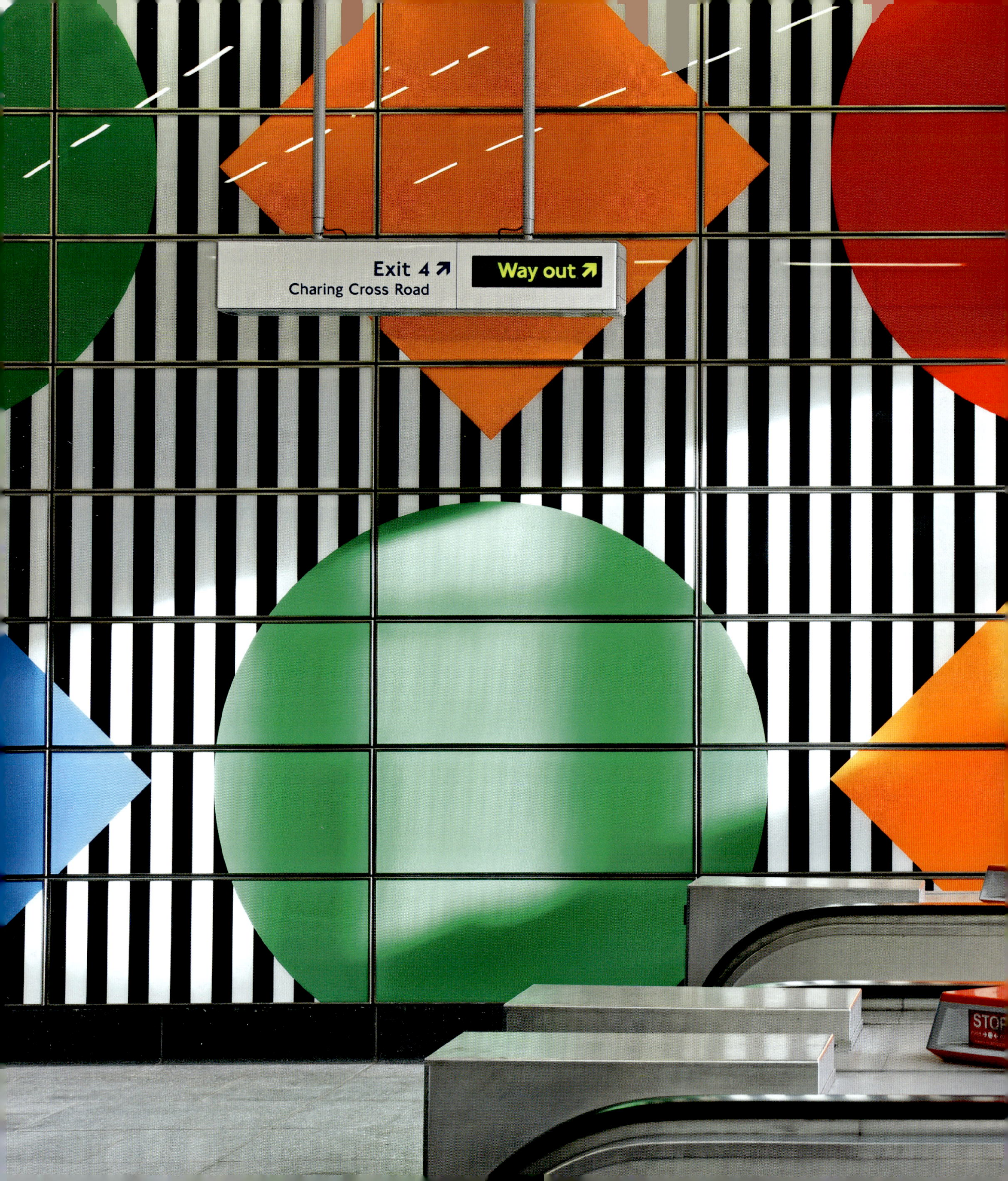

Exit 4
Charing Cross Road
Way out

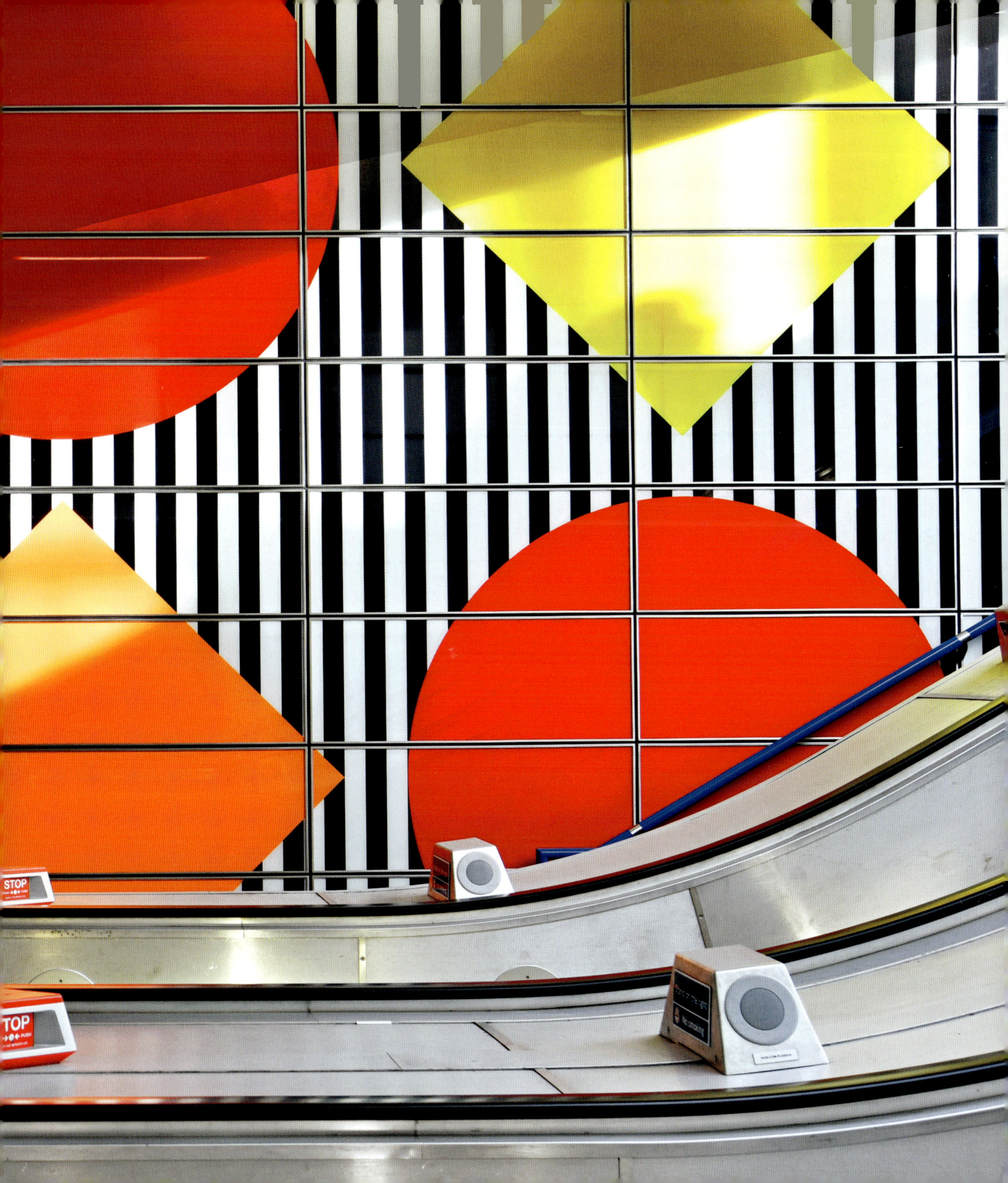

Tamsin Dillon is an independent curator and the former Head of Art on the Underground.

Tim Marlow is Director of Artistic Programmes at the Royal Academy of Arts, London, and a member of the Art on the Underground Advisory Panel.

Hans Ulrich Obrist is Artistic Director of the Serpentine Gallery, London.

Eleanor Pinfield is Head of Art on the Underground.

Mark Wild is Managing Director of London Underground.

Details of art work

Diamonds and Circles, works *in situ*, Tottenham Court Road station, London, 2017

The art work consists of four elements:

The Big Wall, Up and Down, Diamonds and Circles, Black and White, work *in situ*, Oxford Street entrance, Tottenham Court Road station, London, 2015

The Big Wall, Up and Down, Diamonds and Circles, Blue, Green, Orange, Red, Yellow, work *in situ*, Charing Cross Road entrance, Tottenham Court Road station, London, 2016

The Ticket Gate, Transparent Corridor, Diamonds and Circles, White Stripes, work *in situ*, Dominion Theatre entrance, Tottenham Court Road station, London, 2017

In the Window, Diamond and Circle, Blue and Yellow, work *in situ*, Ticket Hall, Tottenham Court Road station, London, 2017

Acknowledgments

We would like to thank the artist, Daniel Buren, for his tireless work on the project since 2007 and his cooperation on this publication.

We also thank the contributors Tamsin Dillon, Tim Marlow, Hans Ulrich Obrist and Mark Wild, and the designers TSOWC / The Studio of Williamson Curran.

Support from within Transport for London has been resolute, especially from Mike Brown MVO, Transport Commissioner and previously Managing Director of London Underground and Rail (2010–15), Sir Peter Hendy (Transport Commissioner 2006–15), and Tim O'Toole (Managing Director, London Underground 2003–9).

This major new work has been driven forward by various members of the Art on the Underground team, in particular Tamsin Dillon, who initiated the commission in 2007 and was Head of Art on the Underground until 2014, and Eleanor Pinfield, who took on that role from 2014.

We would like to thank the Art on the Underground Advisory Panel, with the following members since 2007: John Ball, Jo Baxendale, Matt Carney, Howard Collins, Mark Evers, Steve Gumbrell, Caro Howell, David Hughes, Keith Khan, Julie Lomax, Chris Macleod, David McNeill, Tim Marlow, Judith Nesbitt, Tim O'Toole, Richard Parry, Jacqueline Poncelet, Gareth Powell, Julia Royse, Alex Sainsbury, Justine Simons, Ellie Smith, Mark Titchner, Anna Vickery, Mark Wild.

The project would not have been possible without the support of station architects Hawkins\Brown, who worked with the artist to realize the art work from the initiation of the project. Harbinder Singh Birdi, Partner, has been a key driving force to deliver the project. We would also like to thank the project team that delivered the upgrade works at Tottenham Court Road station; joint venture partnership Taylor Woodrow Bam Nuttall, plaza architects Stanton Williams and NG Bailey, station entrance architects Arcanthus, and Transport for London colleagues.

The artistic intervention at Tottenham Court Road has been a major undertaking, and this publication seeks to draw together its impact. Many people have contributed to its success and we would like to take the opportunity to thank those who have been involved along the way: Lee Almond, Mike Ashworth, Thierry Bal, Dylan Beeson, Rebecca Bell, Kiera Blakey, Chris Bonner, Louise Coysh, Jessica Davies Molloy, Mark Evers, Ralph Freeston, Andrew Grant, Cathy Haynes, Benedict Johnson, Lisson Gallery, Josephine Martin, Chris Phiniefs, Lucianne Quinn, Simon Reynolds, Sally Shaw, Allan Thomson, Jessica Vaughan, Mariam Zulfiqar.

Picture credits

1, 12, 17, 18, 24, 29, 31, 36–7, 40–1, 42–3, 45, 46, 50–1, 52, 53, 54, 55, 58, 64–5, 66, 67, 68, 74–5, 77, 80, 81, 82, 83, 86, 87, 128: Benedict Johnson

6, 8, 13, 22, 23, 38–9, 48–9, 56–7, 59, 60–1, 69, 90–1, 92–3, 95, 97, 102–3, 104, 107, 108–9, 110, 111, 114–15, 116–17, 118, 121, 122–3: Thierry Bal

10 (top), 11, 14, 15 (bottom), 16, 30: Hawkins\Brown

10 (bottom), 19, 20 (top), 25, 26, 27, 28: Daniel Buren Studio

15 (top), 34–5, 70–1, 96, 98–9: Transport for London

21: Iwan Baan / Fondation Louis Vuitton

20: Metropolitan Transportation Authority Arts & Design, New York City. Photo: James and Karla Murray (details); Rob Wilson (overview).

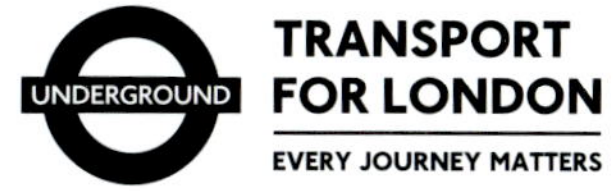

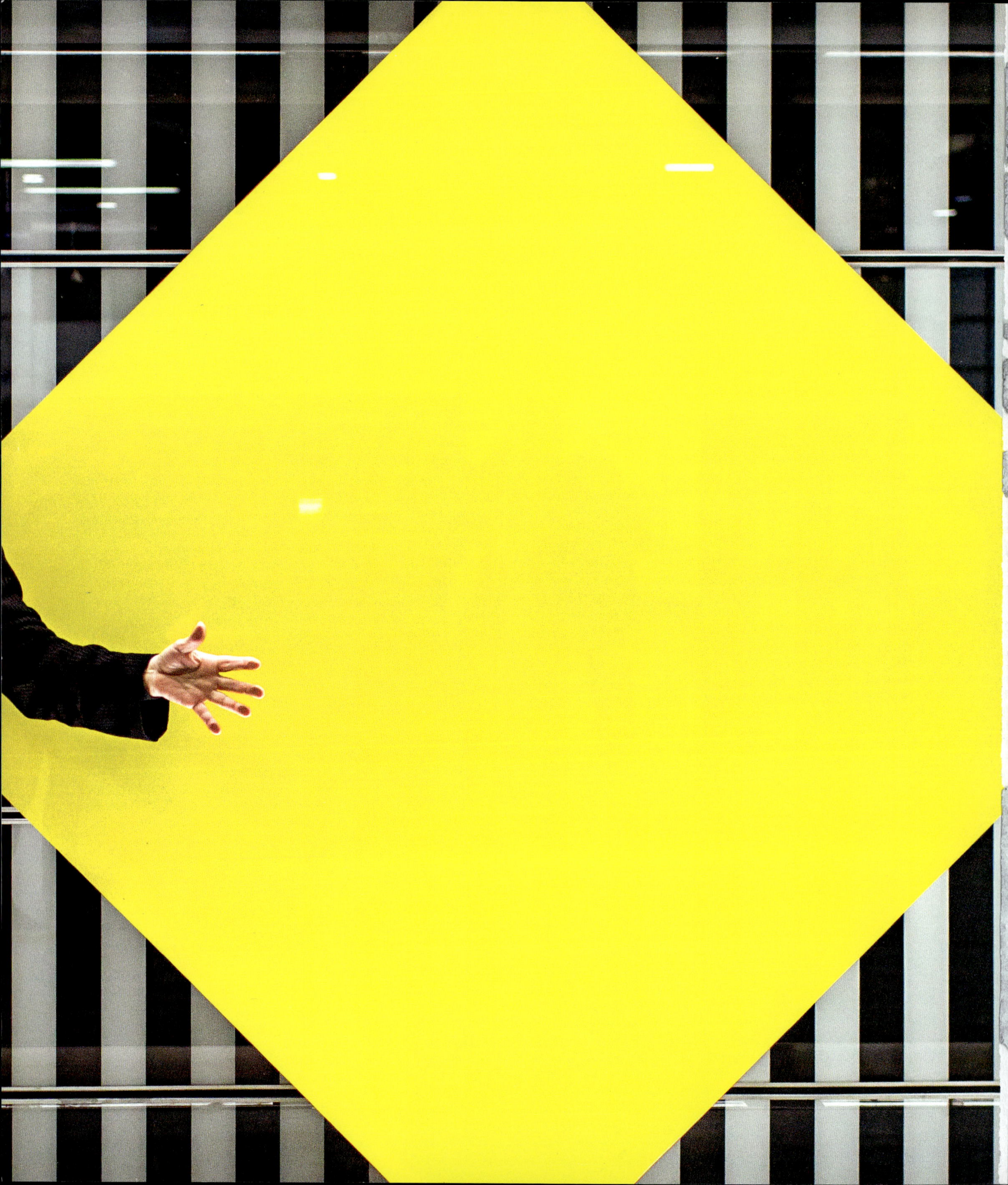